D1716288

This book identifies the main national and international influences on park development in nineteenth-century Britain and relates them to the design and use of municipal and other public parks. Municipal parks made an important contribution to the urban environment and they developed within a social, economic and political context which affected people's attitudes to recreation. The promoters of parks wanted to encourage education and particular forms of recreation, and parks reflected this in their design, buildings, statues, bandstands and planting. Appendices summarise the relevant legislation and provide a chronological descriptive gazetteer of early parks.

PEOPLE'S PARKS

PEOPLE'S PARKS

THE DESIGN AND DEVELOPMENT

OF VICTORIAN PARKS

IN BRITAIN

Hazel Conway

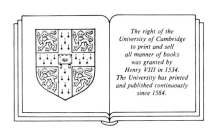

The right of the
University of Cambridge
to print and sell
all manner of books
was granted by
Henry VIII in 1534.
The University has printed
and published continuously
since 1584.

CAMBRIDGE UNIVERSITY PRESS

CAMBRIDGE

NEW YORK   PORT CHESTER

MELBOURNE   SYDNEY

Published by the Press Syndicate of the University of Cambridge
The Pitt Building, Trumpington Street, Cambridge CB2 1RP
40 West 20th Street, New York, NY 10011–4211, USA
10 Stamford Road, Oakleigh, Melbourne 3166, Australia

First published 1991

Printed in Great Britain at
the University Press, Cambridge

British Library cataloguing in publication data
Conway, Hazel
People's parks: the development and design of Victorian Parks.
1. Great Britain. Parks. Design, history
I. Title
711.558

Library of Congress cataloguing in publication data
Conway, Hazel.
People's parks: the development and design of Victorian parks
Hazel Conway.
p.   cm.
Includes bibliographical references and index.
ISBN 0-521-39070-2
1. Parks – Great Britain – History – 19th century. 2. Parks – Great
Britain – Design and construction – History – 19th century.
3. Architecture, Victorian – Great Britain. 4. City and town life –
Great Britain – History – 19th century. I. Title. II. Title:
Victorian parks
SB484.G7C59   1991
711'.558'094109034 – dc20   90-44512

ISBN 0521 39070 2 hardback

The publication of this book has been assisted by a grant from
the Twenty-Seven Foundation

WV

For Zara

Contents

Illustrations

Tables

Graphs

Acknowledgements

So many people have helped me in this project, both directly and indirectly, that it is impossible to mention them all by name. Family and friends have accompanied me on visits to parks, in all sorts of weather, as well as visiting particular parks on my behalf. Among the friends and colleagues that I would particularly like to thank are Rowan Roenisch for her continued encouragement and valued criticism and Patrick Goode for reading the final manuscript. Their suggestions have added clarity to the text, but the final responsibility rests with me. I would also like to thank the following for their kindness and help: John Cook, Brent Elliott, Peter Goodchild, Allan Hart, Pat Havron, Martin Lupton, Geoffrey Martin, John McLaren, Patrick Phillips, John Pugsley, Harry Smolins and Robert Thorne. To the many local historians throughout the country, who have been so patient with my queries, I would like to express my gratitude and finally I would like to thank John Trevitt for the improvements brought by his editing.

The author and publisher would like to thank the following for permission to reproduce illustrations: Alexandra Palace and Park Trust, 27; British Architectural Library, 23; Bath Library, 2; Bradford Libraries, 25, 31; Cleveland County Libraries, 32; Durham County Library, 74; Greater London Photograph Library, 37, 38, 96, 97, 104, 105; Greater London Record Office, 20, 47; Guildhall Library, 1; Liverpool City Council, Libraries and Arts Department, 9, 21, 41, 42; Manchester Public Libraries; Local History Library, 18, 66, 67, 68, 102; The Museum of London, Dustcover, 5, 6, 53, 55, 60, 62, 93, 94, 98; G. A. F. Plunkett and Norfolk Library and Information Service, 51, 54; Nottinghamshire County Library Service, 81; People's Palace Museum (Glasgow Museums), 78, 83; Sunderland Museum and Art Gallery, 64, 79; Wolverhampton Public Libraries, 34, 87, 89; Trafford Leisure Services, 33.

Abbreviations

BRIC	Birkenhead Road and Improvement Committee
CPS	Commons Preservation Society
ILN	*Illustrated London News*
LC	Liverpool Council
LCC	London County Council
MBC	Manchester Borough Council
MCC	Manchester City Council
MPCS	Manchester Parks Committee Scrapbook
MPGA	Metropolitan Public Gardens Association
MPPC	Manchester Public Parks Committee
MSSA	Manchester and Salford Sanitary Association
PRO	Public Record Office
SCPW	Select Committee on Public Walks
VPP	Victoria Park Papers

Introduction

'. . . to sit in the shade on a fine day, and look upon verdure, is the most perfect refreshment', said Fanny, the heroine of *Mansfield Park*, and her feelings strike a chord of recognition, particularly among urban dwellers. Nowadays we visit the country to find verdure, or we walk in our local park, but at the time that Jane Austen was writing, and indeed for the greater part of the nineteenth century, such 'perfect refreshment' was unavailable to the majority of people living in Britain's industrial centres. Today almost every town of any size has a number of open spaces, parks, commons and recreation grounds, which vary in size from several hundred acres to less than one. Their designs range from the simple to the very sophisticated, and they contribute green space to built-up areas and form an important part of the urban environment, whether they be large or small, simple or complex.

My interest in parks generally and municipal parks in particular grew out of my researches in landscape design, my studies of Victorian architecture, and my good fortune in having lived much of my life near public parks. The local park plays an important role in many people's lives even today when there are many other choices of activity and many other places to go to. Municipal parks were brought into being via many complex factors, which in turn influenced their design and use. This is a very rich subject, involving as it does social, economic and political history, recreation, landscape design, architecture, sculpture and the urban environment. There have been many detailed studies of aspects of the Victorian city: working-class housing, suburbanisation, the development of transport, railway stations, public houses, town halls and the activities of the building industry have all had their historians. Municipal parks have by comparison received far less attention, although individual parks have been studied, and there is a wealth of information on the royal parks. It is my hope that this book will make a useful contribution to this area. Perhaps one reason for the lack of attention paid by landscape historians to municipal parks lies in the term 'municipal' itself. By the 1870s 'municipal' had become synonymous with lively pride in local powers and their ability to effect positive change. A century or so later, not only have local authorities lost many of those powers, but the connotations of 'municipal' have become almost the antithesis of what they were formerly.

Municipal parks are a form of public park. The term public park implies free and uninhibited accessibility, but this was not necessarily in fact the case. The royal parks are among the best-known public parks in Britain, but only a limited area of Regent's Park in London was accessible to the public for many years. In other public parks, entrance could be by payment of an entry fee, or for only a restricted period. The tendency both during the nineteenth century and more recently has been to use the term public park very loosely and to examine what was implied by it, a detailed examination is made of some early-nineteenth-century examples. It was important to determine how accessible public parks were to the public, in both the short and long term, in order to establish the advantages and disadvantages of the various types of public park and the significance of the municipal park. Only in the municipal parks was the right of access secured in perpetuity and this is why they form the central focus of this book.

The earliest municipal park so far identified dates from the early years of the seventeenth century, but the main development in Britain occurred during the nineteenth century. As the population increased and urban centres expanded, commons, the traditional places for recreation, were enclosed, new buildings spread over the open spaces in and around the towns and cities, the air grew more polluted and opportunities for recreation in fresh green surroundings dwindled. Official recognition of the need for parks dates from 1833 when the Select Committee on Public Walks presented its report to Parliament. Parks would improve the health of those living in cities and provide accessible open space for recreation. Recreation is associated with time when people are free to follow their own inclinations, and the question of 'rational' recreation was one that occupied the minds of many reformers, among whom the park promoters must be included.

Parks provided a source of fresh air, opportunities for financial investment, a means of diffusing social tensions and improving the physical and moral condition of the urban citizens, and an alternative to the public house and the pleasure garden. They were intended for all sections of society and as a meeting ground where the classes could learn from each other. In this process it was tacitly agreed that certain sections of society were more in need of improvement than others. The park promoters had clear ideas regarding 'appropriate' recreation, and the ways in which this was identified influenced the design and use of the parks themselves. The political and social role of parks was reflected in the planting, the buildings, the statues and the activities permitted within the parks, and they concerned park promoters, designers and reformers throughout the century.

The Select Committee on Public Walks provided the first survey of accessible open space in the major towns and cities of England and recommended action for the future. Between 1833 and 1845, when the park movement became recognisable, some important developments occurred. The Select Committee had recommended a park for the East End of London and this recommendation was acted upon. Benefactors came forward with gifts of parks, one of which was designed by Loudon, one of the most important early public park designers. Manchester became the first of the major industrial centres to acquire parks and a trade union instigated a park development. The economic potential of park development was recognised by both a speculative developer and a local authority, and they commissioned Joseph Paxton to design his first public parks. These initiatives are examined in some detail, as they illustrate the reasons for the development of the various types of public park and introduce two of the main protagonists of the park movement, the benefactor and the local authority.

The creation of municipal parks and the preservation of commons was a gradual process in which local and central government, benefactors, entrepreneurs and local communities were at various times involved, as were reformist and reactionary individuals and groups. For much of the nineteenth century local authorities were severely inhibited by the legislation governing the actions they could undertake, and the 'struggle' to acquire municipal parks required much ingenuity. An understanding of the legislation affecting park development is essential to an understanding of the roles of central and local government, the benefactor and the speculative developer;

the main Acts are summarised in Appendix 1. The park movement began to accelerate during the 1840s and continued to do so thereafter. As a result of legislation enacted at the end of the 1850s, the role of the benefactor increased during the 1860s and 1870s, but the local authorities' role in park development was one of significant and growing importance. Despite the legislation which encouraged benefactors and inhibited the actions of local authorities, more parks were created by the latter than by benefactors in every decade of the century, and in 1875 local authorities acquired full powers enabling them to create and maintain parks.

As local authorities gradually acquired the powers necessary for them to confront some of the major urban problems, so their confidence grew and found expression in civic consciousness. This showed itself not only in the acquisition of parks but also in tangible form in the parks themselves. Since my main aim was to identify the national and international factors that were of greatest significance in promoting the park movement as a whole, it was not possible to examine the individual workings of particular councils in any detail. Nor was it possible to distinguish between the composition of councils in different cities, or in different decades, without losing sight of those factors which provided the main impetus to the movement.

The large number of municipal parks that came into being during the course of the century made it quite unrealistic to attempt to analyse them all in any detail. In order to establish the pattern of park development as a whole during the century, it was important to record the chronology of the main parks developed and to identify the first municipal parks created by the major urban centres. To do this, contact was made with all those towns that had populations of over 25,000 in 1851, in order to find out the date of their first municipal park, its size, the designer and the method by which it was acquired. In addition further information was gained from *The Builder*, the *Gardeners' Chronicle*, the *Illustrated London News* and other key periodicals. The results are summarised in Appendix 2.

After establishing the broad historical framework of municipal park development, my aim was to identify the main influences, both national and international, on the parks themselves. In order to evaluate the significance of park design over a period it was necessary to examine particular aspects such as park layout, architecture, commemorative statuary and planting. Parks were texts which were sometimes subtly coded and at other times more explicit, and in order to deconstruct these texts it was necessary to examine their various components separately. Similar theories underpinned park design, whether it was for a private patron or for a public park, and the major designers worked in both areas. John Claudius Loudon, Joshua Major, Joseph Paxton, William Barron and many others faced the challenge of catering for large numbers of people in public park design, and of providing for a wide range of activities, often within a restricted budget. They therefore had to confront very different problems from those encountered in the design of private estates. The contribution of the major public park designers and those who trained with them are examined in the context of the main changes occurring in design and the problems posed by an increasing number of sports facilities.

Lodges, pagodas, palmhouses, boathouses, refreshment rooms, toilets and shelters provided a variety of facilities and extended the use of the parks in cold and bad weather. They reflected a range of architectural styles, new developments in technology and the concern with 'appropriate' forms of entertainment. Their scale and siting was generally small and informal, but there were important exceptions to this. The precedent for most park buildings lay in earlier architectural developments, but one building type, the bandstand, came to be particularly associated with public parks and for this reason its evolution is examined in some detail.

Parks provided space for marking important events. The erecting of statues, commemorative buildings, drinking fountains and sundials provided opportunities for marking a visit by Queen Victoria, and for celebrating the achievements of local heroes, the civic pride of the local authority and the local and national pride of the citizens. The ways in which this was achieved gave each park its special identity, strengthened the links between local government or local dignitaries and the local park, and provided texts for the enlightenment of the local community. The main influences on the planting of municipal parks were undoubtedly the lavish floral displays at the Crystal Palace Park, Sydenham, and the subsequent development of carpet-bedding. Indeed vivid floral displays and carpet-bedding became as closely identified with parks in the public mind as did bandstands, although both had their critics. These techniques of planting were very labour-intensive, but there were important practical reasons for them that related to the problem of growing plants in an atmosphere that was generally hostile to all living things. Appendix 3 lists the trees and shrubs recommended in the 1880s for their ability to withstand the atmosphere of London.

The activities allowed in the parks reflected prevailing attitudes and the ways in which the benefits of parks were identified, while the park regulations made clear the pastimes that were permitted and those that were not. The use of parks on special holidays has been well documented, as has anti-social behaviour, but the everyday uses for relaxation and playing were poorly documented and the park user's voice was rarely heard. Nevertheless it is possible to gain a picture of how well the parks were used and the evident enjoyment they provided. Among the popular activities were listening to the band, and for males playing sports, but it was only towards the end of the century that sports for women were introduced. Permitted sports tended to be those with middle-class connotations and football was permitted only later in the century.

The Victorian park developed in the context of an expanding population, a changing economy and the growth of transport facilities. The physical impact on the major urban centres showed itself in the changing pattern of use as the century progressed. In central urban areas, manufacturing and residential building were increasingly replaced by commercial and municipal activities and the new retailing techniques which resulted eventually in the department stores. Towards the end of the century it was increasingly recognised that large parks did not solve the problem of access to open space for those living in the densest urban areas. The creation of small recreation grounds and the transformation of disused burial grounds into open space for recreation indicated that a major change in public opinion regarding open space had indeed taken place. During the course of these changes the need for better town planning became evident, and the development and location of parks contributed towards the recognition of that need.

Parks had a role to play in overcoming the worst excesses of urban expansion. Their role as a barrier between different types of housing, their relationship to zoning, and their function as a focus for suburban development, were important to the development of town planning and to the loosening of the texture of the urban environment. These points are referred to, however a comprehensive survey of the contribution of parks to town planning clearly lay outside the scope of this study. To establish the precise nature of the contribution of parks to town planning would involve the analysis of which classes were housed next to any particular park under discussion, and the extent that parks protected middle-class properties from lower-class encroachment. Similarly the role of the park as a barrier, or as a centre for suburban development, would need to be debated with reference to specific places in order to establish the precise nature of their contribution to town planning. These points are referred to, but a comprehensive survey was beyond the scope of this study.

In general, parks in Britain were created as isolated elements, lungs and oases of green, which contrasted with their urban surroundings, but there were exceptions to this. Recognition of the role that parks could play in town planning was implied in H. P. Horner's suggestion for a belt of garden or parkland to prevent the continued urban spread of Liverpool (see p. 58). In Manchester, the importance of the positioning of parks and their relation to the town as a whole was evident in the initial suggestion for the creation of four parks located on the four sides of the town. The recommendation that parks should be created in London to serve the populations of the East End and south of the river was another similar example, though none of these could compare with the replanning of Paris. When this took place under Napoleon III, public parks formed an integral part of the new developments undertaken by Baron Haussmann, Préfect of the Seine (1863–9). It was in this period that the Bois de Boulogne was remodelled and new parks such as the Bois de Vincennes and the Buttes-Chaumont were created. In America the development of public parks had been largely inspired by the British example and by F. L. Olmsted's visits to Birkenhead Park. Although Central Park, New York (1858), his first design and America's first public park, was created as an isolated park, thereafter Olmsted's major contribution lay in the development of the parkway system and the role that parks could play in new town development.

The park movement developed as a result of changing economic and social factors and a legislative framework that gradually gave local authorities powers to confront some of the major problems of urban living: a situation that has been reversed today, with local authority powers becoming increasingly restricted and power more centralised. Some of the parks discussed in this book have disappeared, but most of them are still in existence, although many have been altered. They are now under a number of threats, for what is happening to our parks today reflects what is happening in society, just as it did during the park movement. Some of today's problems stem from the period of the Second World War when, as part of the war effort, park gates and railings were removed, allotments were introduced and parks became the sites for gunnery emplacements and barrage balloons. To this day there are parks that are without their gates and railings and, with no method of securing them after dark, they remain a target for anti-social acts.

After the Second World War the influence of modernism, suspended during the war, extended not only to architecture and town planning but also to parks. Massed displays of flowers and ornate planting were replaced by the equivalent of clean-sweep planning, bold sweeps of grass. This had the added advantage of being cheaper and easier to maintain, but was much less interesting from the park visitor's point of view. This trend away from horticulture was reinforced by the Bains Report (1972) which merged local authority Parks Departments with Recreation Services, Swimming Pools and the Arts, so that instead of having a separate budget park managers then had to compete with these other areas.

Shortages of funds now mean that staff are reduced to the minimum and upkeep presents a continual problem. The results can be seen in the litter, the deteriorating fabric of park buildings and the fountains that no longer work, yet research indicates that evident neglect tends to promote vandalism, whereas a continually cared-for environment tends to suffer less. Since there are so few park keepers and parks are no longer used by large numbers of people, the potential for anti-social activities has increased. The homeless, who must have somewhere to go, constitute a further problem, for if they make a park their 'home' other users tend to keep away.

These parks still have a purpose to serve, for access to open space and greenery is still essential. The ecology movement and the importance of nature conservation have brought new levels of awareness of the role that urban parks can play today, and some local authorities are putting aside wild areas in them, to provide a natural habitat for plants and animals. These are no longer seen as isolated pockets, but are being linked to verges, in order to provide connections between a number of such wild areas. Parks need to cater for the demands of today and deliberate strategies need to be developed in order to encourage more people to use their local parks, for increased numbers will help to ensure that they are safe and enjoyable places to be in. Every park needs its local friends, community-based groups, to put forward ideas for making them attractive places and a thriving natural habitat. If they are not used and if they do not find a satisfactory role in the urban environment of the next century, we may lose them permanently. Today's short-term philosophy that everything must be self-financing has led to attempts to privatise municipal parks by seeking to turn some of them into theme parks, while in Regent's Park the number of villas is being increased. It is my hope that this analysis of Victorian park development will go some way towards alerting people to the real significance of the contribution that parks have made and will provide a signpost for their future.

CHAPTER ONE

Public parks and municipal parks

> The Park rose in terraces from the railway station to a
> street of small villas almost on the ridge of the hill. From
> its gilded gates to its smallest geranium-slips it was brand-
> new, and most of it was red. The keeper's house, the
> bandstand, the kiosks, the balustrades, the shelters – all of
> these assailed the eye with a uniform redness of brick and
> tile which nullified the pallid greens of the turf and the
> frail trees. The immense crowd, in order to circulate,
> moved along in tight processions, inspecting one after
> another the various features of which they had read full
> descriptions in the *Staffordshire Signal* – waterfall, grotto,
> lake, swans, boat, seats, faience, statues – and scanning
> with interest the names of the donors so clearly inscribed
> on such objects of art and craft as from diverse motives
> had been presented to the town by its citizens ... The
> town was proud of its achievement, and it had the right to
> be; for, though this narrow pleasance was in itself
> unlovely, it symbolised the first renaissance of the longing
> for beauty in a district long given up to unredeemed
> ugliness.
>
> Arnold Bennett,
> *Anna of the Five Towns*, 1902

The creation of the municipal park has been seen as a prime
example of the Victorian 'aptitude for passionate reform' and as an
attempt to improve the physical, moral and spiritual condition of the
urban dweller.[1] Protected from the realities of its city surroundings by
gates and railings, it represented an ideal landscape in which the air
was clean, the spirit was refreshed by contact with nature, and the
body was renewed by exercise. Yet such a view is necessarily an
incomplete one for it does not identify the nature of the improvements, nor how they were viewed by the improvers and the benefici-

aries, nor does it tell us how they would be achieved. While the municipal park represented an ideal landscape, it was at the same time a real landscape set in an urban environment and used by real people in various ways.

Municipal parks are public parks, but these were not always as accessible to the public as their name would imply. In order to identify municipal parks to which there was free access, it is important to distinguish between the various forms of public park, but in practice it is not always easy to do so. Landscape gardeners used particular terms precisely, but the park promoters did not. The latter used the terms public park, garden and walk in a variety of ways, so the type of open space and its accessibility could not be deduced from the terms they used. John Claudius Loudon, the landscape gardener and one of the most influential writers on the subject in the first half of the nineteenth century, defined public walks as promenades or roads among trees 'and such other verdant scenery as the situation may afford, heightened and rendered more interesting by art'. As examples he cited the walks in Oxford and public squares.[2] Today the term public walk has fallen out of use, but it persisted for a large part of the nineteenth century: the Public Health Act 1875[3] used it, despite the fact that a Public Parks Act[4] had been passed in 1871.

Loudon defined parks as enclosed spaces of considerable extent such as Hyde Park, 'varied by wood, water, rocks, building, and other objects'. They were interspersed by roads and walks, grazed by sheep, deer and cattle, and 'without flowers or shrubs'. He subdivided gardens into scientific gardens, landscape gardens, gardens for recreation and refreshment, and gardens for burial. Their common feature was that they were enclosed and the turf was kept mown, rather than being grazed. At the time that he was writing, and indeed before he died in 1843, there were insufficient examples of municipal parks for him to attempt a definition.

Public access to open space depends on the status of the space. Normally there is no access to privately owned space and only restricted access to semi-public spaces. Semi-public space includes areas such as the squares of London and other major centres which were normally open only to the residents of the houses facing them, who were key-holders.[5] Bloomsbury Square in London, built for the Earl of Southampton in 1661, Brunswick Square, Grosvenor Square and many other eighteenth-century squares added new neighbourhoods to the city, each with their own semi-public open space.[6] Pleasure gardens, zoos, botanic gardens and, eventually, golf courses, were other forms of semi-public space where entry was normally by payment of a fee, or by membership of a club or society.

ROYAL PARKS

The best-known examples of public parks in Britain are probably the royal parks. Hyde Park has been opened to the public since the 1630s; St James's Park and Green Park were formed by Charles II; and Regent's Park opened in the early years of the nineteenth century. Regent's Park was designed by John Nash between 1811 and 1826, and because of its size (142 hectares), the prestige of the designer and its location in London, it became an important influence on the subsequent development of municipal parks. Figure 1 shows the areas of the park accessible to the public in 1841. The villas in the park were surrounded by trees and shrubs so that they would not be visible to each other and the whole park appeared to 'belong' to each villa. Here Nash was applying the theory of appropriation, or apparent extent, which Humphry Repton, Nash's erstwhile partner, considered to be one of the major sources of pleasure in landscape gardening.[7]

Regent's Park was designed in conjunction with the housing in and around it, for the profitability of the development was as important as beauty, health and convenience. Nash's figure for the potential income from the development was more than double that of the other competing proposal and undoubtedly helped him to secure the commission. This income did not increase as rapidly as Nash had implied it would and by 1826, when the building of the villas in the park was brought to a halt, the income from the ground rents was so far below Nash's estimate that he was questioned by the Commissioners. He recommended that they 'restrain the anxiety for *immediate* Revenue, to give opportunity of selecting a higher class of tenants, remembering, that as the Park increases in beauty it will increase in value, and that the first occupiers will stamp the character of the neighbourhood'.[8] Regent's Park was designed as a public park but it was only gradually opened to the public. At first the roads in the park were open and a contemporary writer noted that the park was bright and animate 'at the fashionable airing hours of the day', indicating in that

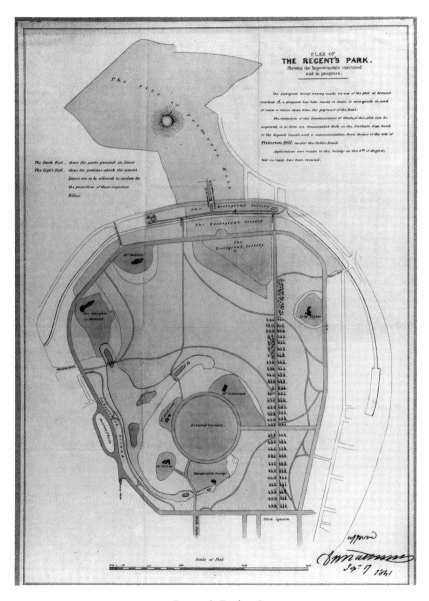

1 Regent's Park, 1841

The dark areas around the buildings were granted on lease and the lessees were allowed to enclose the lighter areas surrounding these 'for the protection of their respective Villas'. The remaining areas were freely open to the public, apart from the Botanical Gardens and the grounds of the Zoological and Toxophilite Societies.

phrase the type of user.[9] When Peter Josef Lenné the German land-scape gardener visited England in 1823, he thought Regent's Park and the other London parks inferior to those on the Continent and intended more for the grazing of cattle than the enjoyment of people. There were no places for refreshment and amusement in Regent's Park, and no seats or shelters for the pedestrian in any of the parks except St James's Park and Kensington Gardens. To enjoy the London parks 'it is necessary to be a man of fortune, and take exercise on horseback or in a carriage'.[10] Lenné also noticed the fences surrounding most of the London parks and squares and contrasted these with the unfenced public parks in Germany.

In 1835 the eastern side of Regent's Park and a strip next to the canal were opened, forming some thirty-six hectares, and in 1841 another thirty-eight hectares were opened. The restricted areas at that date were the surroundings to the villas, a strip of land in front of the southern terraces and the grounds of the Royal Botanic Society (founded 1838), the Toxophilite Society, and the Zoological Society (founded 1824).[11] The main activities in those parts of the park that were open to the public were walking, riding and driving in carriages, and it was not until c.1860 that a gymnasium was opened in the northern corner. In the summer this was crowded with youths and boys and 'A person who seems to have been an old soldier acted as superintendent: before dark the ropes and poles were taken down, and the company soon dispersed.'[12]

Regent's Park only gradually became more accessible to the public. It was not until it became so that it could really qualify as a public park. It was initiated as a royal park and remains one to this day. Its importance to later urban park design lay in the economic lessons to be learnt from the development of a park combined with housing, and in its successful adoption of some of Repton's principles of landscape gardening.

The other London park designed and laid out by John Nash in 1828, as part of the whole Regent's Park and Regent Street scheme, was St James's Park. This was also a royal park, but it was not a new one, for it had been fully accessible and used by the public since the time of Charles II. Indeed both Samuel Pepys and John Evelyn referred to it.[13] Nash's improvements included forming a lake with an island in it, in place of the narrow canal, and picturesque planting of trees and shrubs.

LEASING AND THE ROYAL VICTORIA PARK, BATH

Another way in which public parks could be created was by leasing land, but the problem in this case was the future of the park once the lease had run its full term. The Royal Victoria Park, Bath, which opened in 1830, was the first park to be named Victoria Park. 'Very opportunely for the committee ... her present Majesty, then the youthful Princess Victoria ...' arrived in Bath in October 1830 with HRH Duchess of Kent and they agreed to open the park and name it.[14]

The main reasons for the development of Royal Victoria Park appear to have been economic ones, although they took a very different form from those of Regent's Park. Bath was a spa and two of the tradespeople were concerned 'to make Bath a place of summer residence as well as of winter resort'. The town lacked shady walks and drives and a park would add to its attractions. The site chosen lay to the south-west of the town where common fields, belonging to the freemen of Bath, had been the subject of 'trespass-paths' and their value had as a result depreciated. At that time there was such 'stagnation of trade that one third of the houses in Bath were uninhabited' and even in the best streets there were 'two or three good shops together' which were unlet, and the economic climate was not right for building on the land.

Four hectares were laid out in 1830, at a cost of £7,000–£8,000 which was raised by subscription. The Corporation gave £100 towards the initial outlay and agreed to pay £100 per year for expenses, an undertaking which they carried out until 1835, when the Municipal Corporations Act made such payments illegal. The Corporation also erected a gothic farmhouse (Fig. 2, No. 3). The layout of the park was extremely simple, consisting mainly of a drive, with a belt of trees (25,000 were planted) around the periphery of the site, and various walks crossing the park. It was open 'to all classes, as none are excluded from participating in its benefits'.

Royal Victoria Park was a public park, but not a municipal park, for the Corporation did not own the land but rented it. Its leasehold status would have been for a specific number of years and after the termination of the lease the use of the land for recreation could not be assured. In this instance the recreational use of the land was preserved

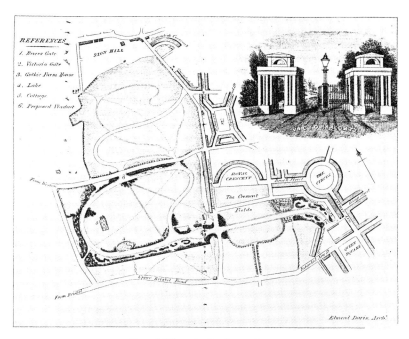

2 Royal Victoria Park, Bath, c.1831.

and Bath still has its Royal Victoria Park, but other later leasehold parks were less fortunate.

MUNICIPAL PARKS

The municipal park is a public park and its advantage over all other forms of public park is that complete control rests with the local authority and the unalienable right of public access for recreation is secured. The term implies that it was an achievement of the municipal corporation and should be associated with the passing of the Municipal Corporations Act 1835,[15] but municipal parks were developed in certain urban centres long before the nineteenth century. The first municipal park so far identified was formed in Exeter, in the early seventeenth century: 'in 1612, Northern-hay [was] levelled, and a pleasant walk made thereon, and upon the Mount over against Gallants-Bower, seats or benches of timber were erected, and at the Cities charge'.[16] The site of two hectares adjacent to the castle walls, seems to have been cared for by the city continuously since that date and the park is still in use today. Its high position on the castle mound provides an excellent view over the northern part of the city. Others were created in Shrewsbury, in Leicester and elsewhere. In Shrewsbury a public walk, known as The Quarry, was laid out along the banks of the Severn in 1719. This area of eight hectares was open to the public at all times and was kept up by the Corporation.[17] In Leicester the New Walk, nine metres wide, was formed by the Corporation in 1785 as a 'promenade for the recreation of the inhabitants'.[18] These, however, were isolated examples, with no discernable pattern to their distribution.

LOCAL GOVERNMENT

Municipal means 'pertaining to the local self-government or corporate government of a city or town' and dates from 1600 according to the *Oxford English Dictionary*. The Municipal Corporations Act 1835 recognised the weakness of existing local government and marked the beginnings of a formal structure for it. The four different types of institution responsible for local government in the 1830s were the Municipal Corporation, the Improvement Commission, which existed in most large towns, the Manorial Court and the Surveyors of Highways. The latter were to be found in every parish or town in the country, but the existence of the other three institutions depended on the local historical background. The Act gave a more liberal constitution to those boroughs that came within its terms, but because of the way in which local government institutions had developed, major towns such as Manchester and Birmingham lay outside the scope of the Act, and they did not achieve municipal incorporation until 1838.[19]

The new Act did not necessarily make the new corporations more effective, for the divided responsibility between the Corporation and the Improvements Commissioners persisted. The latter could hand over their powers, but were not obliged to do so and were in no hurry to end their existence. Birmingham's Town Council in 1838 had less power than the Street Commissioners and it was not until 1851, when the electors were assured that the town could 'be efficiently governed at much smaller cost' by the Corporation, that they handed over their powers.[20]

Despite the weak state of local government, the success of Bath illustrated that it was possible for towns to acquire open spaces for public parks. A few municipal parks were created in the first half of the nineteenth century and Moor Park, Preston, 1833, is the first so far identified, to be formed in an industrial town. The main development of municipal parks, however, occurred in the second half of the century and there are many reasons for this delay, despite the early recognition of the need for parks.

MOOR PARK, PRESTON

Preston Moor lay to the north of the town and was in the 1830s deemed to be in a 'neglected and unprofitable condition'. In 1833 the *Preston Chronicle* published an article on 'The Intended Inclosure and Improvement of Preston Moor', showing the form of the new proposals whereby the area 'shall be so improved and appropriated as to become every way serviceable to the community',[21] a by no means unusual way of justifying enclosure. Preston Moor's proposed enclosure differed from others in that it was undertaken by the Borough Council, who claimed that as various Royal Charters in the Middle Ages had granted the Moor to the burgesses collectively, the Council, acting as a body representing the burgesses, was entitled to make bye-laws controlling the Moor. As it had never been common land, or available for use by anyone except the burgesses, there was no necessity for an Act of Parliament to enclose it. There were some objections to this line of reasoning, but the decision of the Council was not overturned.

Part of the Moor was to be laid out in public walks and drives and part 'if not the whole of the remainder will be made productive of revenue to be devoted to the general improvement of the town'. The few burgesses who had rights of pasturage might not find the new arrangements altogether satisfactory, as their profits would be reduced. The poor freemen, who had never enjoyed such advantages, and the rest of the townspeople would find the new arrangement gave them a 'pleasing source of recreation, and the whole community would benefit from the revenues arising from the improved occupation of the land'. The author of the article was well aware of the Report of the Select Committee on Public Walks for he stated that a suggestion similar to the present design was made 'only a few months ago, when the subject of public walks was before parliament . . .'. The improvements showed roads 'to be laid out in a tasteful manner, so as

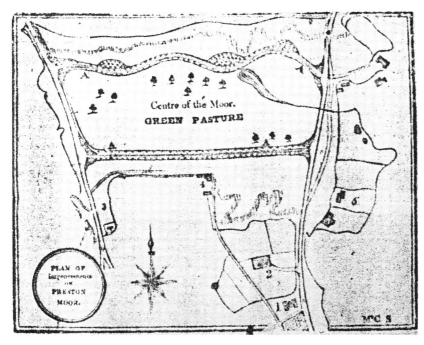

Centre of the Moor.
GREEN PASTURE

PLAN OF
Improvements
ON
PRESTON
MOOR.

3 Intended improvements to Preston Moor, 1833.

to form an agreeable resort for pedestrians, as well as riders', rides planted with trees on either side and a broad gravel way suitable for carriages towards the centre of the moor (Fig. 3). The forty-hectare pasture would, as a result of these improvements, support a larger number of cattle than the present 100 hectares and a pond for the cattle would provide 'a pleasing adjunct to the scenery'. The whole area would be laid out to view, with the cattle contained by a ha-ha, and as the building sites around the moor would be very desirable, 'neat and fancy cottages may be expected to spring up'. On the east side of the moor the Council planned to reserve some eight hectares, for use as a public cemetery or botanic garden. By 1835 the walks, rides and drives had been laid out, Moor Park Avenue on the south side had been planted, a road had been built on the north side to form a boundary, the serpentine walk had been formed and two lodges built on the south and west approaches. The lodge on the north side was built the following year, 1836.[22] The design of Moor Park at that date was not very sophisticated, but it provided a 'pleasing source of recreation' which included walking, riding, driving and playing various games.

19

The main factors influencing the development of Moor Park, Preston, Royal Victoria Park, Bath and Regent's Park were economic ones. These parks illustrate some of the ways in which the term public park was applied: Regent's Park was, and is, a royal park to which the public had gradually increasing access; Royal Victoria Park, Bath was a public park leased by the Corporation of Bath for a specific number of years; and it was only at Moor Park, Preston that the unalienable right of access of the public was assured. Action to secure it took place in 1833, the year which saw the first official recognition of the problem of open space for recreation.

CHAPTER TWO

The need for parks

The aim of the Report of the Select Committee on Public Walks (*SCPW*), 1833[1] was to establish what open space was available for public use in the major towns and to recommend local and national action to ensure adequate provision in the future. Although economic factors had provided the main impetus for the development of the early nineteenth-century parks, they were not stressed in the Report. Its main emphasis was on the physical need for open space and the 'problem' of working-class recreation. The Report was chaired by R. A. Slaney and it was the only one, of all those produced during the century, to focus solely on public walks. Slaney's contribution to the promotion of parks was probably one of the most sustained and effective of all those who were working in this area. Not only did he bring the problem to Parliament's attention in 1833, but some twenty-five years later he was also responsible for promoting the Recreation Grounds Act 1859,[2] an important piece of legislation aimed at stimulating the provision of parks. Slaney had entered Parliament in 1826 as Member for Shrewsbury and had earlier given some indication of where his interests lay in *An Essay on the Beneficial Direction of Rural Expenditure*.[3] This included sections on places of amusement 'for the labouring classes', and on the advantages of public walks and gardens, but was directed at rural rather than urban conditions.

THE PHYSICAL NEED

Until towns had grown considerably there was little physical need to set aside open space specifically for recreation. The existing open spaces of the town square, the market place and the churchyards, remained from medieval times, and most towns were small enough for adjacent spaces such as commons and wasteland to be accessible.

In the mid eighteenth century approximately one person in five lived in a town of any size and the population of England and Wales was of the order of six million. By the beginning of the nineteenth century London was the largest city, with a population of over one million, and other urban centres were growing rapidly. Manchester, Liverpool, Birmingham and Bristol all had, by 1801, populations of over 60,000. Fifty years later the figures for Manchester and Liverpool had reached nearly 400,000, Birmingham was well over 200,000 and 1851 marks the point when the population became equally divided between town and country dwellers. By that date it had reached 18 million.[4] During the second half of the century this population expansion continued and by the time of the census of 1911 it had reached thirty-six million. By that date town dwellers formed 80.1 per cent of the population.

Table 1. *Populations of the major urban centres and resorts (in thousands)*

Cities	1801	1851	1881
Bristol	61	137	307
Birmingham	71	233	401
Leeds	53	172	309
Liverpool	82	376	553
Manchester and Salford	89	367	517
Sheffield	46	135	285
London	1,088	2,491	3,881
Resorts			
Bath	33	54	52
Blackpool	–	3	14
Brighton	7	66	108
Southend-on-Sea	–	–	8

Figures for the period 1801–51 are for the area of towns in 1851 as nearly as possible. The figures for 1881 are those shown in the census of that year (B. R. Mitchell and P. Deane, *Abstract of British Historical Statistics*, 1962).

During this period there was also a marked growth in the smaller towns associated with pleasure resorts. Some, like Bath, which had become well established in the eighteenth century, continued to grow during the first half of the nineteenth century and then gradually declined, but a phenomenon new to the nineteenth century was the growth of the seaside resort. Brighton had a population of 7,000 in 1801 and by 1881 its population stood at 108,000. Other seaside resorts such as Blackpool or Southend-on-Sea grew from virtually nothing at the beginning of the century to populations of 14,000 and 8,000 respectively by 1881. The rate of growth of many of these resorts was greater than that sustained by the major manufacturing and commercial centres.[5]

With the population expansion, the growth of the urban centres and the enclosure of commons, open space for recreation became less accessible. According to a critic writing at the end of the eighteenth century, 'The town of Liverpool affords no walks or amusements in its vicinity, commerce alone appears to engage the attention of the inhabitants.'[6] In Manchester before 1820 there had been many open spaces close to the town centre which everyone could use, and around the town there were fine fields with many footpaths. At that date it was still possible to walk in a circle 'seldom greater than a radius of two miles from the Exchange' and hardly ever meet a busy road. The foundation in 1826 of the Manchester Society for the Preservation of Ancient Footpaths indicates how much these were prized.[7]

COMMONS AND RECREATION

Commons were the traditional places of recreation. Most common land originated as wastelands of the manor, with ownership of the soil vested in the lord of the manor. In the course of time adjoining landowners and their tenants acquired rights such as digging turf, cutting gorse and bracken, and grazing cattle and sheep. Commoners' rights could not be used for sale or profit and because ownership was not absolute, these rights prevented the lord of the manor from selling, enclosing, cultivating or building on the land unless he applied to do so by Act of Parliament. With the growth of population, commons in and near towns were used increasingly for recreation, but that use was not recognised, or protected by law.[8] Recreation was reconcilable with commoners' rights, but the profit to the commoners tended to decrease as a result. Expanding towns also brought increases in land values and in that situation legal rights became important. If the commons were enclosed commoners received no compensation and the townspeople lost their traditional places for recreation.

> The Law locks up the man or woman
> Who steals the goose from off the Common,
> But lets the greater robber loose
> Who steals the Common from the goose.[9]

Fairs, religious meetings, election meetings and a variety of sports took place on commons. In Nottingham, which by the mid 1840s was one of the most densely populated urban centres, 'almost every other man is a cricket-player'. At 5.00 a.m. 'innumerable parties' played cricket in the beautiful meadows surrounding the town, 'and why? Because there is no other town in the kingdom, perhaps, that offers so many advantages in having open spaces in the immediate vicinity of the town.'[10] Those who held rights over the land surrounding Nottingham and wished to retain them used the importance of commons as recreation space as part of their argument to prevent enclosure. If the land was built over, people would no longer be able to use it for recreation; enclosure nevertheless took place in 1845.[11]

Kennington Common, London, one of the many London commons, had provided a place for crowds to gather and listen to popular preachers since the mid eighteenth century. During the early part of the nineteenth century it became a place of assembly for the growing working-class movements and candidates for the first election after the Reform Act 1832 were nominated there. In 1833 the SCPW recommended that the Common could become a park for the south of London, but nothing came of this suggestion. At that date, some 500 tenants of Kennington Manor, owned by the Duchy of Cornwall, had the right to pasture horses and cattle, but by mid century it was far from presenting a delightful rural scene. The grass was 'trodden and soiled by a troop of cows', and the ditch around the common received the waste from the nearby vitriol factory, as well as 'constant contributions from unmentionable conveniences attached to a line of low cottage erections'. It was also the cemetery of 'all the dead puppies and kittens of the vicinity. Their decaying carcases may be seen . . . in all the green and purple tints of putrefaction.'[12] Despite all this, and for the want of anywhere better, the common was used for recreation and on summer days there were numerous games of cricket.

Political meetings continued to be held on Kennington Common, the most famous being held on 10 April 1848, when the supporters of the National Charter, numbering some 25,000, met there. The Char-

4 Chartist meeting, 1848, Kennington Common, with the vitriol factory responsible for polluting the ditch, in the background.

tists formed a procession to carry their petition to Parliament, but only a few delegates were allowed through to Westminster[13] (Fig. 4). How much that particular event inspired the Government to take action to transform the Common into a park, is difficult to say. In 1841 another site for a park in the south of London was proposed, then two years later a plan was put forward to build an ornamental lake and private villas around Kennington Common in a scheme that was similar to that at Regent's Park. Nothing came of that proposal either, and it was not until 1851 that the idea of turning the Common into a park was revived – three years after the Chartist gathering.[14]

Between 1750 and 1850 enclosure by means of private Acts increased.[15] Part of the land was ploughed up to add to the country's productive powers, part of it went to increase the private parks of the lords of the manor and part of it was built on. Whether there really was a gain, was questioned by William Cobbett who wrote of Horton Heath, a common of some sixty hectares:

The cottagers produced from their little bits, in food for themselves, and in things to be sold at market, more than any neighbouring farm of 200 acres

25

... I learnt to hate a system that could lead English gentlemen to disregard matters like these! That could induce them to tear up 'wastes' and sweep away occupiers like those I have described! Wastes indeed! Give a dog an ill name. Was Horton Heath a waste? Was it a 'waste' when a hundred, perhaps, of healthy boys and girls were playing there of a Sunday, instead of creeping about covered with filth in the alleys of a town?[16]

THE SCPW REPORT

The SCPW received evidence of the open space available in London, in towns associated with the major manufacturing industries, and in smaller towns such as Shrewsbury and Norwich, so they were not concerned only with those towns where the factory system was most fully developed, or with the largest urban centres. From this evidence they established that the greatest problems concerning access to open space for recreation occurred in the largest population centres. 'With a rapidly increasing population, lodged for the most part in narrow courts and confined streets, the means of occasional exercise and recreation in the fresh air are every day lessened, and inclosures take place and buildings spread themselves on every side.' Only in the West End of London was there sufficient open space, due to the presence of the royal parks. The situation in Manchester was summed up by Dr J. P. Kay in a letter to the chairman, R. A. Slaney:

at present the entire labouring population of Manchester is without any season of recreation and is ignorant of all amusements, excepting that very small proportion which frequents the theatre. Healthful exercise in the open air is seldom or never taken by the artisans of this town, and their health certainly suffers considerable depression from this deprivation. One reason for this state of the people is, that all the scenes of interest are remote from the town and that the walks which can be enjoyed by the poor are chiefly the turnpike roads, alternately dusty or muddy ... I need not inform you how sad is our labouring population here.[17]

Because the evidence to the Committee did not indicate who was allowed to use the available open spaces, the situation was in fact worse than that presented. The six-hectare Botanic Gardens in Manchester which had opened in 1831, for example, were only open to subscribers who were admitted by ballot.[18] To everyone else 'the brazen gates are closed' and a contemporary wrote:

There is something inconsistent in the rule of an institution which, professing to be established for the enlightenment of our fellow-creatures, is yet forbidden ground for those who most require a participation in its refining influence. Once a year ... the Sunday school children, amounting to several thousands, are permitted to walk through these beautiful grounds; and let it be remembered that on such occasions, not a shrub or flower has been injured ...[19]

Those presenting evidence to the SCPW and other park promoters such as Loudon, saw botanic gardens and cemeteries as examples of public open space and therefore precursors of public parks. They were not concerned with the question of accessibility and so did not differentiate between cemeteries such as the Glasgow Necropolis (1832), which were freely accessible and botanic gardens which generally were not. In Liverpool the Necropolis (1825) and the St James's Cemetery (1829) were 'planted very prettily, and the public are allowed to walk in them very freely', although few did so, but perhaps this was because they were located on the outskirts of the town.[20] By contrast the botanic gardens which opened in this period, such as the Manchester one already mentioned, the Birmingham Botanical Garden, 1831 (J. C. Loudon) and the Sheffield Botanical Garden, 1833 (Robert Marnock) were semi-public spaces with restricted access.

THE CONTINENTAL EXAMPLE

The Committee also included evidence of the public open spaces which had opened on the Continent in the late eighteenth and early nineteenth centuries. The royal parks and gardens of Paris had been opened to the public after the French Revolution. In Germany, the Englischer Garten in Munich had been commissioned by the Elector, Karl Theodor, in 1789 and laid out in 1807 by Friedrich Ludwig von Sckell. The Committee heard that the disused town fortifications of Frankfurt and Magdeburg had provided the opportunity for laying out gardens and promenades, but they seemed unaware that Dorchester's ruined Roman fortifications had been planted with trees and laid out as walks in the early eighteenth century.[21] Magdeburg's park was laid out in 1824 by Peter Josef Lenné, director of the Potsdam gardens, who had visited England the previous year. Lenné particularly noted that the project had been initiated by the municipality of

Magdeburg. 'It is nothing new to me that princes and wealthy private persons should spend large sums on the beautiful art of the garden. But an undertaking of this kind ... by the town authorities, is the first example I have ever encountered.'[22] The Committee concluded that people on the Continent were healthier and more content than English people, because of the existence of these parks, but they made no reference to the comparative rates of industrialisation or urban population growth, or to rates of mortality.[23]

These continental examples provided useful ammunition to the park promoters and when Manchester began to create her parks in 1844, they were again cited as evidence of the benefits that parks could bring. When Mark Philips, MP for Manchester, who had presented evidence to the SCPW, addressed the first public meeting held to raise funds for the Manchester parks, he told them of the continental examples: of the Bruhl terraces (which he called gardens) in Dresden, where the whole population 'enjoy themselves rationally ... all classes mix together', of the former fortifications at Frankfurt, now 'one of the most interesting places of public resort', and of the beautiful promenades formed from the ramparts of Rouen, 'the Manchester of France'.[24]

Others drew attention to certain other lessons that could be learnt from the German example. The Anlage, which had been laid out along the banks of the Rhine by the corporation of the city of Mainz, was free and open to all members of the public every day. 'There are no dogs, or growling keepers at the gate – no surrounding walls coped with broken glass ...', a point that had struck Lenné on his visit to England.[25]

The SCPW Report provided the first general survey of the open space available for public use in the major industrial and commercial centres of England and drew Parliament's attention to the existence of the problem. Although it did not dwell in detail on the effects of enclosure it reinforced the efforts of both J. A. Roebuck and Francis Place in this area. Both were Utilitarians who aimed for 'the greatest happiness for the greatest number', in accordance with Jeremy Bentham's doctrine of Utility. Roebuck recognised that if open space was to be retained for recreation then there must be some limit placed on the activities of speculative builders. He put forward his ideas on open space and town planning in a speech before the Utilitarian Debating Society in 1828: tree-lined boulevards and publicly accessible parks in the towns, and surrounding them commons, maintained by either the state or the local authority, for the benefit of the urban inhabitants.[26] Roebuck was elected Member of Parliament for Bath in 1832 and he used his influence most effectively when the SCPW Report was presented to the House (see Chapter 3).

THE RECREATION 'PROBLEM'

In the early decades of the century, while the physical need for parks was being identified, traditional patterns of recreation had been changing, as indeed they had for some time before the nineteenth century, for they were rooted in an agrarian society. Custom was the feature of small communities and increased mobility had the effect of gradually breaking down rural insularity, while in the new congested cities custom had little place. As the century progressed new forms of recreation became available and the introduction in mid century of cheap fares on the railway extended the horizon in a way that would have been unimaginable in those early decades. Urban growth and enclosure affected the open spaces traditionally associated with popular recreation but the streets still provided possible playing places. The Shrovetide games of football played in the market place and streets of Derby, Kingston-upon-Thames and other places, persisted well into the century[27] despite the Highways Act 1835[28] under which anyone playing football or any other game on the public highway could be fined.

During the 1820s and 1830s there was a growing sense among the middle class that recreation should be associated with improvement: subscription concerts and circulating libraries, for example. Many popular recreations became the target of reformers, moralists and others and the term 'rational recreation' was used to denote those activities that were approved of. The term could imply 're-creation', that is to say, refreshment of the mind and spirit 'necessary for the right development of our being'. There was a clear distinction between rational recreation and those pastimes which involved

throwing off restraint and letting the passions loose ... The more we encourage rational recreation ... the more we lessen sexual licence and its evil consequences, excessive alcohol consumption, the delight in immoral exhibitions, the admiration for torturing animals dependent on us for protection; and above all, the more we diminish the number of human

29

beings that pander to the false pleasures of those who can or will pay for and buy them.

Here rational recreation implied reducing the profit motive. It could also involve investment in education so that people could learn to use their time in creative ways, 'for even the Government cannot be made to see that the cost of a singing master, in the People's education, will be a hundredfold compensated for, by the means it will give the children of doing something better for amusement than pitch and toss, the roaring of obscene songs, and the torturing of little animals'.[29]

One interpretation of rational recreation sees it as an attempt by the middle class to impose their cultural values and thereby achieve social control. Another interpretation sees it in more positive terms as extending cultural experiences more widely, but if this involved middle-class patronage, then it was ultimately a more subtle form of social control.[30] The recreation 'problem' was class specific, as Matthew Arnold indicated in *Culture and Anarchy*. The aristocrats (barbarians), had plenty of room to do what they liked on their estates, that is to say, to hunt, shoot, fish and behave barbarically. The middle class (Philistines), by contrast, were so restricted by their social and religious observances that they had little opportunity for pleasure, and the idea of pleasure for its own sake would in any case have seemed positively sinful. Doing what one liked did not present a problem so long as only the aristocrats and the middle class were involved, but, said Arnold, it 'was getting inconvenient and productive of anarchy now that the populace wants to do what it likes too'.[31] Pleasures which tended to occur on private estates such as the hunting of deer, foxes and hares were successfully ignored by the reformers,[32] while those such as football, which occurred in public places, were increasingly controlled.[33]

THE PUBLIC HOUSE

As urbanisation proceeded and the opportunities for access to open space for recreation for those living in the most congested districts decreased, the public house became an important recreational centre. Together with shops they were among the first local facilities to be provided as towns expanded. In Birmingham in 1848 there was one public house for every 166 inhabitants.[34] In addition to drinking, public houses provided a wide range of facilities: the Star Inn at Bolton, for example, had a museum attached to it as well as a music hall.[35] In Manchester the largest music saloons were the Casino, the Victoria Saloon and the Polytechnic, and entertainment included clog and grotesque dancing, juggling and singing. The Casino catered for some 15,000 people weekly, according to an estimate made in 1853.[36] As well as providing entertainment, public houses provided a meeting place for clubs and for the early trade unions, and on Sundays they were the only places open for recreation. A Frenchman visiting Manchester in 1844 noted that 'The public house is for the operative what the public squares were for the ancients.' Sunday was spent in intoxication because 'bigoted Puritanism . . . is opposed to all innocent recreation . . . the more rigorously the Sabbath is observed, the more frequented are the public houses and the gin shops'.[37] John Finch, an iron merchant of Liverpool, testified to the Select Committee on Drunkenness, making a similar point. 'It is a very absurd thing that on Sunday, especially in Liverpool, all the public houses are open and all the public walks, cemeteries, zoological gardens, and botanical gardens where people might amuse themselves innocently, are closed.'[38] Finch's attitude may have been altruistic, or it may have been influenced by a preference for a sober and diligent workforce.

To social reformers, moralists and those concerned with rational recreation, among whom the park promoters must be included, public houses were seen not only as primary sources of drunkenness, but also as centres of anti-social, if not revolutionary activity, particularly in the late 1830s and the 1840s, the period of Chartist activity. Public houses were patronised almost solely by 'the working class', a term used indiscriminately to include the artisan, the skilled and unskilled labourer, the unemployed and the poor, and they were not frequented by 'neighbours of different ranks'.[39] Consequently there were few opportunities for social contact between the classes, or for reformers to exert their influence.

PLEASURE GARDENS

Semi-public spaces such as botanic and zoological gardens offered few opportunities for social contact between the classes since entry was restricted to members, or by paying an entrance fee. Although entrance to pleasure gardens was not free, their patrons tended to come from a broader cross-section of society. Pleasure gardens opened in London, and in fashionable resorts such as Bath and Cheltenham, during the eighteenth century and the first half of the nineteenth century. Some evolved out of tavern gardens, others were associated with taking the waters, or with tea gardens and all were commercial ventures whose profits came from entrance fees, the sale of alcohol and other refreshments, and their ability to attract customers. It was mainly at night that pleasure gardens came alive and the largest provided complete centres for entertainment with music, drinking, dancing, masquerades, balloon ascents and fireworks.

As the nineteenth century progressed pleasure gardens came under increasing pressure from urban expansion and rising land values. Their fluctuating fortunes also reflected changing patterns of recreation and reformers' attitudes towards it. The entertainment offered by pleasure gardens makes an interesting and dramatic contrast with the pastimes permitted in the new municipal parks. The most famous of all the London pleasure gardens was Vauxhall Gardens (1661) which both John Evelyn and Samuel Pepys visited. By the 1830s its attractions included theatres, supper rooms, walks and gardens, optical illusions and cosmoramas. One of these consisted of a grand moving panorama, 150 metres long and covering some 7,000 square metres of canvas, of views of London, Dover, Brussels and other towns, as seen from the flight of the Nassau balloon. In 1827 a Battle of Waterloo spectacle was added, and in 1839 the gardens were opened twice a week in the mornings for Greek chariot races, Roman races and 'Thessalonian Sports'. By that time it was, according to J. A. Roebuck, 'a scene of disgraceful licentiousness . . . a meeting place for drunkards, pickpockets and prostitutes . . .'[40] By the 1840s Vauxhall was suffering from competition, particularly from Cremorne Gardens in Fulham, and it finally closed in 1859, when the site was let for building.[41]

Cremorne (5 hectares) opened in 1843 and included among its

5 Dancing platform, Cremorne, oil painting by Phoebus Levin.

attractions a 'monster pagoda' surrounded by a circular platform, which could accommodate 4,000 dancers (see Fig. 5). It also featured theatres, a circus, a banqueting hall, an American bowling saloon with American drinks (introduced c.1848), a maze, a gypsies' tent and spacious lawns with flowers and trees. A naval fête staged in 1851 featured a fortress under attack from fourteen ships, one of whose hulls was blown to pieces.[42] Cremorne finally closed in 1877.

As the major industrial centres grew, so pleasure gardens were opened there too. Belle Vue Gardens, Manchester, opened in 1836 and provided a favourite resort for the pleasure seekers of the town and neighbouring districts.[43] Its attractions included luxurious gardens, a zoo and facilities for eating, drinking and dancing. Smaller centres such as Worcester also developed pleasure gardens though in some cases their success was short-lived. Arboretum Gardens, Worcester was acquired by the Worcester Public Pleasure Grounds Co. Ltd. and opened in 1859. The Corporation gave £1,000 towards the costs of laying out the grounds and the public was allowed free access on one day a week, Monday, in return. The Company organised various attractions such as firework shows, tightrope walking and a horticultural show, but the expenses were such that they went into liquidation in 1863. Although various attempts were made to keep the land and make it publicly accessible, these failed and the whole site was sold for building purposes three years later.[44]

BENEFITS OF PARKS

The park promoters, like other reformers, thought that working-class recreations were physically, socially and morally reprehensible. If they were replaced by 'suitable' recreations then many of the 'problems' of working-class behaviour would be solved. The working class would then become thrifty, industrious, docile and moral, in other words like the middle class themselves. 'It has justly been observed that in the same proportion as sources of innocent amusement and healthy recreations are provided for a people, in the same proportion do they become virtuous and happy.'[45] Fears were expressed to the Select Committee on Arts and Manufactures (1836) that if parks were opened to the public then plants would be damaged and destroyed. 'Every nobleman, and every gentleman who allow [sic] people to walk in their gardens find they commit all sorts of indecencies' testified Sir J. D. Paul. When asked by the committee if this had been seen as a problem when St James's Park had opened to the public, he agreed that it had. But when further questioned as to whether the public had 'learned to appreciate the benefit by enjoying it?', he replied 'They are improved.'[46] Not everyone took such a negative view of the public and J. Ashton Yates MP for Liverpool in his evidence to the SCPW told how he had opened his walks along the banks of the Mersey river, which were two and a half miles from the centre of Liverpool, to the public and in twenty years of doing so, had experienced no trouble. No police were on duty, only gardeners.

The SCPW Report noted that if parks were provided there would be 'a better use of the Sunday, and a substitution of innocent amusement at all times for the debasing pleasures now in vogue'[47] (see Fig. 6). Parks would provide a counter attraction to 'the temptations of the tavern and the beerhouse, and their frequent accompaniments of immorality and vice'.[48] Moreover they would reinforce the identity of the family as a unit. Other recreations, particularly those centred on the public house, were, in the park promoters' view, available mainly to the adult male members of the family. Parks would provide

6 View of Victoria Park, London. Watercolour by Joseph Maccoby c.1913.

opportunities for the recreation of all members of the family and so would have a positive role to play in enhancing family togetherness: 'the encouragement of such means of recreation as would afford both fresh air and exercise ... and the institution of public games, museums ... would afford some inducement to the labourer to spend as much time and means with his family as he, in many cases, squanders alone'.[49]

The need for parks was identified in the 1830s against a background of severe social unrest and an increasingly polarising class system between workers and employers. The park promoters clearly saw the creation of parks as part of the political process, indeed according to the SCPW unless parks were provided, 'great mischief must arise'.[50] The Utilitarians thought that the working class saw the nobility and gentry solely as enemies. In the past recognition and respect for class and social order had been fostered by the aristocracy 'mixing' with the lower classes, so they could 'be judged of by speak-

35

ing to the people'.[51] Such contact could occur in parks, and as a result social tensions would be reduced and social harmony promoted. This had the added advantage that sharing recreational experiences was obviously preferable to political power sharing, or to making changes in the economic base of society. This point came over clearly at the large public meeting held in Manchester in 1844, to raise subscriptions for the formation of parks. Mark Philips MP spoke of 'the mutual improvement of all classes' that would result from the opportunities for social contact that parks would provide. All classes would benefit and 'the more they mix with one another ... the more they will understand of one another'.[52] It was generally understood that certain classes were more in need of improvement than others.

At the same meeting, another speaker advocated the introduction of parks, in terms of bread and circuses. It was 'a mere matter of government ... that the more amusements were given to the people, the more contented they were'. Parks would 'conduce to the comfort, health and content of the classes in question' and so provide a safety valve. This view that parks could diffuse class tension and provide a diversion was 'proved' by the reformer, Edwin Chadwick. Chadwick recorded that on the occasion of a holiday given in Manchester to celebrate the Queen's marriage, arrangements were being made for a Chartist meeting 'which greatly alarmed the municipal magistrates'. The Mayor was persuaded to open the zoo, the botanic gardens and the museum 'to the classes who had never before entered them' at the same hour as the meeting, and as a result only 'two or three hundred attended the political meeting' and charges of drunkenness and riot were less than the average.[53] If this action was as effective as Chadwick claimed, it was because those institutions had never, as he said, been opened to the general public before. How effective parks would be when they were accessible all the time was another matter.

In addition to providing a diversion from more pressing problems and fostering respect for class and social order, the SCPW thought that contact between the classes in the parks would promote pride and competition, and hence have a beneficial effect on the country's economy. The cleanliness, neatness and appearance of people would improve because 'a man walking out with his family among his neighbours of different ranks, will naturally be desirous to be properly clothed, and that his wife and children should be also'. This desire, the Committee noted, was similar to that which promoted civilisation and industry, namely the competitive spirit and spirit of pride. An industrious workforce was best promoted by inducement and one of the most powerful inducements was the desire to improve the condition and comfort of the family. So, they argued, the provision of public walks would have a direct effect on the economy of the country, by promoting the spirit of competitiveness. If a small charge was made to the individual or the public, then this would defray the expense of laying out public walks, and the work involved would in addition help to solve the problem of unemployment.[54]

Others disagreed with the whole idea of providing free parks and libraries or 'any kind of [free] amusement for the lower classes ... nothing is more mischievous in the present state of society ... it is a most dangerous principle to introduce'. If the different classes were brought into contact with each other they would make comparisons. The working class would have their feelings of disadvantage reinforced every time they went to a free park or library, and instead of promoting social harmony, social divisiveness would be enhanced: 'as to Peel Park [Salford], I cannot go a dozen yards without seeing the invidious distinction of classes marked out, and the poor man tainted with the boon that is extended to him, which is a very great mischief'.[55] It was in other words advisable for the isolation of the classes to be maintained or more problems might result.

RECOMMENDATIONS

In order to secure public walks 'properly regulated and open to the middle and humbler classes' in the future, the SCPW recommended the removal of certain legal difficulties. As the law then stood, land could not be bequeathed for public use and negotiations involving entailed and corporate property were extremely complex. 'The liberality of individuals, if properly assisted, would provide all that is necessary', and alteration of the law regarding bequests of land would be one way of stimulating such generosity.[56] The SCPW also recommended that when turnpike roads or canals were built near towns above a certain population size, there should be clauses in the relevant Acts to ensure that land up to a breadth of one hundred yards on either side was not built on. This area could provide walks, with trees and seats, and would have the advantage of increasing the value of the adjacent land. The funds could be obtained by public grant, voluntary subscriptions, a low rate, Government assistance, or a combination of all these methods.[57] To improve the facilities for London the SCPW recommended that a park should be formed to serve the East End, and that if Kennington Common was improved it could serve as a park for those living south of the river.

What comes over strongly from the SCPW and the other park promoters is the clear identification of the sector of the population that needed parks most. Although it was important that parks should be available for all, they thought that the poorest people of the community and those who lived in the most densely populated districts had the greatest need. The identification of the social, moral, political and physical benefits which parks could bring proved to be a potent influence on their design and on the entertainments and facilities provided in them. It was, however, some time before the SCPW's recommendations were put into effect.

CHAPTER THREE

Pioneering park development

In the decade following the SCPW Report a number of parks were created but few of them owed a specific debt to the SCPW, and it was not until c.1845 that the park movement became recognisable as such (Appendix 2). In this pioneering period of 1833–45, initiatives important to the developing park movement came from central and local Government, from benefactors and from the community. Parliament took certain rather minimal steps to promote parks generally and it also took action to create parks in London. To promote park development, the SCPW had recommended stimulating 'the liberality of individuals', but before legislation could be introduced to do so, the first benefactors came forward to donate parks in Derby and Sheffield. Norfolk Park, Sheffield (1841), donated by the Duke of Norfolk, was laid out very simply with open spaces for cricket and football and a shady peripheral walk with regularly placed seats,[1] but Derby's design and designer proved more influential. This period saw the successful financial lessons of park development, illustrated at Regent's Park, applied by the speculative developer in Liverpool and by the local authority at Birkenhead. These ventures gave Joseph Paxton his first opportunities for public park design. This period also saw the involvement of the community in park development and Manchester became the first of the major industrial centres to acquire parks, through the 'local exertion and munificence' of its citizens, while the Amicable Society of Wool-sorters of Bradford began developing their pleasure gardens and baths.

PARLIAMENTARY ACTION

The reaction of Parliament to the SCPW Report was influenced by both individuals and groups. James Silk Buckingham, elected MP for

Sheffield in 1832, was among those actively concerned with open space for recreation, and for three years in succession he introduced Bills to establish walks, playgrounds and public baths. Although none was passed his continued pressure was important. In 1833 the influence of the Utilitarians and J. A. Roebuck was much greater than their actual numbers and Roebuck grasped the opportunity presented by the SCPW Report. 'At last we are getting support for our open spaces and trees. I have promises from more than 20 today . . . soon our towns will blossom and the air will be pure.'[2] The anti-enclosure lobby achieved some success with the Enclosure Act 1836,[3] which exempted common fields from enclosure if they lay within a certain radius of large towns (Appendix 1). This was reinforced by Joseph Hume, who proposed that all future Enclosure Bills should make provision for open space for recreation, and this was adopted in a Standing Order of 1839.[4] The ideals of Parliament under the influence of the radicals were high, but the practical achievements in terms of land set aside for recreation were rather small, and in the election of 1837 the radicals were defeated.[5] In 1841 the Government took further action to encourage the provision of public walks and parks near towns by making a grant of £10,000, but because of the restrictions faced by local authorities this was not finally disbursed until 1856.[6]

Although the response to the SCPW Report was favourable, it did not lead to further general action by Parliament until the end of the 1840s, when legislation was passed to promote park development. It did, however, lead to effective local action in 1842, to secure Primrose Hill, near Regent's Park, as an open space[7] and to form Victoria Park to serve the East End of London.[8] Of all the parks that were established in this period, the relationship of Victoria Park to the SCPW was the most direct, for its need had been identified by the SCPW and Bonner's Fields, one of three sites recommended for Victoria Park, was included in the site chosen.[9] Parliament also took the first steps towards forming Battersea Park by authorising a sum of not more than £200,000, in 1846, to form an embankment along the Thames, purchase land and lay out the park. Ten years later Battersea Park opened, after further funds had been granted.[10]

VICTORIA PARK

The poverty and disease of the East End of London had by the 1830s become notorious. The traditional industries such as silk weaving were declining, with poverty and unemployment consequently increasing. At the same time the docks were expanding and the unskilled labour pouring into the area to serve them was creating conditions of massive overcrowding. The statistics recorded by William Farr in his *First Annual Report of the Registrar General of Births, Deaths and Marriages in England 1837–1839*, estimated that the death rate in the East End was twice that of the West End. Farr thought that a park in the East End would not only benefit those living there, but would be more generally beneficial, for epidemics knew no boundaries and his Report reinforced the SCPW's identification of the need for a park to serve this area. Action to secure a park began to take place towards the end of the 1830s when George Frederick Young MP instituted a series of public meetings. At a meeting held by 'public spirited and well-placed gentlemen of Limehouse' it was decided to present a petition to the Queen. The petition of 30,000 signatures was presented to the Queen by the Marquis of Normanby, the Home Secretary, in 1840, and stressed the conditions under which the 400,000 inhabitants of the district lived and the high mortality rate. It then went on to compare these conditions with those of the West End, where due to the 'bounty of your Majesty's predecessors' the public enjoyed the open spaces of the royal parks. Finally the Queen was asked 'to direct that enquiry be made as to the practicality of forming within the Tower Hamlets, a Royal Park ... on a scale commensurate with that of the other Metropolitan Parks:– worthy of bearing the name of your Majesty ...'[11] Funds for the purchase of 110 hectares for 'a Royal Park by the name of Victoria Park' were made available by a Royal Grant from the sale of York House in 1841.[12]

James Pennethorne, Victoria Park's first designer, was architect to the Commissioners of Woods and Forests and had worked with John Nash on Regent's Park in the 1820s, references to which occurred frequently during the development of Victoria Park. Regent's Park had improved the environment for those living nearby, so 'How much more valuable ... must the formation of Victoria Park prove to that mass of the public residing Eastward? – whose occupations are generally of a character most injurious to health, and whose circumstances preclude the possibility of their participation in the advantages so extensively enjoyed by their more wealthy fellow subjects.'[13] The intention behind the development of this park was not only to provide open space for recreation, but also to halt the decline in land values in the district, by building attractive houses in pleasant streets around the park. 'To land and house owners in this eastern district it is of the greatest importance that emigration to the west should be checked, by providing a rational and wholesome place of recreation similar to those enjoyed in the north and western districts.'[14]

Pennethorne recommended locating the park near the Thames, where the population was densest, but a cheaper site to the north, near a less dense population, was chosen.[15] Part of the 1842 purchase included Bonner's Fields, a traditional place for open air meetings and rallies. This was not advanced as an official reason for choosing the site, though it was perhaps implied in the statements presented to the Commissioners, that the expenditure of private capital 'among those through whose labour it had been accumulated ... would produce those many social and political benefits which it is unnecessary to particularize to your Lordships.'[16]

Pennethorne's plans involved the construction of two approach roads to the park, one to the west to link the area to the City, since ease of access would make investment more attractive, the other to the south towards the river. As funds for these roads were not allocated, the building plot did not attract the hoped-for investment, and as they could not be let, they were eventually sold off.[17] With no main approach roads on the London side and the park hidden by blocks of houses, 'Where is Victoria Park, is not an infrequent question, even within 100 yards of the gate!'[18] Nearly a decade later this situation had hardly improved. 'This park has been miserably managed as to approaches; there is really not a respectable road for a vehicle, *even now*, – in 1855.'[19] The main problem was the limited finances allowed for the development of Victoria Park. The Treasury had hoped for a return similar to that at Regent's Park, but the project did not attract sufficient investment, due in part to the lack of funding for the access roads. The difficulties of attracting developers illustrated that a park location attractive to investment was essential if such a project were to succeed and that the successful development of a park with housing could not necessarily be assured.

Victoria Park was a royal park and royal parks may be divided into two types: those that are still royal parks today, for example Regent's Park and Hyde Park, and those that ultimately became municipal parks. The changing status of the latter related to the way in which the local government of London was organised in this period. Royal parks and other crown lands were placed 'in the care of the nation' on the accession of each monarch. Land which provided a source of revenue was managed by the Commissioners of Woods and Forests, and Victoria Park was managed by them until 1854. It then passed to the Commissioners of Works and Public Buildings who had responsibility for royal parks and other crown land that did not provide revenue. In 1855 the Metropolitan Board of Works was formed to replace the old local bodies, such as the vestries, the district boards and the boards of guardians, which had been responsible for the local government of London, but as Victoria Park was a royal park it did not come under their control and expenses for it continued to be borne by the Treasury. This situation continued until 1887 when with the passing of the Public Parks and Works (Metropolis) Act,[20] Victoria Park and the other London parks that had been formed in the interim passed to the Metropolitan Board of Works. In so doing they changed their status from royal parks maintained by the Treasury to that of municipal parks maintained by the rates. The following year, 1888, the London County Council came into being and in 1892 the LCC created its Parks Department and all London parks except the royal parks came under its control.[21]

LOUDON, STRUTT AND DERBY ARBORETUM

While the creation of Victoria Park was directly linked to the recommendations of the SCPW, the donation of Derby Arboretum (1840) seems to have been inspired more by the 1836 Enclosure Act.

The town of Derby was growing fast and Joseph Strutt, the textile manufacturer, decided that as there were no commons or wasteland near Derby that could be set aside as open spaces for recreation 'With a view of further promoting the same objects, I have determined to appropriate a piece of land . . .'[22] The project received wide publicity not only by virtue of the donor's position, but also through the writings of its designer, J. C. Loudon. Loudon's contribution to the theory and practice of landscape gardening is well known, but until recently little has been known about his commitment to social

43

reform.[23] Loudon had been taught by Jeremy Bentham, who remained an important influence, and he became concerned with such issues as education, town planning, working-class housing and clean air. Although he was never in a position to put his ideas into practical effect Loudon wrote letters, petitioned those who were in a position to effect changes and joined the Metropolitan Improvements Society which was set up in 1842. There he met such influential figures as Joseph Hume, Sir Charles Barry and Edwin Chadwick. Above all, it was as editor of the *Gardeners' Magazine*, the *Magazine of Natural History* and the *Architectural Magazine* that he had a forum from which to promote his concerns.

In *An Encyclopaedia of Gardening*, 1822, Loudon began advocating the creation of public open spaces in Britain. He observed that almost every town of consequence on the Continent had its promenades for pedestrians and for those on horseback, but British towns did not and he recommended that London should have a circular promenade extending from Hyde Park to Greenwich Park in the south-east. This promenade could cross the river at Greenwich, by means of a cast iron colonnade, at the site of the present pedestrian tunnel.[24] In 1829, Loudon joined in the protest against the proposal to enclose the common land of Hampstead Heath, on the north side of London, and in 'Hints for Breathing Places' published in the *Gardeners' Magazine* in the same year, he proposed that provision for public open space be made in all enclosure bills. This was some six years before Hume succeeded in his amendment. Loudon also proposed that London should have a series of green belts one mile wide, alternating with built-up zones of a similar width and stretching as far as the sea.[25] In 1831 Loudon was invited to prepare designs for the Birmingham Botanical Gardens and some four years later he was invited to design his first public park in Gravesend, Kent. The Terrace Garden, Gravesend, which he described in 'Design for a Public Garden, made for an English Corporate Town', was an attempt to show what could be achieved on a site 'not much exceeding three acres, and very unfavourably circumstanced, at the least expense', although it overlooked the river on one side.[26] Loudon created interest within the garden by increasing the contours of the ground and by the planting. The walks were made as long as possible, within such a restricted space, and the views varied along them. Figure 7 shows a walk (to the right of the entrance) which made a complete circuit of the garden,

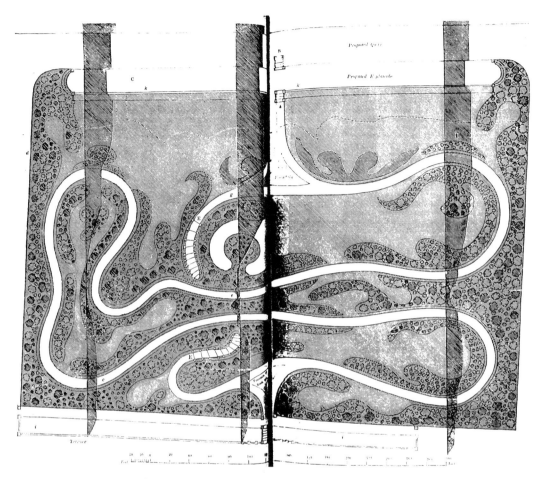

7 J. C. Loudon, Terrace Garden, Gravesend, plan 1836.

while the other walk passed under it, through a twenty metre tunnel to the esplanade. Loudon planted an extensive collection of trees and shrubs and concealed the boundaries, except at the main entrance and by the riverside, and he went on to develop many of these techniques further in his design for Derby Arboretum. The Terrace Garden was intended for both recreation and education and was privately owned, but no longer exists, for in 1875 the land was sold for building development.[27]

In Derby Arboretum Loudon had much more scope for combining his social and landscape ideals and he considered it to be the most important commission of his career.[28] The site was on the outskirts of

45

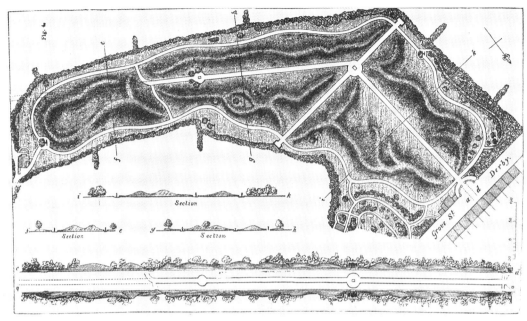

8 J. C. Loudon, Derby Arboretum showing the profile of the ground.

Derby, building was spreading and as there was no prospect worth taking into consideration Loudon decided that 'the whole interest of the garden should be contained within itself'. To conceal the surroundings as far as possible, he raised up undulating mounds of soil two or three metres high, which disguised the boundaries of the site and prevented people walking on the various paths from seeing each other (as shown in Fig. 8). This preserved the illusion that the Arboretum was much larger than it was in reality. Houses were not developed in conjunction with the Arboretum, as they had been at Regent's Park.

Derby Arboretum illustrated the role of the benefactor and the problems that such gifts presented to local authorities. At that date local authorities could not use the rates to acquire parks or to maintain them even if they were gifts. Application had to be made to Parliament, a costly and lengthy process. In order to maintain the Arboretum funds were raised by subscriptions and by charging admission fees. It was Strutt's intention that his gift should 'be open to all classes of the public . . . on every Sunday, and also on at least one other day in every week'. The public were admitted free on Sundays, except during the morning service, and on Wednesdays from dawn to dusk throughout the year, consequently Derby Arboretum was a semi-public park, not a freely accessible public one. The *Westminster Review* commented, '... is it not preposterous, does it not seem incredible, that the ratepayers of Derby, through their representatives in the Town Council cannot, after receiving this noble gift, vote from their own funds one, two or three hundred pounds per annum, to preserve the property from deterioration and fulfil the intention of the donor? yet it is so'.[29] It was not until the end of the 1840s that this situation was rectified, and it was not until 1882 that there was free access to the Arboretum.[30]

PAXTON'S FIRST PARKS

In contrast to Derby Arboretum, Prince's Park, Liverpool (1842–4) was a speculative development by Richard Vaughan Yates who had acquired the site from the Earl of Sefton for £50,000. The Yates were a Liverpool landowning family and the intention was to develop a park and housing. The park would enhance the value of the building land and improve the amenity of the area for the middle-class residents, while the rental from the housing would pay for the park maintenance[31] (Fig. 9). From the point of view of the growing park movement, the project was significant in two ways: it provided a further demonstration of the economic potential of a park and housing development, and it was Joseph Paxton's first public park design. Paxton's abilities as a landscape gardener had been well established by his work for the Duke of Devonshire at Chatsworth and this was a new opportunity for his talents that Richard Vaughan Yates offered. The 'residents of the villas and terraces only, were to have access to the park' and the plan clearly shows Repton's theory of appropriation, with the park acting as an extension to the gardens of the houses.[32] A contemporary report noted that it was designed for 'a private individual, under restrictions, but probably not for general convenience' so it would be more accurately termed a semi-public, rather than a public park.[33] Prince's Park remained privately owned until 1908 when it became a municipal park under the control of the Corporation of Liverpool.

When the Birkenhead Commissioners, just across the Mersey, were considering a similar exercise in 1842, it was perhaps not surprising that their thoughts should also turn to Joseph Paxton. Geographical proximity was reinforced by Paxton's direct connection with one of the members of the Commission, Thomas Brassey, whom Paxton had met via the launching of the *Horticultural Register* in 1831.[34]

After the Napoleonic Wars Birkenhead had become a place of residence for the wealthy merchants of Liverpool, but industrial features began to appear with the building of the Laird's shipyards in 1824. In 1842 Birkenhead's Improvement Commissioners promoted a private Bill to enable them to purchase land 'for the Recreation of the Inhabitants . . . not being less than Seventy Statute Acres', but the motives were not entirely altruistic and while they were awaiting Royal Assent there was speculation in the land involved. Some twelve months before Royal Assent was given in April 1843,[35] key members of the Improvement Commissioners, including Thomas Brassey, together with Birkenhead's largest landowner, Richard Price, and William Laird of Laird's shipyards, had become the owners of the

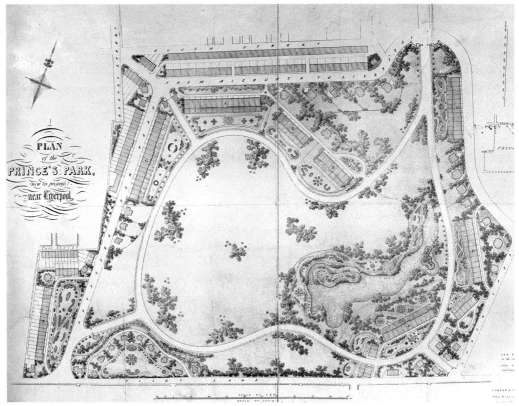

48   9 J. Paxton, Prince's Park, Liverpool, c.1842.

land proposed for the park and of the land surrounding it. The Act stipulated not less than twenty-eight hectares and the Commissioners acquired 90 hectares, out of which 50 hectares were set aside for the park and the rest sold for building sites.[36] The choice of the site, located as it was between the artisan and the wealthier quarters of the town, could be interpreted as a response to the effects of industrialisation on residential amenities.[37] It certainly proved financially attractive to those who had invested in it, since there was a more than seven-fold increase in the value of the building land between 1842 and 1845, over its first cost. The cost of building land in 1842 and 1843 was between '£230 and £250 per acre, averaging a shilling a yard'. The Park Commissioners approved the plans and elevations for the detached villas and terraces and fixed the rental value. All houses were to be set back eighteen metres from the road and no buildings for trade were to be allowed. In June 1845 a large proportion of the land surrounding the drives was offered for sale and about 'ninety thousand yards were sold, at prices varying from seven to fifteen shillings per yard'. The expectations of the park promoters were well satisfied and the sale 'reimburse[d] the township for the original cost, and the expense of laying out, planting and draining, etc'.[38]

Birkenhead Park opened to the public in 1847. It was a municipal park acquired and maintained by the local authority out of public funds, and in terms of its influence on later park development was one of Paxton's most important landscape designs (see Chapter 5). Birkenhead was not the first town to acquire a municipal park in the nineteenth century, Preston qualifies for that position, but it was the first to apply to Parliament for powers to use public funds for that purpose and the first to recoup the costs of park development successfully.

THE COMMUNITY AND THE MANCHESTER PARKS

Preston was the first industrial town of any size to acquire a municipal park, but Manchester must take the credit for being the first of the major industrial centres to do so. Land for parks was acquired in 1845 and Philips Park and Queen's Park in Manchester, and Peel Park in Salford, were officially opened to the public in 1846. The whole community was involved in the fund-raising for the Manchester parks, and it was a comparatively rare example of working people

49

taking an active part in park development, for this was not a strong feature of the park movement generally.

Mark Philips, one of the two Members of Parliament for Manchester, had first raised the subject of open spaces with the Mayor in 1843[39] and a provisional committee was set up to prepare a plan of action and to find out what other towns had done.[40] This committee recommended that Manchester should acquire four parks, each of at least eight hectares, and one on each side of the town so that they would be as accessible as possible. The cost, they thought, would be approximately £25,000. The next step was to organise a large public meeting in the town hall, in August of the following year, to raise subscriptions. This was attended by the major dignitaries who agreed that the acquisition of parks for exercise and active sports 'would contribute greatly to the health, rational enjoyment, kindly intercourse, and good morals of all classes of our industrious population'.[41] Provided the people of Manchester contributed generously to the project, Mark Philips thought that it might be possible to secure a grant from Parliament. A Public Walks, Parks, Gardens and Play-Grounds Committee was appointed to raise funds, select and purchase sites, lay them out and then convey them to the borough 'for the free use and enjoyment of the inhabitants in perpetuity'. One of the first actions of this Committee was to call for contributions from the inhabitants of Manchester. The rich were appealed to in terms of their duty and responsibility and the less affluent were called upon to make some sacrifice and practice self-denial, while the poor were assured that no sum was too small.[42] This was followed by the setting up of canvassing committees.

The next large meeting, held in the Free Trade Hall, was called by working people and some 5,000 attended. There the address stressed the value of health to the poor, who possessed nothing else of value, and compared the human body to a machine which needed oiling and looking after if it was to work well. As oil was to machinery, so pure air was to the human frame, 'it prevents the friction and corrosion of parts [and] removes impurities from the blood ... Bad air fills the body with impurities, and impedes its proper action; just as bad oil clogs and hinders the progress of machinery.'[43] After comparing the mortality rate in Manchester with the lower rates elsewhere, the address concluded that what Manchester needed was more oxygen: 'A greater amount of vegetation, open spaces for ventilation, active recreation and exercise, so as to oblige us to breathe the greatest amount of oxygen to purify the blood.' These general meetings were followed by local meetings held in the principal mills and workshops and by Christmas 1845 subscriptions had reached £32,470 2s 5d.[44]

The energy and enthusiasm of the fund-raising was noted by L. Faucher, the French visitor to Manchester:

A pleasing feature in this movement is the united exertion of the different classes of society in one common object. The *millionaire* has cheerfully come forward, and acknowledged by princely donations, the moral claims of his poorer fellow-townsmen upon the capital which they have assisted in creating; and the working classes have organized themselves into districts and canvassing committees in support of the same object.[45]

While the fund-raising was progressing the Public Parks Committee applied for and was awarded a £3,000 grant from the Government, provided a surveyor inspected the way in which the money was spent, and provided the local subscriptions reached £30,000.[46] Three sites of approximately twelve hectares were purchased: Queen's Park lay one and a half miles from the poorest districts on the north-east of Manchester; Philips Park, to the east, lay near 'a population of at least 50,000 chiefly of classes most needing ... a public park' and Peel Park, to the west, lay one mile from the Manchester Exchange 'and convenient for the whole of Salford'.[47] Since Peel Park was in the middle of Salford this was handed over to Salford after the official opening of all three parks in 1846[48] (see Fig. 10).

Unlike Birkenhead, the local authority of Manchester was not involved in the process of park acquisition, other than in the sense that they backed the project and individual members of the Council contributed to the fund-raising. The whole scheme was an exercise in local fund-raising supplemented by a government grant. The emphasis throughout the acquisition of the Manchester parks was on the physical, social, moral and political benefits of parks, for their economic potential was not a factor. The money raised for the sites did not include the land surrounding the parks, so there was no opportunity for housing development.

The reasons why Manchester was the first of the major industrial centres to develop municipal parks are complex. Manchester had been drafting a local sanitary code in the 1840s and her reputation for local reform was growing. Parks could be seen as part of that process. The

Peterloo massacre of 1819 had occurred in Manchester and the town was a strong centre for Chartist activity in the 1840s, but so were many other towns, so it would be unwise to relate the development of parks too closely to those particular events. Similarly although the development of parks was evidently given a high priority in Manchester, it does not follow that the need for social control was given a higher priority there than elsewhere. Contact between the classes could be minimised, indeed the layout of the town seemed designed for that purpose, as Engels described so graphically:

the town itself is peculiarly built, so that a person may live in it for years, and go in and out daily without coming into contact with a working-people's quarter or even with workers, that is, so long as he confines himself to his business or to pleasure walks. This chiefly arises from the fact, that ... the working-people's quarters are sharply separated from the sections of the city reserved for the middle class; or, if this does not succeed, they are concealed with the cloak of charity ... And the finest part of the arrangement is this,

10 Opening of Queen's Park, Manchester, 1846
The park was created out of the site of the Hendham Hall estate. Spectators on the roof of the Hall had an excellent view of the opening ceremony.

that the members of this money aristocracy can take the shortest road through the middle of all the labouring districts to their places of business, without ever seeing that they are in the midst of the grimy misery that lurks to the right and the left. For the thoroughfares leading from the Exchange in all directions of the city are lined, on both sides, with an almost unbroken series of shops, and are so kept in the hands of the middle and lower bourgeoisie, which, out of self-interest, cares for a decent and cleanly external appearance and *can* care for it. True these shops bear some relation to the districts that lie behind them, and are more elegant in the commercial and residential quarters than when they hide grimy working-men's dwellings; but they suffice to conceal from the eyes of wealthy men and women of strong stomachs and weak nerves, the misery and grime which form the complement of their wealth.[49]

In *The Condition of the Working Class in England* Engels vividly recorded living conditions in Manchester, but these were not significantly better in any of the other major centres, as Dr William Farr's statistics on life expectancy in various towns underlined. During the 1840s, while the pioneering parks were being developed, the Sanitary Reformers were making systematic reports of urban conditions. Nothing brought home the insanitary nature of towns more than the statistics on life expectancy published by Farr, in his reports to the Registrar-General.[50] These reports, which formed part of many official investigations, indicated that the higher the population density, the higher the mortality rate. Clean water, adequate sewage disposal and fresh air to ventilate the crowded cities were prime essentials. Parks had a role to play as lungs, in the provision of fresh air, for it was thought that 'noxious vapours' were one source of disease and it was important for air to circulate.[51]

While many agreed that the provision of open spaces in or near towns was desirable, there were others who thought that facilities such as bath houses were more important. 'Free public baths seem even more desirable than free public walks, inasmuch as the employment of the poor generally necessitates some kind of exercise, however partial, whilst the almost universal neglect of personal ablution is without any such remedy.'[52] The Woolsorters' Baths and Gardens in Bradford would have merited this critic's approval, for they provided hot and cold baths and a swimming pool, as well as pleasure gardens.

THE WOOLSORTERS' GARDENS, BRADFORD

In 1844 the Amicable Society of Woolsorters of Bradford took a twenty-one year lease on a small farm, out of the sight and the smoke of the factories and less than two miles from the town. The idea for the project arose in a period of depression, and it aimed to provide employment for the Society's members by cultivating part of the land, and funds for the Society, by selling the vegetables in the local markets. Another aim was to provide the public with pleasure gardens, baths and a swimming bath, for in one of the four fields there was a spring. Bradford at the time had 'but one warm bath', which was expensive and 'entirely out of reach of the working people'. To fund the project the Society applied to the wealthy inhabitants for subscriptions, raising several hundred pounds. Queen Victoria subscribed £100, while others presented flowers and shrubs.[53]

The site was laid out by William Barratt of Wakefield and the gardens, with the buildings complete, opened on 20 May 1846. Ninety metres beyond the rustic entrance visitors came to the bath house, 'a miniature resemblance of the seraglio at Constantinople'. This provided hot and cold baths and was the home of the curator. Behind it was a series of ornamental pools whose filtered water supplied the baths, and beyond them was a Chinese pavilion, with refreshments and tea. To the right of this was the swimming bath for men, approached through an artificial tunnel and sheltered from view. At different points in the gardens were 'Moss Cottages', or shelters for relaxation and refreshment. Subsequently other attractions such as a monkey-house and a dancing saloon were added, but the gardens seem to have had a struggle to attract visitors and they eventually closed in 1862, before the lease had run out.[54] This venture is the only example so far discovered of a trade union becoming so directly involved in open space for recreation.

The clearest summary of the position regarding the physical need for parks and open spaces was presented in the *Second Report on the State of Large Towns and Populous Districts*, published in 1845, in the aftermath of the great cholera epidemic.[55] This found that park initiatives were by 1845 'numerous and combined enough to render them a movement'. Manchester was 'making active exertions', Oldham was 'organising resources for public walks' and in Bolton, Stockport, Aston, Blackburn and several other towns 'a movement is beginning'. It was recognised that parks could serve as lungs to refresh the exhausted air of the city.

every city has its public pulmonary organs – its instruments of popular respiration – as essential to the mass of the citizens as is to individuals the air they breathe. Paris boasts her Boulevards ... her Bois de Boulogne, – Madrid her far-famed Prado ... and the mighty Babylon pours her pent-up population through the various avenues of her Parks. Well, indeed, and happily, have these been designated 'The Lungs of London'.

This emphasis on the role of parks as lungs related to the work of the sanitary reformers and to the increasing recognition that 'The prime essentials to human existence in crowded cities are pure water, pure air, through drainage and thorough ventilation ...'[56] Public opinion 'is gradually awakening to a sense of the importance of open spaces for air and exercise, as a necessary sanatory [sic] provision, for the inhabitants of all large towns'.[57]

The *Second Report* did not think that the difficulties in providing open space for recreation were as great as many had thought: 'In many cases local exertion and munificence would accomplish the object if some assistance was given.' To provide this assistance it recommended altering the law, providing compensation and empowering local administrative bodies to raise the necessary funds for the care of parks, once they had been established, recommendations which were very similar to those made twelve years before by the SCPW.

CHAPTER FOUR

The park movement

In the years following the *Second Report on the State of Large Towns and Populous Districts*, the park movement in Britain was affected by local, national and international developments. Parks in turn had a part to play in urban and suburban development, but it was only in the last decades of the nineteenth century that the problems of town planning and of park location were confronted (see Chapter 10). The legislation governing the actions permitted to local authorities provided the framework within which they could develop parks. The weak state of local government persisted for much of the century and it was not until 1875 that local authorities gained full powers to develop and manage parks. Of the 187 incorporated towns in 1845, only twenty-nine town councils had exclusive powers to act on matters of drainage, cleansing and paving. In 62 towns neither the councils nor the Commissioners exercised such powers, consequently these towns were left without the means for improving their sanitation, streets or water.[1] A further weakness came from the problem that as towns expanded, local government areas did not keep pace with them. Consequently many growing urban districts did not come within any corporation and their administration fell to parish authorities and county justices with their even weaker powers. It was only gradually that the full machinery of local government came into being, and with it came an increasing sense of civic consciousness that showed itself in magnificent town halls, libraries, concert halls and parks. It is against this difficult background that the park movement must be placed.

One of the first actions of Parliament in the early years of the park movement was to pass the General Enclosure Act 1845.[2] Ostensibly this was intended to safeguard open space near towns, for if commons were within certain distances of large towns a proportion of the enclosed land had to be set aside for recreation (see Appendix 1). The effects of the Act, however, proved more detrimental than the previous practice of enclosure under private Acts and less land, proportionally, was set aside for recreation.[3] Another important piece of legislation passed in this period was the Towns Improvement Clauses Act 1847,[4] which consolidated within one Act provisions usually contained in local Acts for town improvements. This Act simplified the procedures for local authorities to acquire land for parks, provided the site was not more than three miles from the principal market or from the offices of the Commissioners. Local authorities were still unable to maintain parks that had been given to them, as the example of Derby Arboretum had illustrated, and this anomaly was rectified in the Public Health Act 1848.[5]

LOCAL GOVERNMENT INITIATIVES

In the period 1845 to 1859, local authorities acquired parks by a variety of methods and much ingenuity was shown in overcoming the difficulties. In certain instances they were the beneficiaries of local generosity and Manchester's method of raising money by subscription, so that none of the costs of acquisition were met by the municipality, was adopted by Bradford. The initiative for acquiring Peel Park (1850) came largely from Sir Titus Salt the textile magnate, who contributed £1,000 to the project and persuaded other wealthy residents to subscribe. The 22 hectare Bolton House estate, which was already planted, lay on the boundaries of Bradford and Bolton and was acquired for £12,000.[6] A few towns, including Bradford, successfully applied for a grant from the Government fund of £10,000, but the sums involved were very small.[7]

If the pioneering period of park development of 1833–45 is compared with the following period 1845–59, when further important legislation was passed, a considerable acceleration in park creation can be seen (Appendix 2). More than three times the number of parks were opened in this later period and local authority activity was increasing, despite the difficulties, while the number of gifts remained steady. These parks were located mainly in the north-west of England, in towns associated with the major industries, a geographical distribution which reflected the main thrust of the SCPW's investigations.

Manchester and London's pioneering achievements were soon followed by the other major urban centres. Glasgow successfully adopted a method similar to the one used by Birkenhead and D. M'Lellan, writing at the end of the century, noted 'the great tact and carefulness' that the Corporation had shown in their purchases of land. The 'able and skilful manner' in which the land around the parks had been leased had enabled the original purchase money to be recouped.[8] The first site for developing a park with housing around was acquired in 1852 for £78,000 and Joseph Paxton was invited to prepare the design for Kelvingrove Park. Five years later the Council purchased the site for Queen's Park, which was also laid out by Paxton. The surrounding land was leased for housing and the park opened in 1862.[9]

Local authority action to provide parks in Liverpool dated from the mid 1840s. With the example of Edinburgh New Town before them, rather than the local example of Prince's Park, the Health of Towns Association advocated rebuilding the town, starting with the worst slums. They also thought that all future town extensions should be planned, instead of taking place piecemeal.[10] The Improvements Committee called for plans in 1850 and H. P. Horner's plan was selected. This recommended improving the roads and links with the city centre and preventing the spread of Liverpool by providing a 'belt of garden or parkland' around it.[11] Under this plan nine parks would be formed, with further building taking place beyond them, but the Corporation decided not to implement it because of the cost. Two parks were subsequently opened, Wavertree Park (1856) and Shiel Park (1862), and then in 1864 a Commission of Enquiry was set up to consider the question of parks for the north of the town. Eleven sites were visited[12] and under the Liverpool Improvement Act 1865[13] a loan of £500,000 was raised and powers granted to create three parks, Newsham, Stanley and Sefton Parks, financed out of the rates. In all three projects the land included sites for building development, in order to recoup costs. These sites were almost equidistant from the pier-head and, with the botanic gardens and Prince's Park, in effect formed a ring of parks, so they were a step in the direction of Horner's belt of parkland (see Fig. 11).

RECREATION TIME

The growth of the park movement in the late 1840s and the 1850s was not solely the result of the 1840s legislation, for there were other important factors such as the increased concern with recreation as a result of the Ten Hour Act 1847[14] and the growing Saturday Half-Holiday Movement. The prospect of increased opportunities for

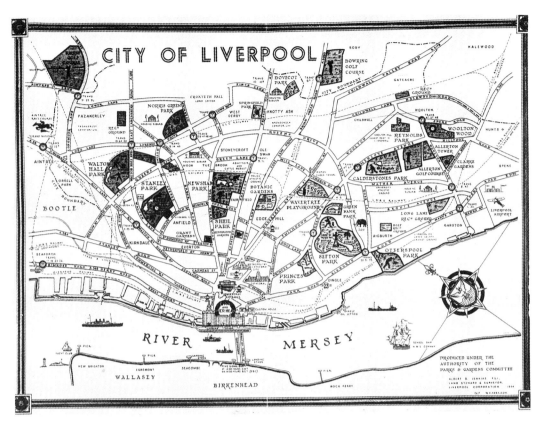

11 Liverpool parks, 1934. The inner ring was formed 1841–72, the outer parks were added later.

recreation became the target of the Temperance Movement, the Sabbatarians and reformers concerned with rational recreation. The Temperance Movement sought to transform social behaviour and to exert pressure in Parliament through the Central Association for Stopping the Sale of Intoxicating Liquor on Sundays, but they were not successful, and public houses remained open on Sundays while places of 'innocent amusement' such as museums were closed.[15] The Sabbatarians, who were not anti-drink, were concerned that Sundays should be kept for religious observance, and the influence of both movements could be clearly seen in the facilities available in parks and in the pastimes permitted on Sundays (see Chapters 6 and 9).

The changes to the length of the working day and week introduced by the Ten Hour Act focused attention on the question of recreation. In Bolton, for example, the physical and moral 'training' of those who worked in the factories was discussed as a result of the passing of the Act. Robert Heywood, a prominent citizen and alderman, suggested that the town should acquire a park to encourage the effective use of recreation and two were opened in 1866.[16] Others questioned the relevance of parks to those whose working day was so long:

Parks are well for those only who can have time to perambulate them, and baths are of little use to such dirty people as do not leave work until eight o'clock at night. We protest that it is a mere burlesque upon philanthropy, to make provision for these benefits, with a continuance of twelve hours' labour and fifteen hours' occupation for every manufacturing operative above thirteen years of age.[17]

Recreation depended on the time available so it was linked to the whole question of holidays and the length of the working day and week. For the majority of the population the time available for recreation increased only gradually during the century, although the pattern of holidays changed. Three types of 'holiday' were identified in the various Reports on employment in the manufacturing industries: 'holidays' that were enforced by employers (though the term would hardly be used in that way today) due to the state of the industry, when employees were laid off or sacked; time taken off by employees without the agreement of the employer; and time off recognised by both parties.[18] The Factory Act 1833[19] gave young workers below 18 and above 13 years old the first statutory holidays of four days a year, or eight half-days, with a whole day at Christmas and on Good Friday, but there were many variations between regions and trades. It was not until the passing of the Bank Holiday Act 1871[20] that existing holidays were increased to include Boxing Day, Easter Monday, Whit Monday and the first Monday in August. By the end of the century most of the traditional holidays had been replaced by these official ones and skilled workers were in addition allowed one week's holiday with pay. Unskilled and semi-skilled workers, however, were often not even paid for the four Bank Holidays.

One of the questions discussed by employers and reformers was whether it was in the interests of employees to have more unpaid holidays. Although they agreed that the existing holidays were inadequate for the millions who laboured six days a week, they thought no problem more difficult than 'the affording of more holidays to the working classes, without at the same time diminishing their hours of subsistence'. Since holidays were unpaid, some reformers thought it more appropriate to give people opportunities to be in the fresh air by providing accessible parks. '[In] the shade of trees, by the margin of fair waters, and in the grateful freshness of grass . . . let there be no town or district without its people's park. Happily this idea has been recognised.'[21] This was a rather optimistic view, since the problem of park provision could hardly be said to have been solved by that date, 1863.

THE WORKING DAY

The concept of a Normal Working Day of ten hours (sixty hours a week) had been established by the London engineers in 1836. This concept was appropriate for factories and workshops with an established pattern of work but not for those working on piece rates, in small workshops, or on shifts in the continuous process industries. Nor was it applicable to domestic workers or those in the transport industries. Their hours remained well above those established by the Normal Day.[22] For women and children under eighteen, the Ten Hour Act brought the working day in the textile factories down to sixty hours, with work stopping on Saturday at 2.00 p.m. A gradual decrease in the Normal Working Day was achieved during the course of the century, for the trade union movement provided the organisational framework within which shorter hours could be negotiated effectively, when economic conditions were favourable. This decrease implied an increase in time for recreation, but such an increase did not necessarily follow because of the amount of overtime worked.

Park use was related to location and to the availability and cost of other forms of recreation. Since parks tended to be open from dawn to dusk, the changes in the length of the working day were likely to have affected park use only during the summer months, whereas the changes in the length of the working week affected the opportunities for recreation at the weekend and particularly on Sundays.

THE WORKING WEEK

The Saturday Half-Holiday Movement was concerned not only with the cessation of work at 1.00 p.m. on Saturday, but also with the early payment of wages. 'We may have early payment of wages without Saturday leisure, but we cannot have Saturday leisure without early payment of wages.'[23] An active Half-Holiday Movement had begun among the Manchester clerks and warehouse workers in 1843. The movement was backed by the Sabbatarians who thought it would enable working people, other than shop-workers, to do their domestic chores, shop and even relax by going on excursions on Saturday and so leave Sunday free for religious duties. Others were concerned with the burden that would be placed on women and advocated a half-holiday on either Monday or Wednesday. The Saturday Half-Holiday would 'isolate the husband in his enjoyment' while his wife made the preparations for Sunday. How would Sunday be preserved if 'the wife is taken from her domestic duties . . . to some scene of pleasure? Or is it intended that the husband should enjoy the selfish hours by himself . . . ?' If everyone was to benefit 'the social relations of the workman should be especially considered, and the claims of his wife and children, be more carefully provided for than even his own'.[24]

Throughout the 1850s the Saturday Half-Holiday Movement increased steadily, particularly in Manchester and the north of England. In the Midlands and the south, where the factory system of production was not so fully developed, traditional patterns of work and recreation persisted into the 1860s and 1870s. The Ten Hour Act and the Saturday Half-Holiday Movement redirected attention toward the recreation 'problem', as well as raising questions about appropriate Sunday activities and the use of parks on that day, and these concerns persisted throughout the rest of the century.

BENEFACTORS AND BENEFITS

Local authority initiatives to acquire parks during the 1840s and 1850s took place within a framework of restrictions that impeded, rather than enhanced, their effectiveness. No common strategy could be evolved, since each situation was different, and the local authorities availed themselves of opportunities to acquire parks whenever they presented themselves. This situation was not greatly enhanced by the important legislation of 1859 and 1860 that was directed towards benefactors.

As towns expanded, landowners had become involved in the increasing market for building, laying out roads, negotiating housing leases and, in some instances, park development. The role of the benefactor in park development was greatly enhanced at the end of the 1850s by two important pieces of legislation. The Recreation Grounds Act 1859,[25] introduced by R. A. Slaney, the Chairman of the Select Committee on Public Walks, encouraged the donation to local authorities of money or land for recreation. This was followed by the Public Improvements Act 1860[26] which gave local authorities powers to acquire, hold and manage open spaces out of the rates. A limit of 6d in the pound was stipulated, but before the rate could be levied, half the estimated cost of the improvement had to be raised by private subscription, donation, or other means. Local authorities could not borrow money in order to carry out the purposes of the Act. The enhanced role of the benefactor can be seen from the growth in gifts of parks in the 1860s and 1870s (see Graph 2, and Appendix 2).

Benefactors came from the ranks of local dignitaries, landowners and successful entrepreneurs. Among the aristocratic landowners whose names are perpetuated in that of a park we find the Norfolks of Sheffield, the Calthorpes of Birmingham, the Seftons of Liverpool

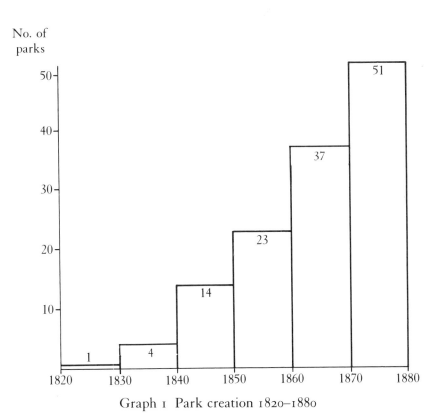

Graph 1 Park creation 1820–1880

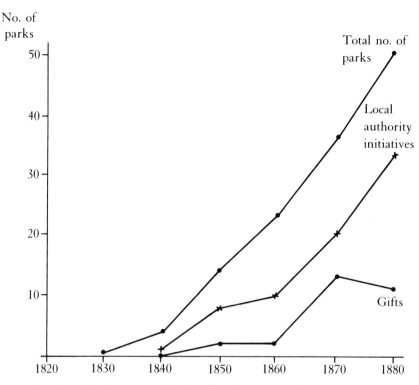

Graph 2 Parks created by local authorities and as a result of gifts

and the Dartmouths of West Bromwich. A successful entrepreneur Alexander Kay, gave his name to Kay Park, Kilmarnock, and Saltaire town and park commemorate the successful alpaca manufacturer Sir Titus Salt. Sir Francis Crossley of Dean Clough Mills preferred the more democratic name People's Park for his gift to Halifax, while Henry Bolckow the steel magnate in Middlesbrough named his gift Albert Park after the Prince. The benefactor's role in park develop-ment took two main forms, that of philanthropy and that of self-interest. Park gifts ranged in size from the three-quarters hectare of Derbyshire Recreation Ground in Bolton to the thirty hectares of Jesmond Dene, donated to Newcastle-upon-Tyne in 1883 by the armaments manufacturer, Lord Armstrong. Derby Arboretum, the gift of Joseph Strutt in 1840, was an early example of philanthropy, for Strutt donated the four and a half hectare site for the park and did not retain any interest in the land surrounding it. Similarly Mrs Jane Stanley, who donated Stanley Recreation Ground to Peterborough in 1860 in memory of her husband, and Mrs Locke, who donated Locke

Park, Barnsley in 1872 in memory of her husband Joseph Locke the engineer, did not retain any interest in the land surrounding those sites.

Benefactors were not slow in recognising the financial opportunities presented by a combination of philanthropy and self-interest. In general that self-interest was best promoted by the donor retaining an interest in the land surrounding a park. When, for example, Lord Vernon gave Vernon Park to Stockport, he stipulated that 'A sufficient plot of land be reserved ... for building purposes.'[27] Henry Bolckow, who donated the thirty hectare site for Albert Park in 1868, reserved three sides of the park for building 'villa residences'.[28]

Benefactors were not always successful in their ventures, as Z. C. Pearson, twice mayor of Hull, discovered. Pearson gave the eleven hectare site for Pearson Park in 1860, retaining four hectares on the north, south and east sides of the site for building purposes. There the 'most notable developments in middle class housing' occurred, but the project seems to have run into difficulties, for at the time of the formal opening of the park Mr Pearson's financial affairs were being investigated by the London Bankruptcy Court and he was unable to be present.[29]

These gifts tended to be seen as acts of generosity to the local community, whether or not the benefactors had gained directly from the transaction, though there were occasions, such as that concerning Sefton Park, Liverpool, when this was questioned publicly. Sefton Park had by 1890 cost the ratepayers some £292,266. The land had been bought from Lord Sefton for £250,000 and that sum, invested at 4 per cent, had given him a return of £10,000 per annum. This 'was a very good thing for him', as a witness to the Parliamentary Enquiry on the Liverpool Corporation Bill held in 1890 stated. At that same Enquiry the City Surveyor reported that not only had Lord Sefton received this return, but the construction of the park had also improved the value of his estates nearby. He had enjoyed this greatly increased income for the past twenty years and his only contribution 'has been to drive a four-in-hand and live in the lap of luxury' while the people of Liverpool had been 'toiling and sweating in order to make ends meet'.[30]

Similarly the question of how benefactors had achieved the position from which they could be so generous was rarely asked. If, however, they were not disposed to act in a fashion appropriate to their standing, they could be heavily censured, and this indeed occurred in Birmingham. Birmingham obtained its first parks by leasing them. In 1845 funds were raised for public walks, but were used instead in 1846 to buy baths.[31] In 1850 the Council made an unsuccessful offer to buy Aston Hall Park, and then five years later they were offered Adderley Park as a gift provided they laid it out and gave the donor, Charles Bowyer Adderley, a voice in how it should be run. This the Council declined, but when the donor pointed out that he was virtually making a free gift, the Council accepted the gift on a lease of 999 years at a peppercorn rent of five shillings per year, and the park opened in 1856.[32] That same year the Council received an offer from Lord Calthorpe, Birmingham's major landowner, of a lease, on an experimental basis, of eight to twelve hectares of land for recreation, for one year, at a rent of £3 per acre.[33] The Council was not overwhelmed by this and requested clarification and modifications. Calthorpe Park was officially opened on 1 June 1857 (Fig. 12), with the Council renting the park for £5 per annum, but without any legal agreement, a position which remained unchanged until Lord Calthorpe's death in 1868. There were dangers inherent in this situation:

The Calthorpe and Saltley [i.e. Adderley] Parks, useful as they are . . . are not the property of the town, and only their *use* is given by their proprietors; they may at any time be reclaimed and taken from the town. This is not a thing likely to occur, but there is nothing absolutely to prevent it. What is needed . . . is the unalienable right to such parks . . .[34]

This unlikely event of a park being reclaimed occurred when the new Lord Calthorpe took up his inheritance in 1870. In May of that year his lordship's agents wrote asking for part of Calthorpe Park to be returned since he wished to let the land for building, although this ran counter to his father's wishes. Poor quality land, that was unlikely to be built on because of its location, was offered in exchange. This led to severe criticisms by both the Council and the press. The peer was reminded in no uncertain terms of the duties that wealth and position brought, and how that wealth had been created out of the industry of the people of Birmingham. Under this pressure he was persuaded not to proceed and he divested himself of all existing and future interests in the land.[35]

Birmingham acquired its first municipal park, Aston Hall Park, in

1864. Renewed attempts to realise this project dated from 1857 when George Dawson, the non-conformist lecturer, politician and preacher, chaired a meeting 'to get Birmingham a park worthy of its name.'[36] A limited company was formed to raise money by selling 40,000 shares of one guinea each.[37] By 1858 more than 18,000 shares had been applied for and the park opened to the public in that year. Since the purchase had not been completed an entrance fee was charged until 1864, when the Council completed the purchase of the site, and the company was wound up two years later.[38] It could be argued that this mode of raising funds was related to middle- and ruling-class experience and appealed to the middle-class aspirations of Birmingham's artisans. The basis of production in Birmingham was small-scale workshops and there was a large proportion of artisans among the working-class population. Some historians have

INAUGURATION OF CALTHORPE PARK : THE DUKE OF CAMBRIDGE PLANTING A TREE.

12 Opening of Calthorpe Park, Birmingham, 1857
The Duke of Cambridge planting a tree, with various dignitaries looking on.
Mounted soldiers face the crowd in the background.

identified Birmingham as a place where cooperation between masters and working people was fostered as a result of these small-scale workshops and artisans were 'more petty bourgeois than proletarian'.[39] There is also evidence that contradicts that view[40] and it would be unwise to deduce that this method of fund-raising was a direct result of the structure of work in Birmingham.

The increased number of parks donated during the 1860s and thereafter indicates that the legislation of 1859 and 1860 was successful in encouraging benefactors to come forward, but there were other significant events that occurred during the 1860s which added to the growing pressure for parks and provided a direct stimulus to park development particularly in Lancashire.

THE COTTON FAMINE

Lancashire depended on America for 80 per cent of her raw cotton and over 1,000 million pounds were imported annually. In 1861, as a result of the American Civil War, the southern ports of America were under blockade and cotton imports to Britain plummeted. Initially this increased the price of manufactured cotton goods and manufacturers benefited as stocks were sold off, but soon unemployment rose rapidly. In Preston the 25,000 people employed in 76 cotton mills were all put out of work in 1864. In Blackburn, out of 74 mills, 30 were closed, 18 ran full time, 16 ran short time, and 15,000 workers were made unemployed. In Oldham where there was a variety of industry, 5,000 were unemployed. In all it was estimated that some half-million people lost their source of livelihood as a direct result of the cotton famine.[41]

Various Acts were passed to provide relief to those areas most affected, and local authorities were empowered to borrow money in order to improve or provide drains, sewers, roads, waterworks, parks, recreation grounds and cemeteries.[42] Four towns borrowed money to undertake work on parks: Bolton (£1,000), Blackburn (£1,350), Oldham (£18,000 and £5,700), and Preston (£3,000).[43] Oldham used these funds to buy the 26 hectare site for Alexandra Park,[44] while the other towns used unemployed cotton workers in park construction. Heywood Recreation Ground in Bolton was laid out,[45] while at Blackburn the scarped slope of the hill in Corporation Park was improved and a carriage drive to the top of the hill constructed[46] (see Fig. 13). In Preston 629 unemployed cotton workers, out of the 25,000 out of work, levelled and made the roads in Avenham, Miller and Moor Parks.[47] Edward Milner was asked by the Council to make a report on these parks in 1864[48] and they were then laid out according to his designs.[49] Unemployed workers had also been used in park construction before the passing of these Acts. In the trade depressions of 1816, 1819, and 1826, for example, when unemployment was widespread in Glasgow, a few out of the thousands unemployed were given work on draining, levelling and raising Glasgow Green.[50] Although the cotton famine did not provide a major stimulus to general park development, its effects were of significant local importance. A more general stimulus to the park movement came from the work of the Commons Preservation Society.

13 Employment of Lancashire operatives under the Public Works Act, at Revidge Hill, Corporation Park, Blackburn, 1864. This was extremely hard work for men used to working indoors in the cotton industry.

CHAPTER FIVE

Design and designers

In a sense the design of each park was the solution to the particular
factors affecting each individual project. Parks ranged in size from
fractions of a hectare to several hundred hectares, and they were
created out of a wide variety of sites which included commons,
wasteland, infill and marginal land such as disused quarries. Some
parks were created out of sites that were already partly laid out if they
had previously been private parks and gardens, while others such as
Moor Park, Preston, were not fully laid out until many years after
they actually opened as parks. Despite this, it is possible to see certain
broad changes in design during the course of the nineteenth century.

The most important influence on landscape design at the beginning of the nineteenth century was Humphry Repton. It was his
theories that influenced John Nash in his revised designs for Regent's
Park and his ideas were kept alive well into the nineteenth century by
John Claudius Loudon. It was Repton who first attempted to draw up
the fundamental principles of landscape gardening and to analyse the
sources of pleasure in it. Although the problems of public park design
were very different from those involved in the design of private
parks, many of his principles, particularly those concerning picturesque beauty, variety, novelty, contrast, appropriation and animation, were influential in the early phase of urban park design in the
1840s. Picturesque beauty encouraged curiosity and this in turn
meant that all the significant features of a design should not be
immediately visible. Novelty and contrast also stimulated curiosity
and were important elements of the picturesque. Appropriation
involved enhancing the apparent extent of an owner's private property and this was applied to public parks, where it was important to
give the appearance of as large an extent of park as possible. Other
sources of pleasure identified by Repton included the changing
seasons, and animation which enlivened the scene by means of the

movement of water or animals, or smoke from distant dwellings, although smoke was hardly a positive factor for urban park designers and park keepers.[1]

Apart from Repton and Loudon, the other major figure during the first decades of the park movement is undoubtedly Joseph Paxton. Paxton's first public park was Prince's Park, Liverpool (1842), his first municipal venture Birkenhead Park (1842–7), but the Crystal Palace Park, Sydenham (1855), which was a speculative development, was his most influential park design. One of the problems confronting the designers of public parks was how to accommodate large numbers of people and at the same time preserve a feeling of space and quiet contact with nature. Another problem concerned the location of an increasing range of activities, such as sports and music, which had to be reconciled with the prevailing contemporary ideals of landscape design. The fullest opportunities for designers to develop their ideas occurred in those parks which were not already laid out when they were acquired and some important examples from the 1840s show how Loudon, Paxton and others resolved these problems. In the 1850s and 1860s Paxton's design for the Crystal Palace Park became a major influence, while in the 1870s the introduction of French principles of park design at Sefton Park, Liverpool, seemed to point to a solution of the problem of accommodating sports and playgrounds.

In some instances designers were chosen by competition (Appendix 2), but the role of competitions in this area was not nearly so important as it was in the area of public architecture. The majority of municipal parks were not designed by competition and it was only after 1875 that competitions became more important.

THE PARKS OF THE 1840s

Loudon thought that 'a prevailing error in most public gardens' was the lack of unity of expression. Walks crossed in all directions, providing a puzzle to the visitor, whereas if the principle of unity was applied then each garden would feature one main walk from which 'every material object in the garden may be seen in a general way'. From this walk 'small episodical walks' would branch off to other areas. These would never be broader than one third of the main walk, so there would be no confusion between the main and the subsidiary

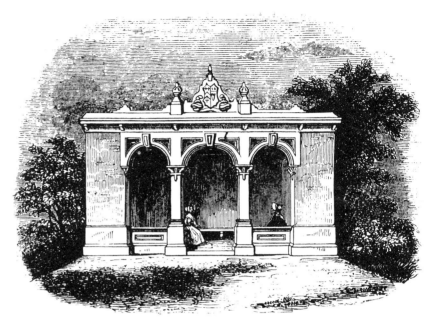

14 Pavilion, designed by E. R. Lamb, Derby Arboretum.

walks, and they would join the main walks at right angles 'so as not to seem to invite the stranger to walk in them'.[2] At Derby Arboretum he put these principles into practice.

Joseph Strutt, the donor, wished to preserve the existing garden, trees and buildings and minimise the expense of maintenance. A design featuring trees and shrubs 'in the manner of a common pleasure-ground' would tend to become boring after one or two visits and a botanic garden would prove expensive.[3] An arboretum featuring a collection of foreign and native trees and shrubs, one example of each, with its name displayed, would provide beauty, variety, interest and education in all seasons of the year. Figure 8 shows how Loudon combined axial symmetry with informal paths and planting. A broad central walk provides the spine of the design and at the junction of the central gravel walk and the main cross walk was a statue on a pedestal, since 'a straight walk without a terminating object is felt to be deficient in meaning'. Pavilions providing seats and shelter performed the same function at the ends of the cross walks; an example is shown in Fig. 14. The subsidiary walks took the visitor around the periphery of the site, and the undulating ground and planting promoted the illusion of solitude and obscured the boundary, so concealing the apparent extent of the site. Loudon also wanted to create hollows and winding valleys, but the soil and difficulties of drainage prevented this; however flat spaces were left for tents as Strutt wished. Unlike later park designers, Loudon was not required to incorporate a wide range of facilities within his design.

There were 350 seats in the Arboretum and Loudon gave detailed instructions on how they should be placed, so that the extent of the park was not made obvious. This meant that those seated should not be able to see both exits from where they were sitting, nor should they be able to see both boundaries. For interest, comfort and security he recommended that the seats should face a view or a feature, or be positioned in gravelled recesses by the side of walks where passers-by would provide interest (see Fig. 15). Some should be open to the sun for winter use, others should be under the shade of trees, but the majority, which would be used in the summer, should face east, west or north. Loudon's concern with comfort and security can also be seen in his suggestion that the seats placed on the grass should be backed by trees and shrubs so that no one could easily come up close to them from behind; or alternatively double seats with a common back could be provided. All fixed seats should have footboards for the comfort of invalids and the aged.[4] Such attention to the detail of positioning seats

15 The seats in Derby Arboretum, c.1900, were not recessed as Loudon recommended.

16 Cast iron seat backed by shrubs. Of the many designs available, this was among the most lavish.

was not the rule and when Kemp reported on the number and position of seats in Birkenhead Park in 1857 he only gave the most general indication as to where and how they were placed. Out of a total of 72 seats, nearly half were positioned by the walks around the lower lake[5] (Fig. 16).

Loudon also considered the problem of accommodating variety, with the conflicting need for unity of expression. In order to keep visitors' interest alive there should be variety and 'one kind of scene must succeed another', but to give the coherent effect necessary for unity of expression, these scenes should be related according to some principle recognisable by the visitor.

In a zoological garden, the visiter [sic] should not be led from a cage of canary birds to a den of lions, without passing through the intermediate gradations of birds and of quadrupeds; and, in a botanical garden, he should not pass at once from plants of the torrid, to those of the frigid, zone . . . In a picturesque garden, level, rocky, hilly, and lake scenery should not follow each other at random, nor in such a manner as to produce violent contrasts, but according to consistency and truth.[6]

The planting of the trees in the Arboretum gave Loudon an opportunity to put this principle into practice, though there was less scope for him to create a variety of picturesque scenery. This principle was applied in many of the larger parks of the middle decades of the century, sometimes more successfully than others.

THE COMPETITION FOR THE MANCHESTER PARKS

In the design of municipal parks it was the benefactor, or the local authority, who decided on the facilities to be included, rarely the designer. The first municipal parks to be designed as the result of a competition were the Manchester parks, and the Public Parks Committee's clearly stated objective was 'to provide the greatest variety of rational recreations for the greatest possible number'.[7] By November 1844 the Committee had unanimously agreed upon the facilities that the new parks should offer: gymnasia, one or more fountains of pure water, numerous seats, spaces for active sports such as quoits, skittles and archery, and buildings for refreshments. The competition for the best set of plans, together with estimates for laying out the sites already purchased, offered a first prize of fifty guineas and a second prize of twenty-five guineas. Although these entries have not been found, comments on them throw interesting light on the subject of public park design at this time.

The information sent to competitors included the names and sizes of the three sites, two of which were already partially laid out. The total cost of laying out, planting, fencing and draining, including the provision of seats for all three sites, was to be about £4,000, but this figure did not include the cost of lodges and other buildings. The instructions to the competitors was that plans should indicate the sites of the playgrounds, archery grounds, quoit and skittle alleys, refreshment rooms, fountains, lodges and retiring places. A carriage drive around the parks was desirable, but it should not cut across the sites. Above all the Committee stressed that the designers should pay 'utmost regard . . . for the promenading of large numbers of persons' and remember that they were sketching '*a park* for the *public*, to be constantly accessible, and not a private pleasure ground'.[8]

Over one hundred designs were received and put on display to the public for four days, 27–30 October 1845. The estimates of costs varied from £2,000 to £9,000 and the problem of comparing the plans was considerable since they were drawn in differing scales, with various modes of presentation. Some were in pencil, some in india ink, some had a sepia tint, others were in colour. Most showed ground plans, but there were some bird's-eye views which showed the groves and arbours 'in a most engaging way'. Some designs emphasised the artificial lakes, others the fountains, and in some the planting was so close 'as to resemble a maze'. Others filled every area with walks and hedges, leaving only small patches of grass between, so that there was no large open space where crowds could gather. Few gave elevations for the lodges or refreshment rooms. Since each site was only about twelve hectares it was important to make the most of the space available and contemporary critics felt that straight lines should be avoided: 'winding curves, or what are called 'serpentines' seem naturally to present themselves. Yet some of the plans look like the laying-out of streets of the city, rather than the walks and places of exercise and sport in a park'.[9] Despite the problems in comparing all the entries, these were initially reduced to nine and subsequently to three. The winner was Joshua Major & Son of Knowstrop near Leeds, and the second prize went to H. Bigland & Co. of Manchester.[10]

Under the agreement between Joshua Major and the Public Parks Committee, Major would superintend the laying out of the parks, 'with such alterations as the Committee may from time to time suggest'. He was to make at least one visit per week and was to send one or two people to take charge in his absence until the project was completed. His fee on completion would be £200, and the wages of those sent by Major to superintend the contractor's work would be paid by the Committee at the rate of one guinea per week.[11] Funds for the project were certainly not lavish, for in December that year the Committee called for donations of articles likely to be of use in the parks, 'particularly Stone, Flags, Bricks, Timber, Derbyshire Spar, Shrubbery Plants, Forest Trees, Iron Railings, Gates, etc. etc.'[12]

Since Queen's Park and Peel Park were already partially laid out, it was only at Philips Park that Major really had a free hand to design the whole site.[13] Figure 17 shows the plans for the three parks. Philips Park, like the other parks, featured open ground of five to six hectares, where meetings could be held and games played. One of the open spaces was clearly identified as a cricket ground, and Major considered the opportunities for playing football but there is no record of it being played in any of the three parks. The other games were located in separate sites around the periphery of the parks in the pleasure ground, where the winding paths and varied shrubs, trees, flowers and lawn provided partially hidden recesses for them[14] (see Fig. 102). The archery ground of Peel Park is more visible and with the footpath passing behind the target, perhaps such visibility was essential to safety (Fig. 18).[15] Labyrinths or mazes were included in both Queen's Park and Philips Park, but ten years later it was recommended that they be removed because of problems of upkeep.

Several alterations were made to Major's designs within two years of the official opening in 1846, particularly to Philips Park. This was the boldest and most romantic of the three parks, 'with much broken ground, and a pretty little amphitheatre sloping down to the river Medlock'. In the original design, the skittle and archery grounds were located in the valley of the park by the banks of the Medlock, 'the most beautiful part of the park'.[16] By 1849 these had been moved and the area laid out as flower gardens. Where formerly there had been 'men shouting under the excitement of the skittle ground or the unrestrained merriment of the factory girls who used the swings. It is now quiet and tranquil ...' This excitement and merriment were relocated to the edge of the park where they would be less audible and intrusive.

The Manchester Public Parks Committee were well content with Major's designs, but elsewhere contemporary critics made adverse comments and the controversy, which was published in the *Gardeners' Chronicle*, continued for some time. Much was made of the 'profusion of angles' and straight lines to be found in the walks and flower beds, the thinness of the grass verges of the walks and the niggardly scale of such features as the water and rocks.[17] Major countered these criticisms both in the *Gardeners' Chronicle*, and later in his book, *The Theory and Practice of Landscape Gardening*. The angles and the narrow grass verges were, he replied, mainly confined to those areas 'appropriated to youthful games and athletic exercises'. Later he agreed that the provision of a games area necessarily imposed limits on artistic display,[18] and this indeed pinpoints the conflict posed by, on the one hand, the ideals of landscape design and, on the other, the practicalities of designing for a large number of people and a wide range of activities including sports and games.

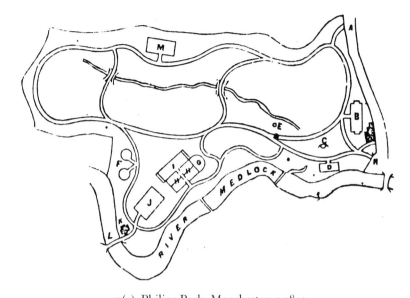

17(a) Philips Park, Manchester, c.1849
B Girls' ball and shuttlecock ground; C Shuttlecocks and skipping ropes;
D Quoit alley; E Girls' shuttlecocks; F Boys' circular swings; GHH Skittle
alley; I Archery; M Gymnasium

VICTORIA PARK, LONDON

Of all the London parks, Victoria Park was the one which 'in the variety of its features, and in all its arrangements, may be held to be the best ...'[19] However it was some time after it opened that it acquired those features. The initial design of 1841 by James Pennethorne was hardly more than a sketch and showed little planting and no lakes.[20] The plan published two years later showed more detail but still no lakes[21] (Fig. 19). By 1845 some 3,000 deciduous trees, 1,000 evergreens and 1,000 coarse shrubs including lilac, spirea, ribes, Guelder rose and tamarisk, were being planted, and the public had started using the park.[22] The planting took the form of a scientific arboretum 'so as to combine amusement and information of the highest class'.[23] Pennethorne thought that lakes were 'almost an integral and indispensible part of a Royal Park' and two lakes were excavated in 1846, the gravel from them being used in the park construction.[24] He also suggested buying a pagoda, which stood at Hyde Park Corner and was for sale for £800, for the larger island in the western lake, where it would be 'extremely ornamental and useful'.[25]

17(b) Queen's Park, Manchester, c.1849
C Rosarium; D Cricket ground; E Pond filled up; F Circular swings; I Ball
and shuttlecocks; K Skipping rope and swing grounds; N Shuttlecocks;
OOPP Quoit and skittle alleys; Q Archery

When John Gibson, who had worked with Paxton at Chatsworth, was appointed superintendent of Victoria Park in 1849, he instituted a number of improvements. He increased the plantations, extended and widened the western lake so that it was less like a canal, raised mounds on the northern side of that lake and generally increased the diversity of the landscape.[26] The effect of these improvements can be seen in Fig. 20. By 1863 there were two bathing lakes in the eastern part of the park, two gymnasia, and the planting was generally much richer. Unlike the Manchester/Salford Parks, or the early Paxton parks, the design of Victoria Park evolved over a number of years.

THE EARLY PAXTON PARKS

Paxton could almost be said to have had the monopoly of laying out urban and municipal parks. He was involved in designing and laying out parks at Birkenhead, Glasgow, Halifax, Dundee, Dunfermline, Liverpool and London and his influence extended through the people

85

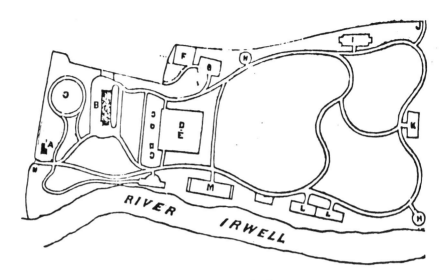

17(c) Peel Park, Salford, c.1849
FG Quoit alley; H Circular swings; I Skipping ropes; K Gymnasium;
LL Skittle alleys; M Archery

18 Archery ground, Peel Park, Salford, c.1850.

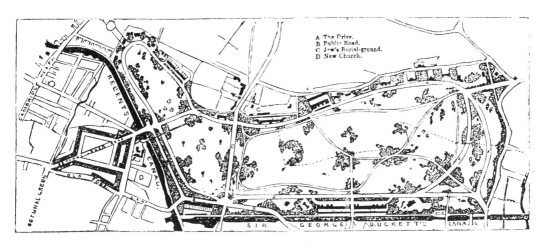

A The Price.
B Public Road.
C Jew's Burial-ground.
D New Church.

19 Victoria Park, London, 1843.

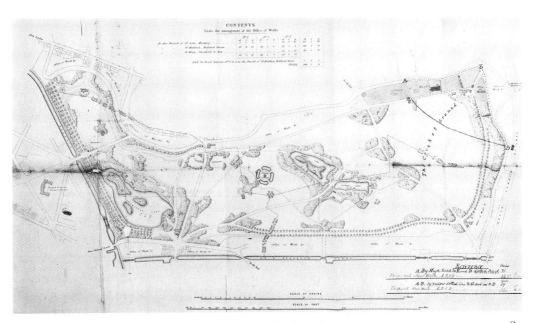

20 Victoria Park, 1863.

who trained with him and subsequently went on to design parks themselves. Edward Milner worked with Paxton on Prince's Park, Liverpool (1843), Crystal Palace Park, Sydenham (1852–6) and the People's Park, Halifax (1856–7), before going on to set up his own practice and design municipal parks at Preston and private parks at Glossop and Buxton. In the last phase of his career he became director of the Crystal Palace School of Gardening. Edward Kemp was trained at Chatsworth and supervised the construction of Birkenhead Park for Paxton. He set up his own practice in 1847 and went on to design Hesketh Park, Southport (1868) and Stanley Park, Liverpool (1870). John Gibson had also worked at Chatsworth before being appointed superintendent of Victoria Park, London. He worked with Pennethorne on the design of Battersea Park, London (1856), subsequently becoming overseer of the London royal parks in 1871.

The national importance of Paxton's work as a landscape designer has been well established and an analysis of the design of his early parks illustrates how particular features were accommodated within his designs. If Prince's Park, Liverpool, (Fig. 9) is compared with Birkenhead Park (Fig. 21) the similarities become apparent, particu-

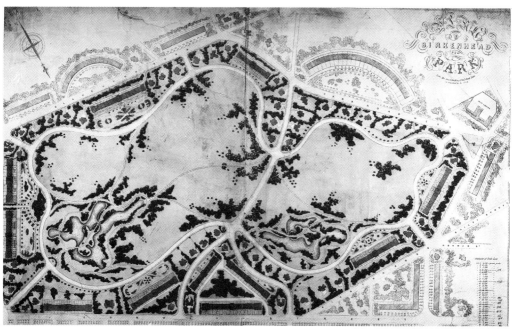

21 Birkenhead Park, c.1845.

larly if the latter is considered as effectively two parks, divided by
Ashfield Road running from north-east to south-west. Both feature
short terraces of housing that appear to be within the boundaries of
the parks, and the lakes provide the focal point of interest within the
parks. The islands in the lakes prevent the whole expanse of water
being taken in at a glance, so its extent is not evident. The edges of the
lakes are well planted so that they are not obvious and the footpaths
around them vary in their distance from the lake edges, so that a
variety of views is presented. Birkenhead Park differs from Prince's
Park in the broken ground introduced around both lakes. Mounds
and rocky formations created partly out of the lake excavations
enclose the area around the lakes, adding to the privacy of that part of
the park and to the variety of the landscape. In both parks open grass
contrasted with small-scale, more intimate, planting. The areas of
formal planting and the layout of the footpaths near the park
boundaries, reflect the formality of the crescents and terraces of
housing facing the park, and contrast with the informal planting and
winding footpaths of the inner areas of the parks. Unlike Derby
Arboretum, there are no straight walks terminated by small buildings
within the parks.

A major difference between the two parks, apart from their size,
was the circulation system, which was very sophisticated at Birkenhead Park. Paxton provided for through traffic across the park (Ashfield Road), pleasure traffic within the park and a separate circulation
system for pedestrians. F. L. Olmsted, the American landscape
designer, visited Birkenhead Park in 1850 and again in 1859, and in
the designs he created with Calvert Vaux for Central Park, New
York, he developed many of the ideas present at Birkenhead Park.
He wrote vividly of his first visit and of the features he found most
interesting. The main entrance (Fig. 42) he found too heavy and
awkward, but a short distance up the avenue he found a 'thick,
diversified, luxuriant garden . . . a perfection I never before dreamed
of', consisting of winding paths, varying surfaces and a variety of
shrubs and flowers set in borders of green turf.[27] About a quarter of a
mile from the entrance he came to an open field of densely mown
grass where cricket was being played, and beyond this a large
meadow with sheep, where women and children were playing. He
was fully aware of the significance of the project, for in America at
that time there was nothing comparable. At the same time he also

noted such practical features as the drainage, the macadamised road surfaces, the buildings and the circulation system.

By 1845 the park had been laid out and Paxton, concerned that 'the peculiar characteristics of the place' be developed, suggested that Edward Kemp, who had trained at Chatsworth, be retained as head gardener, with free accommodation in one of the lodges, as was 'the almost invariable custom'. He also thought that the park overlooker should live in a lodge in the centre of the park as 'it is the usual practice in good gardens'.[28] In other words the standards appropriate to the maintenance of private property should be applied to Birkenhead's municipal park. Paxton's concern with maintenance also included the costs of upkeep and 'provided the return from the Grassland be appropriated to the use of the Park, as of Course it will be, £1,000 a year will enable the Superintendent to maintain it in the highest possible order'.[29] The grass was let for grazing, and Kemp recommended that the hay should be auctioned and this was agreed.[30]

The features that the Manchester/Salford parks, Victoria Park and the two Paxton parks had in common were the variety and diversity of the design and planting, together with areas of open grass. In the Manchester/Salford parks Joshua Major accommodated various sports within his designs right from the outset, but Paxton's plan of Birkenhead Park gave no indication of any sports facilities and the open spaces were not identified with any specific activities. In May 1846 the Birkenhead Cricket Club asked the Birkenhead Road and Improvement Committee (BRIC), who were responsible for the park, for the use of a smooth portion. This request was referred to Kemp, who was instructed to consult with Paxton on the matter.[31] At that date it was evidently not clear to the Committee how Paxton intended the open spaces to be used. By the time the park was officially opened in 1847, both cricket and archery grounds had been established.[32] The archery grounds received official approval in 1850,[33] and in 1854 the quoit ground was positioned behind the cricket tent.[34] By 1857 there were three cricket grounds in addition to the quoiting ground,[35] and football was allowed in 1861.[36] Initiatives for the sports in Birkenhead Park came from the community, and they were accommodated within Paxton's design rather than being included from the outset. Apart from the main entrance to Birkenhead Park, none of these parks of the 1840s included any formal features either in their layout or in their buildings. These were introduced during the succeeding decades and one of the major influences was the Crystal Palace Park at Sydenham.

When the Crystal Palace was built in Hyde Park in 1851, no major alterations were made to the landscape around it and the engravings reproduced in the *Illustrated London News* showed how the scale of the trees and the size of the Serpentine seemed to form a perfect setting according to picturesque principles. When it was decided in 1852 to move the Crystal Palace, Paxton, with the directors of the newly formed Crystal Palace Co., purchased a site near Sydenham. Their intention was to create a pleasure garden whose costs would be met by the entry fees and whose great advantage would be that it could be used in all kinds of weather. Unlike existing pleasure gardens, the new Crystal Palace would offer 'Refined recreation, calculated to elevate the intellect, to instruct the mind, and to improve the heart ... [of] the millions who have now no other incentives to pleasure but such as the gin palace, the dancing saloon and the ale-house afford them'.[37] Despite these high-minded sentiments alcohol was sold there.

The new Crystal Palace, which opened in 1854, was an altered and enlarged version of the original one. It was sited on the top of a hill, so Paxton was faced with the problem of designing an appropriate setting for it. His solution was to adopt Italian principles of garden design for the area nearest the Crystal Palace and create a series of grand terraces as shown in Fig. 22, with a view over the park and a magnificent display of waterworks. The latter were opened by Queen Victoria in 1856 and consisted of fountains, cascades and water temples. Like the Crystal Palace, the domed water temples were structures of iron and glass, but a calm day was necessary in order to see the 'glassy films in tinted shades'. On the occasion of the official opening, unfortunately, it was gusty and the wind 'drove the sparkling element ... over ten thousand dresses in an instant'.[38]

Below the axially displayed fountains and terraces was an open space bounded by informally planted trees, and beyond these were two lakes whose forms were similar to those in Paxton's earlier parks (see Fig. 23). On the islands was a collection of prehistoric animals which formed part of the educational attractions of the park, and

22 Plan of Crystal Palace Park, 1856
This plan, which was not to scale, shows the formal elements and the transition
to informal planting further away from the Crystal Palace.

nearby was a section of geological strata featuring a seam of coal (see
Chapter 7).

23 Crystal Palace Park, Sydenham, watercolour by James Duffield Harding.

The strong formal elements introduced at Sydenham were on a much smaller scale in Paxton's next municipal park, The People's Park, Halifax (1857) shown in Fig. 24. The park is symmetrical about its east/west axis with a terrace from which it was possible to see to the moors beyond the town. Beyond the central fountain the design becomes informal with lakes and trees. In order to shut out views of the immediate surroundings Paxton, like Loudon, raised mounds around the periphery of the park and the entrances are reached by winding paths, between rocky outcrops, so that the park proper is not immediately visible. The benefactor, Francis Crossley, expressly forbad the playing of any games in this park so Paxton did not have to make any provision for them within his design.[39]

Terraces not only provided a vantage point, pavilions for shelter and a place to display statuary and urns, but they were also a focus for festivities. Their symmetry introduced a formal element into park design that contrasted with the informal layout of the more distant parts of the park and some of them were very imposing edifices. At Peel Park, Bradford (Fig. 25), the terrace was 410 metres long[40] while at Stanley Park, Liverpool, the red sandstone terrace appeared like 'the advance work of a formidable citadel'. To the park users, terraces provided a practical purpose as well as a vantage point, for they

24 People's Park, Halifax, 1857
There is little to indicate that this is a public, rather than a private park, apart
from the numbers of people present. The pavilion appears to be at one end of
the terrace, instead of in the centre, but the enthusiasm for the project can be
gauged from the exaggerated height of the fountain.

offered shelter and in between the showers the raised surface dried
quickly and so could be walked along while the paths under the trees
were still dripping.

Paxton's plan for Queen's Park, Glasgow (1860) also showed a
strong formal element whose focus was a covered winter garden, but
this was not built. Although a 'handsome esplanade' with a 'commanding granite stair' was built instead, this did not provide the
emphasis to the design that the winter garden would have provided.[41]
This formal element might almost be termed a characteristic of
Paxton's parks and some of the parks designed by those who trained
with Paxton also showed formal features. Battersea Park (1856),
designed initially by Pennethorne and subsequently by John Gibson,
showed such features in its central avenue and formal vista.
Elsewhere informality remained the key to the design of most parks
in the 1850s and 1860s. The People's Park (later named Mobray
Park) in Sunderland opened in the same year, 1857, as its namesake
in Halifax. The site in Halifax had been fields, whereas the Sunderland site had been a quarry for building stone which made it unsuit-

able for building development. Instead of this feature being incorporated into the design of the park, the ground was levelled and laid out as walks, but the whole design seems to have lacked clarity in its layout[42] (see Fig. 26). In London, Alexander McKenzie laid out the grounds of the Alexandra Palace from 1863, so that they were in complete contrast to those of the Crystal Palace. He emphasised informality and there was hardly a straight line to be seen (as Fig. 27 shows). This informality can also be seen in Edward Milner's design for Moor Park, Preston (1864) (shown in Fig. 28), which was very similar in feeling to Edward Kemp's design of Stanley Park, Liverpool, a decade later (see Fig. 29). Both featured central areas of open grass with peripheral planting and the only hint of formality is the large terrace on the southern side of Stanley Park.

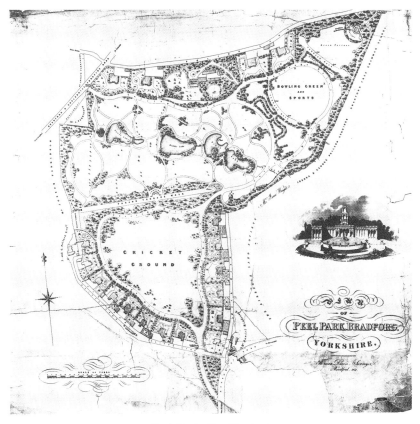

25 Peel Park, Bradford, 1854.

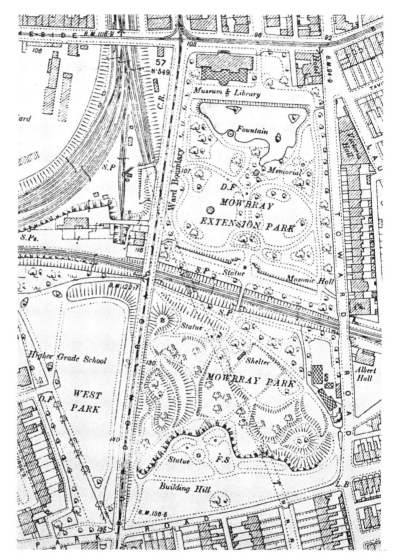

26 People's Park, later named Mobray Park, Sunderland. Mobray Extension Park north of the railway line was added later.

THE INFLUENCE OF FRENCH DESIGN

The dominating influence on park design in the first decades of the park movement in Britain was Joseph Paxton. Meanwhile in France Jean-Claude-Adolphe Alphand, a French engineer and landscape architect, had been laying out the parks of Paris. The sweeping improvements and redesign of Paris undertaken by Baron Haussmann

27 Alexandra Palace, watercolour by Alfred Meeson, c.1863. The only straight line visible is on the left, where trees line the route to the central entrance of the Palace.

for Napoleon III included parks and boulevards, and Alphand had been invited to join Haussmann in 1853. The Bois de Boulogne, the Parc Monceau, the Buttes-Chaumont and the Parc Montsouris were among the parks laid out by Alphand, who was advised by Barillet-Deschamps on the planting and design, and assisted by a young landscape architect, Edouard André, whom Alphand had invited to join the team.[43] It was André who introduced Parisian principles of park design to Britain and the first park in Britain to show that influence was Sefton Park, Liverpool (1872). The competition for the design of this park was won in 1867 by Edouard André and Lewis Hornblower of Liverpool, who had earlier contributed to the design of various buildings in Birkenhead Park. The second prize was won by Edward Milner with Joseph Newton. The Council drew up a list of points to guide the competitors, which included preserving

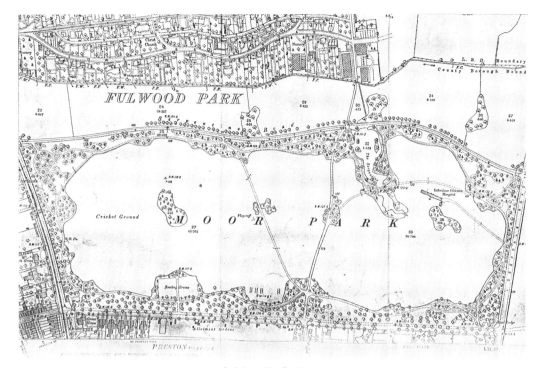

28 Moor Park, Preston.

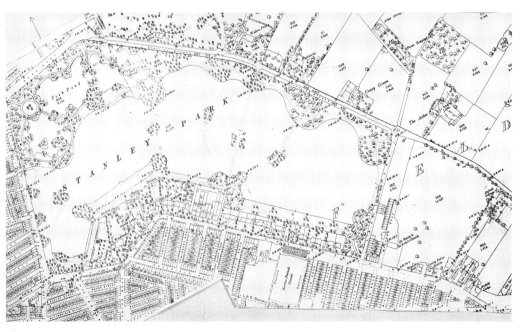

29 Stanley Park, Liverpool.

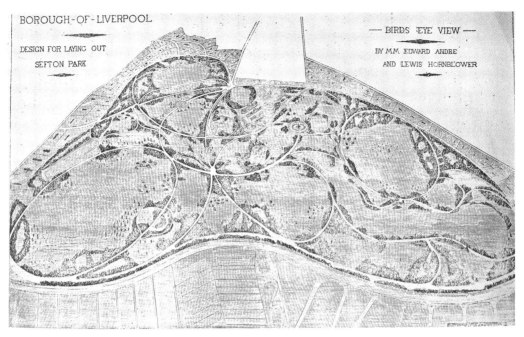

BOROUGH-OF-LIVERPOOL

DESIGN FOR LAYING OUT
SEFTON PARK

— BIRDS EYE VIEW —

BY MM. EDWARD ANDRE
AND LEWIS HORNBLOWER

30 Sefton Park, Liverpool, 1867.

the longest vistas in the park so as to increase its apparent size and positioning churches, bandstands and refreshment pavilions as points of interest to terminate those vistas. The walks in the park should provide ready communication to all parts and there should be open ground for cricket and military reviews. Outside the park the building sites should be arranged so that there was maximum return with the least damage to the ornamental character of the park.[44]

The problem faced by André was that the site was completely barren but very undulating. A valley ran down the centre of the park, joined by another from the eastern side, and both had a drop of about thirteen metres. This suggested a series of cascades leading to a main lake in the south of the site (as shown in Fig. 30). At commanding points it was intended to place a variety of buildings, but many of those proposed were not constructed and the botanic gardens, formal garden and grand conservatory, which would have cost an additional £40,000, did not materialise.[45] The most important innovation was André's layout of the paths and drives within the park. These enclosed a series of open spaces for a variety of activities, screened by peripheral planting which potentially offered a solution to the

99

problem of accommodating different sports. The similarities between the design of Sefton Park and Alphand's design of the Buttes-Chaumont and the Parc Monsouris in particular are striking and are evidence of André's debt to Alphand.

SPORTS AND PLAYGROUNDS

The provision for sports and playgrounds varied from park to park and in those which included sports the design problems were resolved in one of three main ways. The pragmatic approach, adopted in Birkenhead, was to add sports facilities piecemeal, as they were demanded, and to fit them into the existing design as conveniently as possible. The separatist approach involved segregating the sports ground and the pleasure ground and treating them as two separate entities, while the integrated approach, adopted by Joshua Major, involved designing for a range of sports and play facilities from the outset. In a sense the pragmatic approach must affect most parks in the long term, for unless they are radically redesigned, all new uses must be accommodated within the existing design. The interesting question, however, is how designers responded to the problem of providing for sports and playgrounds in new parks.

In some instances the solution of separating the sports and playgrounds from the pleasure ground evolved out of the features of the particular site. At Victoria Park, Portsmouth (1878) the railway line ran right through the five-hectare site. The designer, Alexander McKenzie, positioned the playground with its swings, croquet and quoits, south of the line, while the pleasure ground, where users had to keep off the grass, was on the other side of the line.[46] In Bolton, Heywood Recreation Ground was laid out in 1866 in two portions, separated by a central walk. The larger portion of the three and a half hectares consisted of a bowling green, cricket grounds, gymnasia, and 'other facilities for public enjoyment' and the smaller portion featured a raised terrace with flower beds and intersecting walks.[47] William Gay in his design for Saltaire Park (1871) (see Fig. 31) went some way towards overcoming this separation. The northern portion of the park featured walks and flower beds with the croquet ground and bowling green 'cut in elegant designs ... approached by gracefully winding walks, the intervals being beautified by shrubs and trees'.[48] The rectangular site for the bowling green is clearly visible on the

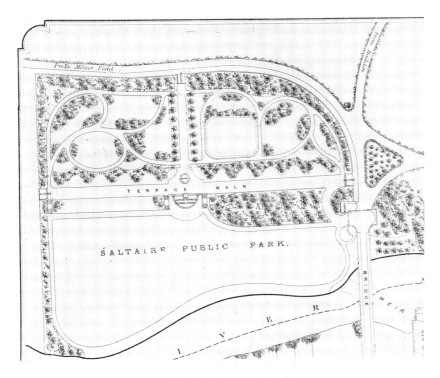

31 Saltaire Public Park, 1881.

plan. South of the broad gravelled terrace walk was an open area for cricket and other sports. In separating the sports and playgrounds from the pleasure ground, designers were in effect avoiding the difficulties posed by these very different park facilities. The reality of these difficulties becomes more apparent if some of the less successful solutions are compared with some of the more successful ones.

APPROACHES TO INTEGRATION

The approach of Joshua Major to the problem of accommodating sports and playgrounds was to provide a centrally positioned open space for sports such as cricket and to position activities requiring smaller spaces around the periphery of the parks, where they could be screened by planting. The need for separating activities and screening them seems to have been generally accepted, and when Broadfield Park in Rochdale was created in 1871, the boys' playground and gymnasium was placed at the edge of the park and separated from the rest of the park by a thick belt of planting, which gave privacy to the boys and prevented the playground from becoming 'too prominent an object to those . . . whose tastes lay in another direction'.[49] The girls' playground was screened by a thickly planted bank of earth. Activities requiring small spaces lent themselves to this solution; it was the sports needing large spaces that posed the problem. Peel Park, Bradford (1850) illustrates a successful solution to this problem, while Albert Park, Middlesbrough (1868) would seem rather less successful.

Peel Park, Bradford, acquired largely on the initiative of Sir Titus Salt, was created out of the 23 hectares that formed the grounds of Bolton House[50] which is located on the northern boundary, and the pleasure ground, with its series of lakes, is immediately south of it (Fig. 25). The parade terrace walk separates the pleasure ground from the cricket ground, while the bowling green and sports ground to the north-west are screened by trees. Although the sports areas are clearly separated from the pleasure ground, they are linked by carriage drives and the unity of the whole is reinforced by the planting around the boundary of the park.

A rather different solution can be seen in Albert Park, Middlesbrough (1868). Here there was no pleasure garden already in existence and William Barratt, the landscape gardener of Wakefield, divided the thirty hectares into four areas with cross-walks planted with avenues of trees (as shown in Fig. 32). The bowling green, croquet lawn and maze, appear on the plan interspersed with clumps of trees and bushes and the whole area has a rather scattered look. The ground falls away to the east and the archery ground is positioned between two low hills. Near it a sunken walk leads down to the lower lake.[51] The mixture of formal avenues, winding paths and scattered planting seems to be neither one thing nor the other, and although a number of sports facilities are included they seem to have got in the way of the overall design, rather than becoming the logic from which the design was evolved.

THE INFLUENCE OF SEFTON PARK

It was Edouard André's Parisian principles of park design at Sefton Park, Liverpool (1872) that provided a logical solution to the problem of accommodating sports and playgrounds. Ellipses and arcs of circles provided spaces for such different facilities as a cricket ground, review ground, bird park, deer park and a botanic garden, but frag-

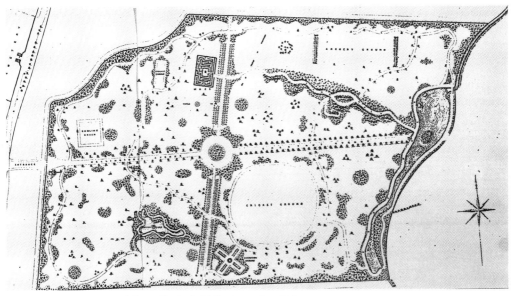

32 Albert Park, Middlesbrough, 1868.

mentation is prevented by the skill with which the spaces are inter-related and held within a tight frame.

In the decade following the opening of Sefton Park, many parks were opened in which there were no, or only a few, sports facilities. Of the parks in which a significant attempt was made to integrate a range of sports facilities into the whole design of the park, two stand out, Stamford Park, Altrincham and West Park, Wolverhampton. Stamford Park (Fig. 33) was designed by John Shaw of Manchester in 1879 and laid out by his son, also called John Shaw. The six-hectare basically rectangular site provides for playgrounds, tennis, croquet, football and cricket within a design based on ellipses, circles and teardrops. Even the bathing pond is elliptical, as is the football pitch. Each area is clearly bounded by paths and the planting is such that there is a partial feeling of enclosure, with occasional views across to other areas of the park.

A competition for the design of West Park, Wolverhampton was held in 1879 and the Council invited estimates not exceeding £5,000. Out of the 27 designs submitted, three were selected for further examination and the first prize of £50 was awarded to Richard Vertegans of Chad Valley Nurseries, Birmingham.[52] The geometrical element in the design of West Park (Fig. 34) is not so apparent as that

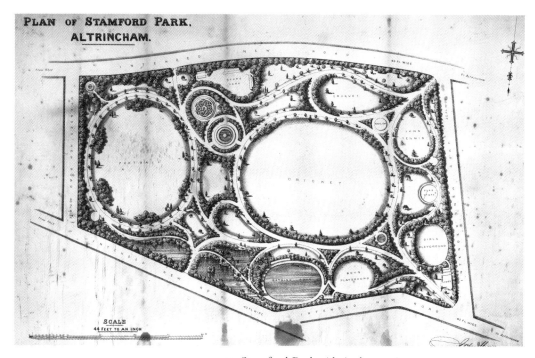

33 Stamford Park, Altrincham, 1879.

in Stamford Park, but a similar principle of enclosing grounds for different activities is applied. Archery ground, bowling green, cricket and volunteer drill grounds are all given their distinct areas within a kidney-shaped site. No provision was made for football in this plan. Superficially it might seem that the two parks have much in common, for both provide separate areas for the different activities offered in the parks. The organisational principles behind the two designs are, however, very different. In Stamford Park ellipses and teardrops make the most of the space within a basically rectangular site but the park user is not encouraged to take any one route in preference to any other. By contrast there is a strong axial element running north to south through the centre of West Park and this forms the spine of the design with the open spaces flowing from it.

William Barron introduced a simple axial plan, with a fountain as the focal point, in his design for Locke Park, Barnsley (1877) (see Fig. 35). In 1878 he won the competition for the design of Abbey Park, Leicester and *The Builder* reported that as the public already had a large recreation ground and cricket ground in the immediate vicinity

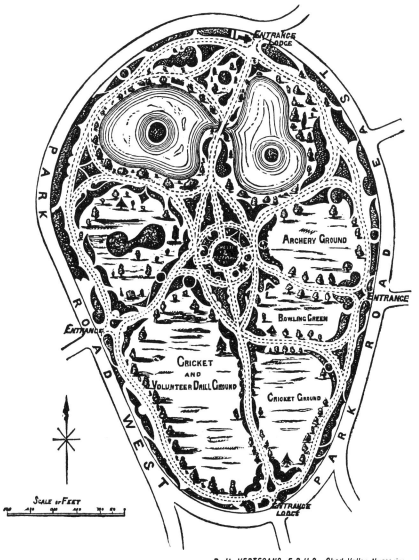

R. H. VERTEGANS, F.R.H.S., Chad Valley Nurseries.

34 West Park, Wolverhampton, 1879.

'the whole 60 acres of the new park is treated as a pleasure ground'[53] (Fig. 36). That statement, together with an examination of the plan, might lead one to conclude that all sports were banished from Abbey Park, but this was not so. Although no indication is given on the plan of particular activities, *The Builder* noted that the design included an 'archery ground, lawn tennis, cricket ground, and bowling green', as

35 Locke Park, Barnsley.

well as an American garden and a rose garden. What is significant is the skill with which Barron accommodated this range of sports within his axial plan.

The long-term solution to the problem of the design of sports grounds lay neither in Barron's solution, nor in André's. This was partly because the principle of enclosing areas for a number of different activities tended to be overtaken by the increasing demand for sports facilities. As the emphasis on active sports grew, the problem of incorporating large spaces, particularly for a number of football pitches or cricket grounds, resulted in prairie-like spaces that were too large to be enclosed by planting. By 1898 Victoria Park in London had 32 cricket pitches and 37 lawn tennis courts.[54] The difficulties of handling such areas in a way that would preserve the feeling of enclosure proved impossible and increasingly the solution was to separate the sports facilities. In the 1880s the emphasis on small accessible recreation grounds located in the inner city areas where they were most needed was one response to this problem; the growth of football and cricket clubs with their own facilities was another.

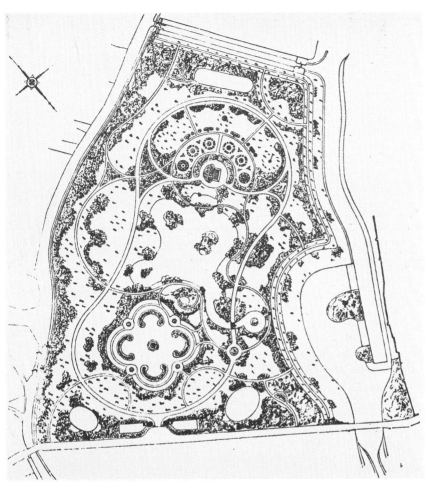

36 Abbey Park, Leicester.

CHAPTER SIX

Lodges, bandstands and the cultivation of virtue

The lodge by the main entrance gates, with the park regulations displayed prominently nearby, is often the first building to greet the park visitor. This was the home of the superintendent responsible for seeing that order was kept in the park and for opening and closing the main gates, morning and evening. The importance of the role of the park superintendent could be emphasised by the scale of the lodge and this in turn reinforced the significance of the park as a place apart. Pennethorne clearly recognised this when he recommended that the main lodge at Victoria Park, erected in 1847, ought 'to contain more conveniences and to be more important in appearance than the other lodges'.[1] 'Elizabethan in character' and built of brick with stone dressings, this was a substantial and imposing building[2] (shown in Fig. 37). A decade later, three more lodges were erected at the other park entrances, but even the largest of these was less imposing than the main lodge[3] (an example is shown in Fig. 38).

Park buildings fall into three main categories: those needed for maintenance, those intended for the park users, and commemorative buildings and structures, which will be the subject of the next chapter. The prototype of most park buildings lay elsewhere, for lodges, shelters, boathouses and pagodas had been a feature of the private parks of the eighteenth century and earlier, while palm houses and conservatories had developed in the early decades of the nineteenth century. The one building that became so closely identified with public parks that it came almost to signify them, was the bandstand, although it too was built elsewhere. Refreshment rooms, toilets, drinking fountains and shelters made it practicable to spend considerable time in the parks, which would otherwise have been impossible, but the need for such facilities had not always been recognised. C. H. J. Smith, the Scottish theorist and practitioner of landscape gardening, who was writing on public parks in 1852, was evidently

37 Main entrance, Victoria Park, London, 1846 (J. Pennethorne).

38 Molesworth Lodge, Victoria Park, c.1856
A picturesque cottage with varied rooflines and wall planes.

not concerned with the comfort of the park users, nor with the question of bad weather. He thought that a superintendent's house, cottages for the gate-keepers and a greenhouse for the propagation and protection of plants would suffice.[4]

In the early stages of the park movement, the design and siting of park buildings were the subject of two virtually opposing principles. The picturesque demand for variety, with buildings set within the landscape, vied with the classical demand for regularity and buildings which were the focus of their surroundings or terminated a vista. Derby Arboretum with its formally positioned pavilions (Fig. 8) and its picturesque 'Elizabethan' and 'Tudor' style lodges, with their steeply pitched roofs and tall chimneys, provided an example of both these principles (see Figs. 39, 40). Some parks were created from sites already featuring large buildings and these, by virtue of their size, formed the main focus of the area of the park in which they were situated, but this did not necessarily mean that the landscape around them was designed to reinforce their importance. Neither in Queen's Park, Manchester nor in Peel Park, Salford did Joshua Major reinforce the significance of the large buildings that he had inherited, by the layout of the landscape around (see Fig. 17b and Fig. 17c).

In some parks with an axial layout, such as the People's Park, Halifax and the Crystal Palace Park, the focus of the axial route was a terrace with buildings. But terraces did not necessarily become the focus of an axial layout, as the example of Peel Park, Bradford shows (Fig. 25). In order to preserve the verdant qualities of the landscape, as a contrast to its urban surroundings, the buildings introduced into the parks were, until the 1870s, generally small-scale and picturesquely positioned so that they were ensconced by trees, or lay low in a fold in the terrain, merging with their surroundings rather than dominating them.

A different attitude to the siting of buildings was evident at Sefton Park, Liverpool (1872), when the Council's guide to competitors suggested that the buildings should be positioned at points of interest and to close vistas.[5] André intended that ornamental buildings should be erected at commanding spots, in a way that was quite different from park practice hitherto, and Lewis Hornblower put forward his

39 Main entrance lodge 'in the Elizabethan style' (E. R. Lamb), Derby Arboretum.

40 East lodge, (E. R. Lamb), Derby Arboretum, showing the public room which visitors could use, on the right.

ideas for some substantial buildings. His proposal for a stone central lodge with French Second Empire detailing, inspired perhaps by André's Parisian principles of park design, was replaced by a cottage orné built beside the main entrance and his other proposals were not built.[6] Except for the palm house, the buildings that were subsequently erected were not positioned to close vistas, although the boathouse (Fig. 41) did have a commanding position beside the lake. With the introduction of increasing formality in park design, seen in Barron's design for Abbey Park, Leicester (1882) (Fig. 36), the siting of buildings tended to become more formal. The refreshment pavilion in Abbey Park is sited at the top of a slight hill with the footpaths and the planting reinforcing its dominant position.

LODGES

The buildings necessary for park maintenance included the lodges for the park keepers, toolsheds, stores, and glasshouses for raising and keeping plants. These would generally be located behind the scenes, rather than forming a part of the park accessible to the public. In Birkenhead Park the buildings designed by Lewis Hornblower and

41 Boathouse, Sefton Park
The timber-framed construction reflects the interest in Old English
architecture.

42 Main entrance, (Robertson and Hornblower), Birkenhead Park, 1847.

John Robertson reflected both picturesque and neo-classical tendencies and the grandest of them was the main entrance (see Fig. 42). John Robertson had contributed designs for lodges to J. C. Loudon's *Encyclopaedia of Cottage, Farm and Villa Architecture and Furniture* of 1839 before going on to become involved in the design of the picturesque model village of Edensor, near Chatsworth. The entrance to Birkenhead Park consisted of two lodges linked by a triple arcaded screen, with giant unfluted Ionic columns. The central archway was for carriages, the two flanking ones for pedestrians, and the whole formed a triumphal arch, a commemorative structure. In this instance the event that was being commemorated was neither a royal visit, nor a military victory, nor the munificence of a local dignitary, but the efforts of the Birkenhead Road and Improvement Committee in creating the park. This entrance was an isolated feature for there was no imposing approach outside the park, but its classical features were reflected in certain of the lodges and in the so-called boathouse/bandstand which housed the boat used for maintaining the lake. Even at the opening of the park this does not appear to have been used as a bandstand (shown in Fig. 43) (see Chapter 9).

43 Boathouse/bandstand, Birkenhead Park.

The formation of a triumphal arch by integrating the lodges with the main entrance gate was not a solution that was widely adopted. Lodges, like the other park buildings, provided an opportunity for architectural variety and those in Birkenhead Park provided an excellent illustration of this. Despite its name, the Gothic Lodge was Tudor in style, with stone quoins and mullions, and ornamental chimney stacks. The Italian Lodge, with its arcaded belvedere tower, was more aptly named, as was the Castellated Lodge (shown in Fig. 44). The Norman Lodges were a pair of axially symmetrical Greek Revival buildings flanking the entrance, each with a Doric porch *in antis*, and the Central Lodge also featured many classical references in its pilastered upper storey, rusticated ground floor and balustraded roofline.

Throughout the century lodge design tended either to reflect what was happening in architecture elsewhere, or else to refer to local architecture, within an aesthetic that was predominantly picturesque. In Grosvenor Park, Chester (1867) the black and white entrance lodge (John Douglas) reflected the half-timbered architecture characteristic of the ancient town and included carvings of the Norman Earls of Chester. By contrast a Tudor style was chosen for Pearson

44 Castellated Lodge, (Robertson and Hornblower) Birkenhead Park.

Park, Hull (1863) and a Swiss style for the main lodge at Mesnes Park, Wigan (1878).

An important exception to this was the Prince Consort's Lodge designed by Henry Roberts and re-erected in Kennington Park in 1852 (see Fig. 45). This had been designed by Henry Roberts for the Great Exhibition of 1851 as Model Houses for Families, and it had been erected in Hyde Park. These Model Houses were part of Roberts' work for the Society for Improving the Condition of the Labouring Classes, whose President was Prince Albert. The houses consisted of four flats, on two floors, each with its own front door. Inside there was very generous accommodation by the standards of the day: a living room, three bedrooms, one for the parents and two for the children, a scullery, a w.c. and an entrance lobby. The exterior walls were constructed of the hollow bricks, patented by Roberts, which made the construction cheaper, provided better heat and sound insulation and reduced the fire risk.[7] Many examples of Henry Roberts' design were built up and down the country, as part of the effort by philanthropic individuals and groups to provide well-designed affordable housing. In the case of the Kennington Park example, the initial intention was to provide a museum of 'Articles relating to Cottage economy', perhaps because the building had originally been erected for exhibition purposes, but this idea did not come to anything.

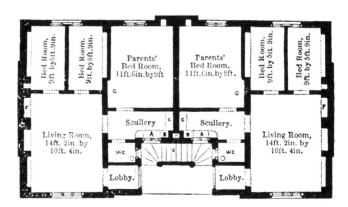

45 Model Houses for Four Families (Henry Roberts). Erected in Hyde Park, at
the Exhibition, 1851 and subsequently erected in Kennington Park.

46 'Matilda', drinking fountain, near Regent's Park (Sculptor, Joseph Durham). Presented by Matilda Kent, the wife of a local churchwarden and erected by the Metropolitan Drinking Fountain Association in 1878.

DRINKING FOUNTAINS

If parks were to be used for any length of time some method of slaking the thirst was essential, otherwise children were seen 'flocking round the cabstand, and drinking with the horses out of their pails'.[8] One solution was to provide free drinking fountains. These could be donated by individuals, whose generosity was usually recorded on the gift, by public subscription, or by organisations such as the Metropolitan Free Drinking Fountain Association set up in 1859 by Samuel Gurney, a Quaker member of parliament and nephew of Elizabeth Fry. The Association was closely connected with the Temperance Movement and it aimed to provide drinking fountains of pure cold water in public places (see Fig. 46 for an example). It was in effect a radical challenge to the free-market private water companies and London's heavily polluted and inadequate water supply. The first fountains were made of cast iron, but later, in the 1870s, grand granite fountains were supplied. The Association began also supplying cattle troughs in 1867 and this was when it changed its name to the Metropolitan Drinking Fountain and Cattle Trough Association[9].

Drinking fountains provided an ideal opportunity for education, for praising the delights of water and for promoting the values of temperance. In the People's Park, Halifax the drinking fountain had 'Thank God for Water' inscribed on one side and on the other 'Water is Best'. Nearby, the sundial, presented by the Mayor in 1878, had 'first the moments, then the day, time by moments, melts away' written around its face and warned against idleness. The obelisk in Sefton Park, Liverpool commemorating Samuel Smith, Merchant, MP, Christian philanthropist and friend of India has at its base some fine bas reliefs and the inscription above the drinking jet reads 'He who drinks here shall still thirst, but he who drinks of God shall thirst no more.'

One of the most imposing drinking fountains was the Victoria Fountain, donated by Miss (later Baroness) Angela Burdett-Coutts, designed by Henry Darbishire and installed in 1862 in Victoria Park, London where it is still a major feature (see Fig. 47). Angela Burdett-Coutts was a wealthy philanthropist, who was described by Charles Dickens as 'that Lady Bountiful, at once wise, gentle and charitable'. With Henry Darbishire, who had been involved in designing working-class accommodation for the Peabody Trust, she built housing (1860–2) and the huge elaborate Columbia Market (1866–8) in the East End of London (demolished 1958–66), as well as Holly Village, a picturesque group of eight cottages ornés in Highgate, North London. The Victoria Fountain had piers of red Aberdeen granite supporting slender pointed arches and a cupola covered in green and purple slates with four inset clock dials. Under the cupola, in the high groined vault, are four cherubs seated on dolphins, and above the water taps is the inscription 'Temperance is a bridle of gold.' Higher up the inscriptions read 'The earth is the Lord's and all that therein is' and 'The Victoria Fountain'.

Sometimes these fountains were erected elsewhere first and subsequently moved to the parks. The drinking fountain at one end of Clapham Common, London was erected near London Bridge by the Temperance Society in 1884 and shows a woman offering water to a man bent over a crutch (see Fig. 48). It was moved to the Common in 1895.[10] Another solution to the problem of thirst was to allow vendors of soft drinks such as lemonade and ginger beer into the parks, but the bye-laws of many parks prohibited this. A third alternative was the provision of refreshment rooms.

THE VICTORIA
DRINKING-FOUNTAIN
VICTORIA PARK   GIVEN TO THE PEOPLE
BY MISS BURDETT COUTTS.
HEIGHT 58FT 7IN — BASE 40FT 9IN — OPENED JUNE, 1862

47 Victoria Fountain, Victoria Park, 1862 (Henry Darbishire). Set against
rising ground with hills and trees. In reality it sits on a grass plain.

48 Drinking Fountain, Clapham Common (Sculptor A. von Kréling, memorial
designed by Charles Barry)

REFRESHMENT ROOMS AND MUSEUMS

The types of building allowed in parks, and the use of existing buildings, related to the whole question of recreation and to the regulation of activities in the parks. In Derby Arboretum Strutt was concerned with the practical needs of the park users, for each lodge provided a room where the public could sit and eat their own refreshments without any charge, or else lunch was provided at the cost of the provisions[11] (Fig. 40). There were also 'proper yards and conveniences' for public use, separate from those used by the occupants of the lodges.[12] Such facilities were not always readily agreed to and soon after the Manchester parks had been created, the Public Parks Committee discussed the need for public conveniences. With no nearby facilities 'the importance of securing females from all possible intrusion' needed to be considered.[13] The Honorary Secretary of the Committee charged with setting up the parks disagreed with the idea of female toilets. 'It is not desirable at any time to have too much accommodation of this kind, nor are the public parks the proper places for such matters. Besides I do not think that too much encouragement should be given to such occupation and I conceive that there is indelicacy in the very idea.'[14] The Council nevertheless decided that toilets should be built in the Manchester parks. Cast iron manufacturers provided designs for a variety of park buildings and Fig. 49 shows a Walter Macfarlane & Co.'s design for urinals.

Where substantial buildings were already in existence a common solution was to provide refreshment rooms in them. In Peel Park, Salford the 'very large mansion', which had been the residence of the High Sheriff of the County, housed refreshment rooms, a library and a museum.[15] The library containing 7,000 volumes opened in January 1850, and a museum of natural history, the following June.[16] C. H. J. Smith, citing the success of the museum in Peel Park, recommended that large buildings in parks should be used for picture galleries, museums of natural history or museums of antiquities.[17] Such uses would reinforce the educational role of the parks, but the question of financing them could present difficulties.

In 1855 the Manchester Public Parks Committee recommended reading rooms in both Queen's Park and Philips Park. They commended the idea of museums in refreshment houses, but thought that 'the means of accomplishing them and affording their upkeep

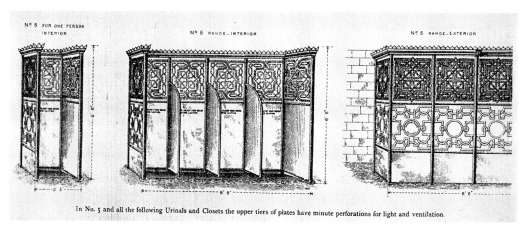

N.º 5 FOR ONE PERSON
INTERIOR

N.º 5 RANGE—INTERIOR

N.º 5 RANGE—EXTERIOR

In No. 5 and all the following Urinals and Closets the upper tiers of plates have minute perforations for light and ventilation.

49 Urinals, (c.1880) (Walter Macfarlane)

represented great difficulties'.[18] They also considered establishing a library in each park but thought that the location was inappropriate. In 1864 a museum, which was open every day except Sunday and Christmas Day, opened in Queen's Park, and the 'importance of imparting popular information has been kept strictly in view'. On the anniversary of its opening the following year, it was noted that the average attendance had been 764 people per day and the total attendance was 239,156.[19] Under the Public Health Act 1875 museums, a conservatory or a free library were allowed to be built in parks. Manchester's record in this area has been sustained and today branches of the City Art Gallery are located in five municipal parks.

Refreshments were not necessarily housed in imposing buildings and Fig. 50 (bottom left) shows the modest wooden refreshment saloon in Victoria Park. In Chapel Field Gardens, Norwich, the thatched tea pavilion reflected the influence of the English domestic Revival and the revival of Old English and vernacular forms of architecture (Fig. 51).

Since parks were seen as an alternative form of recreation to the public house, alcohol was not usually sold, but there were exceptions to this rule and in Roundhay Park, Leeds the question of alcohol became a test of strength between the Temperance and the non-Temperance members of the Council. When Roundhay Park was acquired in 1872, the Council wanted to encourage people to use the park, which was five miles from the centre of town, and one method of doing so was to allow the sale of alcohol. There had been

50 Views of Victoria Park, 1873.

51 Thatched tea pavilion, c.1880, Chapel Field Gardens, Norwich.

Temperance members on Leeds Town Council since the early 1860s and their spokesman, George Tatham, a Quaker leather manufacturer, was naturally against the proposal, so the Council decided to ban the sale of spirits but to allow the sale of other forms of alcohol. The following year the Council planned to let Roundhay Mansion as a hotel and Tatham organised a petition from more than 11,000 people calling for a complete ban on the sale of alcohol there. Thereafter the annual debate in Leeds Council on the renewal of the Roundhay Hotel licence became a battle between the Temperance and the other members of the Council, but the Temperance members achieved only a short-lived triumph in 1884.[20]

Not only was the sale of alcohol prohibited in the majority of municipal parks, in addition the refreshment rooms in some of them were closed during Sunday church services.[21] By contrast alcohol was sold in the Crystal Palace Park, a semi-public park and 'Twenty-two years of experience show how the millions appreciate such a place of wholesome recreation and refinement ... Upward of thirty millions have been there, and not one in a million have been reported by the police as being drunk and disorderly'.[22] Evidently if visitors paid an entrance fee, as they did to enter the Crystal Palace Park, it was all right to consume alcohol, but if the park was freely available, it was not. The absence of alcohol and the exhortations on the drinking fountains illustrate how opportunities were taken in the municipal parks to promote education and cultivate virtue. That this was an effective way of changing behaviour was 'proved' statistically in Macclesfield. West Park had opened in Macclesfield in 1854 and it was noted that three years later cases of 'drunkenness and disorderly conduct' had decreased by 23%, the use of profane language by 60%, gambling by 50% and summary charges of every class by 26%. Although there were other opportunities for rational recreation in Macclesfield, such as the Sunday Schools and the Mechanics Institutions, these had been in existence for years, whereas 'the park has existed just for the period that has witnessed such a remarkable decrease of those offences which are committed by persons exposed entirely to debasing pleasures, having no means of innocent recreation'.[23] A similar point was made about the civilising role of the Victoria Fountain. By the early 1870s this had a well-planted garden around it, with 'pieces of water' between each of the large flowerbeds and planted vases at each corner, 'all tending to make the crystal streams more inviting'. This commentator thought that 'If such magnificent donations were more common, we might be sure of having our streets as well as our parks much freer from the effects of strong drink'.[24]

PAGODAS AND BANDSTANDS

The diversity of buildings for public use present in Victoria Park by 1873 can be seen in Fig. 50. They included a Chinese pagoda, a rustic seat with a bandstand behind it, boathouses and a refreshment saloon. In addition there was a Moorish/Romanesque arcade, designed by Pennethorne as a shelter from the rain (shown in Fig. 52) and the Victoria drinking fountain. Garden buildings in the Chinese taste had become fashionable in England in the late 1740s and early 1750s, although they never became as fashionable as chinoiserie furniture and decoration. A Chinese summerhouse had been built at Stowe in 1746 and one designed by Thomas Anson was built at Shugborough in 1747 together with a Chinese bridge. By 1750 there were Chinese

52 Arcade, Victoria Park (J. Pennethorne) damaged during the Second World War and subsequently demolished.

pavilions in the London pleasure gardens of Ranelagh and Vauxhall. The Chinese taste in architecture was promoted by the publication of pattern books and by the first translation into English in 1752 of a description of the gardens of the Imperial Summer Palace outside Peking.[25] Sir William Chambers became a keen advocate of the Chinese taste in landscape gardening and his design for the pagoda in Kew Gardens (1761–2) still survives, although much altered.[26]

Interest in the pagoda continued into the early decades of the nineteenth century and one seven storeys high, designed by John Nash, was set up in the middle of a bridge over the canal in St James's Park, to celebrate a victory over Napoleon in 1814. This wooden structure formed the centre of a firework display, but unfortunately it caught fire and fell into the water. At Alton Towers, Staffordshire the Earl of Shrewsbury built a little duck pagoda, an open three-storey structure with the ground floor set aside for waterfowl, between 1814 and 1827,[27] and Loudon included an illustration of a five-storey pagoda/fountain standing on a pond in Alton Towers in his *Encyclopaedia of Cottage, Farm and Villa Architecture* of 1835.[28] The pagodas that were installed in Victoria Park and in Birkenhead Park represented further examples of the continuing interest in this particular form of garden building. The Victoria Park pagoda was installed on an island in the ornamental lake in 1848, with the idea that either the Eastern Literary and Scientific Institution could become tenants, or else that it could serve as a boathouse[29] (see Fig. 53). In Birkenhead Park the pagoda served as a shelter and was also sited on an island, reached by means of the Chinese bridge.[30] Pagodas were not widely built in parks in the following decades, but one of the most imposing of those to be erected was the two-storey cast-iron pagoda in Chapel Field Gardens, Norwich, erected in 1880. This had been designed by Thomas Jekyll and exhibited at the Paris and Philadelphia Exhibitions of 1876[31] (shown in Fig. 54). Pagodas also served as commemorative structures and as one of the influences on the development of the bandstand.

The idea that musicians should be positioned on a raised platform had been established in the pleasure gardens of the eighteenth century and in Vauxhall Gardens in 1737 there was a circular two-storey masonry pavilion, with the orchestra positioned in the upper storey.[32] With the availability of new materials, masonry could be replaced by cast iron and the bandhouse in the centre of the dancing platform in Cremorne Pleasure Gardens (1847), was in the form of a 'monster pagoda', with slender columns of cast iron[33], accommodating up to fifty players (see Fig. 5). When the Royal Horticultural Society Gardens, Kensington opened in 1861, they included two band houses, as they were then termed, but these were of a different form (see Fig. 55). 'Light and tasteful in design', these were circular-domed constructions of iron and wood, with the wood covered in zinc.[34] One of them was moved to Clapham Common in 1890 where it stands to this day (see Fig. 56). Like the Cremorne pagoda, these bandstands were on raised platforms, but instead of being based on the design of a pagoda, they were based on that of a kiosk or open pavilion common in Turkey and the Near East. The Crimean War (1854–6) had been fully reported at the time, the press carried detailed accounts, nearly every issue of the *Illustrated London News* illustrated aspects of the conflict, and in 1855 visitors to the Surrey Zoological Gardens in London could 'experience' Sebastopol for themselves. In these pleasure gardens was a large model of Sebastopol, created from maps and drawings, with the fleets blockading the harbour, the forts, the Malakov Tower, the Redan and other places familiar from the reports of the seige. To add verisimilitude a number of troops invalided out

53 Pagoda in Victoria Park, removed after the Second World War.
Watercolour by Joseph Maccoby, c.1913.

54 Pagoda, 1880, Chapel Field Gardens, Norwich.
Removed and replaced by a brick shelter in 1948.

55 Royal Horticultural Society Gardens and the Great International Exhibition, Kensington. Chromolithograph, Leighton, 1862.

56 RHS bandstand on Clapham Common.

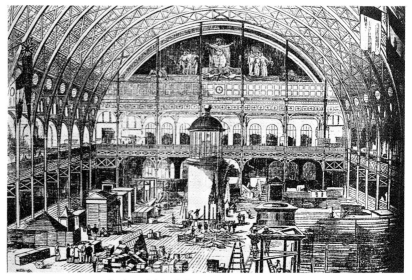

57 Industrial Exhibition Building, Paris, 1855.

of the Crimea mimed sorties, attacks and manoeuvres, 'aided by the pyrotechnical resources peculiar to the establishment'.[35]

The RHS Gardens with their large conservatory and the two bandstands were designed by Captain Francis Fowke of the Royal Engineers. If Fowke had been involved in the Crimean War (1854–6), or in the organisation of the Selimye Barracks, the site of Florence Nightingale's hospital at Scutari/Kadiköy, he could have seen examples of this particular pavilion form, but in 1854 he had been sent to Paris where he was placed in charge of the machinery for the Paris Exhibition of 1855 and he remained there until 1857. Fowke's first direct contact with the pavilion form of bandstand probably stemmed from the Paris Exhibition which opened, after some delay, in May 1855. In the centre of the Industrial Exhibition building was such a pavilion, raised on high (see Fig. 57). On Fowke's return to England he became an inspector of the Science and Art Department and in that capacity he designed galleries, museums, the buildings for the International Exhibition of 1862, the main quadrangle of what is now the Victoria and Albert Museum and the Royal Albert Hall. He died in 1865, and according to Sir Henry Cole had been near to solving the problem of the decorative use of iron for structural purposes.[36]

Music had been played in the parks in the 1850s, before bandstands

were introduced, but bandstands gave a focus to this activity and they
became very popular. When Victoria Park, Portsmouth opened in
1878, the attractions that were singled out in the description of the
opening ceremony were the drinking fountain with its twelve metre
diameter basin, the bandstand and the children's playground.[37] Until
1890 the only municipal parks in London to feature bandstands were
Finsbury, Southwark, Battersea and Victoria Park, but this situation
changed after the LCC came into office[38] (see, for example, Fig. 58).
By the end of the century bandstands had become such a feature of
parks that they had 'acquired the quality of almost sacred pre-
cedents.'[39] Indeed 'no park large or small, is considered complete
without one' and bandstands seemed to symbolise happy hours of
entertainment.[40] Visitors either sat down to listen to a concert or else
strolled around, and the bandstand was rarely the focus for dancing,
as it had been in the pleasure garden. Music was seen as an important
moral influence and 'musical cultivation is the safest and surest
Method of popular culture', so in this view the bandstand became a
further aspect of the reforming potential of parks.[41]

Manufacturers provided a wide range of designs and Walter Macfarlane & Co., Glasgow published illustrations of their bandstands,
giving details of where particular designs were erected.[42] Some of the
designs, which combined a bandstand with a clock tower, were very

58 Bandstand and shelter, Myatt's Fields, London, c.1890.

59 Bandstand with clock-tower, Chalkwell Park, Southend-on-Sea.

elaborate indeed (for example Fig. 59). Information from other manufacturers was not so readily available and although the two-volume 1875 catalogue of the Coalbrookdale Co. had a section on Garden and Park Embellishments, this gave no illustrations of band-stands. Archives for the period in question have not survived, but extant drawings and photographs indicate that bandstands were in production from c.1870. Although there are no details of where and to whom the Coalbrookdale bandstands were supplied, Greenwich Park, London features one which was installed c.1880. Iron manufac-turers did not have a monopoly in this area as Fig. 50 indicates, and the bandstand in Victoria Park was a rustic bandstand, not a cast iron one, as was the bandstand in Brockwell Park (Fig. 60).

Despite their popularity bandstands had their critics, and Reginald Blomfield, the architect, thought that they were among the 'most

60 Rustic bandstand, Brockwell Park, c.1910.

distressing' features of parks because of their ornate designs.[43] Nevertheless bandstands continued to be built in parks until the 1930s. In
the post-war period tastes changed and as the fabric of the surviving
bandstands deteriorated they tended to be removed rather than
restored. Latterly recognition of the merits of bandstands has led
either to restoration *in situ* or to preservation by dismantling them
and re-erecting them in museums. The Walter Macfarlane bandstand, for example, that had been erected in Saltwell Park, Gateshead
in 1907, was dismantled in 1975 and now stands in a partly recreated
park in the Beamish Museum in County Durham.

PALM HOUSES

During the latter part of the nineteenth century palm houses also
began to make a significant appearance in municipal parks. The use
of glass in horticulture had been well established, but it was the
introduction of new and tender plants from warmer climates that
provided a major impetus for improvement in the early nineteenth

133

century. In order for plants to thrive under glass it was important that the maximum amount of sunlight should be transmitted, and this occurred if the sun's rays passed through at right angles to the glass. The problem was that the angle of the sun's rays varied with the latitude, the season and the time of day, so major scientists and horticulturalists experimented and calculated what the optimum form of the glass house should be. In 1815 Sir George Stuart Mackenzie wrote an open letter to Sir Joseph Banks, the President of the Royal Society, giving the results of his calculations of the quantity of sun's rays throughout the day and throughout the year. As a result of these calculations he proposed that a glass half-hemisphere, set against a plain wall, would provide the best results, and he suggested that the glazing bars should be of cast iron in order to maximise the glass surface.[44] Others suggested improvements to this curvilinear design, and Loudon suggested that a peak at the top of the dome would help to shed water. More significant for the subsequent development of the palm house was Loudon's invention of a wrought iron glazing bar which opened up the opportunities for new forms. 'Imagine', wrote Loudon, '. . . a row of detached sections of spherical bodies of an almost perfect transparence . . . and the construction of the edifice combining the greatest strength and durability – what will be the expression?'[45] W. and D. Bailey of Holborn acquired the rights to Loudon's invention and their business thrived as a result.

The subsequent development of the palm house relates closely to the designs of Loudon and others and to the well-known series of experiments carried out by Paxton at Chatsworth, which culminated in the design of the Crystal Palace. The Crystal Palace and the earlier Palm Stove built in Kew in 1844–8 (Decimus Burton and Richard Turner, Dublin) provided magnificent examples of the possibilities of such iron, glass and wooden structures. Palm houses provided a climate in which to grow rare and exotic plants and their sheltered environment could be used at all times of the year. If local authorities were slow to take advantage of these new opportunities this was, at least in part, related to the costs of building and maintenance. Neither of the winter gardens proposed by Paxton for Kelvingrove Park (1854) and Queen's Park (1862) in Glasgow were built and the short-lived enthusiasm for large conservatories, which the Crystal Palace inspired among private patrons, seems to have been retained subsequently only by the nouveaux riches.[46] If funds were raised locally,

61 Palm House, Sefton Park (Mackenzie and Moncur).

or if patrons were prepared to donate a palm house, that was another matter.

In Liverpool the palm houses in both Sefton Park (shown in Fig. 61) and Stanley Park were the gift of Henry Yates Thompson, who had inherited a large part of the £2 million fortune left by his father Samuel Thompson, a banker. The palm houses were designed and built by Mackenzie and Moncur, and opened in 1896 and 1899 respectively. The Stanley Park palm house, known as the Gladstone Conservatory in commemoration of the Prime Minister, cost £10,000.[47] These were large scale buildings, but because palm houses were predominantly of glass they did not dominate their surroundings in the way that masonry structures did. Palm houses introduced visitors to a wide range of sub-tropical and tropical plants and the experience of light and foliage inside was quite different from that outside. 'A breath of the Orient is imparted and the visitor is transported, as it were, into a fairyland of graceful palms, orange, cotton and banana trees and sub-tropical plants in profusion[48] (see Fig. 62). Above all, palm houses extended the use of the park in bad weather in a way that was quite different from that offered by the traditional shelters. For the poor and the unemployed they had the additional advantage of being warm at all times of the year, though some park

135

62 Interior of conservatory in Finsbury Park, London, c.1910.

keepers did not see it as part of their job to share this warm environment with such disadvantaged members of society. In the 1930s the
destitute Helen Forrester recalled crawling, with her younger sister
and baby brother, under the creepers in Sefton Park palm house to
keep warm. If discovered, they would be thrown out by the gardeners
– 'We don't want . . . no dirty ragamuffins in here.'[49]

Despite the fact that Paxton's proposed palm houses for his
Glasgow parks were not built, magnificent glass buildings were built
in other Glasgow parks. The Glasgow Botanic Gardens had been laid
out in 1839 but some half century later were in financial decline. In
1871 the directors agreed that John Kibble's large conservatory should
be moved from his gardens at Coulport and re-erected in the Botanic
Gardens and in exchange Mr Kibble would receive a free lease to use
the building for public meetings, concerts and 'entertainments of an
elevating character'. This arrangement did not prove successful and
in 1891 the Glasgow Corporation took over the Kibble Palace for use
as a winter garden and the Botanic Gardens became a public park.[50]

On Glasgow Green the People's Palace and winter garden, which opened in 1898, formed part of Glasgow's programme of municipal provision, which was already extensive. The idea of a People's Palace was not a new one for in 1863 a Henry Roberts (not Henry Roberts the architect) published a proposal for a people's palace and gardens as a means of providing employment for cotton industry workers unemployed as a result of the cotton famine.[51] His proposal came to nothing but the idea received further stimulus from Sir Walter Besant's popular novel *All Sorts and Conditions of Men* published in 1882. Besant thought that the free provision of music, painting, singing and dancing in centres of rational recreation would bring joy and happiness and as a result political disagreements would decline. This was rather different from the bread and circuses argument, for he thought that sufficient exposure to these cultural activities would lead to a withering of political consciousness. People's Palaces were built in London's East End and in other towns in both Europe and America, although their promoters did not necessarily embrace Besant's thesis. Glasgow's People's Palace was for those living in the deprived area of the East End of Glasgow and the intention was that it should feature a museum, picture gallery, winter garden and music hall all under one roof, with the winter garden acting as both a

63 Interior of Winter Gardens, Glasgow.

conservatory and a hall for music. The People's Palace was designed by the City Engineer, A. B. Macdonald, of red sandstone and the winter gardens, 54 by 36 metres and 18 metres high, were designed in part by William Baird of Temple Iron Works, with the construction by Boyd and Son of Paisley. Local tradition claimed that the profile of the winter gardens was in effect the inverted hull of Lord Nelson's flagship the 'Victory', in deference to the monument to Lord Nelson (1806), the first in the country to be dedicated to him and the first monument to be erected on Glasgow Green[52] (Fig. 63 shows the interior of the Winter Gardens).

Many winter gardens and palm houses were damaged or destroyed during the Second World War and those that survived suffered from problems due to deterioration and the high costs of maintenance. Some, such as the Sefton Park palm house and the large wood and glass John Neild conservatory erected in Stamford Park, Stalybridge/Ashton-under-Lyme in 1907, have been restored (see Fig. 64). Another solution to the problem of maintenance costs has been a change of use, and the Gladstone Conservatory in Stanley Park

64 John Neild Conservatory, Stamford Park, Stalybridge/Ashton-under-Lyme, 1907.

65 Shelter, Alexandra Park, Plymouth (c.1880).

reopened in 1989 after complete renovation including double glazing, as a fully licensed social centre, with restaurants, bars and music.

Throughout the park movement variety remained the key to the design of park buildings, even in those parks created in the last years of the century, when formality became a more significant part of park design. Some of the constructions such as the refreshment houses, the drinking fountains and the bandstands became closely associated with opportunities for the cultivation of virtue, while others such as the lodges proclaimed a hierarchy of importance. Cast iron manufacturers such as Walter Macfarlane provided virtually a complete range of park furnishings from elaborate entrance gates and the railings encircling the park to seats, shelters, bandstands, ornamental fountains and clock towers (see, for example, Fig. 65). Costs could be kept low if a design was manufactured in sufficient quantity, for the principles of prefabrication were an inherent part of cast iron production. Other features that subsequently found a resting place in the parks were the statues, ruins and relics displaced as a result of building or road improvements. In Victoria Park two alcoves which had formed part of Taylor and Dance's London Bridge dating from c.1760 were moved there when the bridge was rebuilt. In Derby

Arboretum the Market Cross or headless stone had once stood in Derby Market Place where it was used for goods about to be transferred from seller to buyer at the time of the plague in 1665,[53] while the Norman archway in Mobray Park, Sunderland came from the courtyard of Bishopwearmouth Rectory when this was demolished in 1856.[54] These fragments and statues posed a problem for the park superintendents who had to decide how best to accommodate them within the existing park design. The pedestals and plinths of statues could 'become the favourite place for the young children of the neighbourhood', but inappropriate to the dignity of the figure commemorated.[55] Rather than fencing the statue off, a preferred solution was to introduce planting around the statue to inhibit access. The preservation of these local historic features by moving them to parks was not just a question of keeping them from destruction, it was also an important means of reinforcing the sense of local identity and local pride.

CHAPTER SEVEN

Local pride and patriotism

Public parks provide space for marking local, national and international events and achievements. A visit by the Queen, the virtues of particular individuals, the achievements of industry and local government, and Britain's imperial role, were celebrated, sometimes in very ingenious ways. The most readily recognisable characters on that stage were those whose statues commanded prominent positions: royalty, MPs, benefactors, dignitaries and local heroes.

By mid century the expanding railway network was making travel quicker, safer and far less exhausting and, until the death of Prince Albert in 1861, Queen Victoria travelled extensively throughout the kingdom, visiting towns and opening new buildings and parks. Such visits were cause for great local celebration, to be remembered with pride. The statues of the Queen that were erected in public parks during the 1850s and 1860s were commissioned largely, if not wholly, in response to a royal visit. On the occasion of her first visit to Peel Park, Salford in 1851, the Queen was greeted by more than 80,000 children and their teachers and a marble statue sculpted by Matthew Noble was erected (Fig. 66). The second visit in 1857 was commemorated by the building of the Victoria Arch[1] (Fig. 67). Similarly when the Queen and Prince Albert visited Pearson Park, Hull in 1854 the event was commemorated by two statues, that of the Queen being unveiled in 1863 and that of the Prince Consort some time later.[2]

After the death of the Prince Consort the Queen went into deep mourning and was rarely seen, except to unveil memorials to him. Salford was one of the first towns to consider erecting a memorial to Prince Albert and the statue, by Matthew Noble, was unveiled in 1864 (Fig. 68). In the 1870s the Queen began to resume public life again and Birmingham was among the places she visited in 1877, in order to lay the first stone of the new Law Courts. She arrived by

66 Queen Victoria, 1851 (Matthew Noble), Peel Park, Salford.

train at Small Heath Station and was first driven slowly round Small Heath Park, before going on to the city centre. The public were excluded from the park that day, but the seven metre wide carriage drive was lined by nearly 50,000 cheering children. This event was commemorated by renaming the park Victoria Park and by a stained glass window in the Great Hall of the Law Courts, which showed the scene in the park.[3] With the Golden Jubilee of 1887 came renewed interest generally in commissioning statues of Queen Victoria, and this was reinforced by the Diamond Jubilee, a decade later, and by the death of the Queen in 1901. Indeed it was in the period after 1887 that the greatest number of statues of the Queen were erected and a number of parks acquired their statues then. Others, such as the equestrian statue of Prince Albert in Albert Park, Halifax were moved to parks as a result of road alterations. Some of these statues were private gifts, others were paid for out of municipal funds, but the majority of them were erected by public subscription.[4]

Public subscription was one of the ways of involving the community and if a transient event such as a royal visit was recorded by a memorial, it could more readily be remembered with pride. Commemorative statuary was a way of enhancing the honour of the crown, or of local heroes, and of reinforcing their status, while the reflected glory added lustre to the locality. Physically elevated on plinths, these statues looked down on the park visitors who were invited, both literally and metaphorically, to look up to them and compare their own position and achievements. In Peel Park, Salford, in addition to the statues of the Queen and Prince Albert, there were statues of the Prime Minister, Sir Robert Peel, and of the local MP Joseph Brotherton, carved by Matthew Noble.[5] No other Prime Minister seems to have been commemorated by having parks named after him. Local MPs, local aristocrats, entrepreneurs and park donors formed a major group of those commemorated and in certain instances two or more of these qualifications were combined in one person. Sir Francis Crossley, for example, was the donor of the

67 Victoria Arch, Peel Park, Salford, 1857.

68 Prince Albert, 1864, (Matthew Noble), Peel Park, Salford.

People's Park, Halifax, owner of Dean Clough Mills and MP for the West Riding of Yorkshire. His statue was erected by public subscription and installed in the pavilion on the terrace in 1860 – 'As a tribute of gratitude and respect to One whose Public Benefactions and Private Virtues Deserve to be remembered', as the plinth records. Over the entrance to the pavilion is the somewhat equivocal inscription, 'Bless the Lord who daily loadeth us with benefits', while on the adjacent pavilions are inscribed texts from the Bible: 'The rich and poor meet together – the Lord is the maker of them all' and 'Let no man seek his own, but every man another's wealth'.

Obelisks, fountains and a variety of buildings, some of them very

grand indeed, served to commemorate achievements. Richard
Vaughan Yates, the founder of Prince's Park, Liverpool is commemorated by an obelisk erected in the park by public subscription in
1858.[6] Fountain Gardens, Paisley was donated by Thomas Coats in
1868 and a grand cast-iron ornamental fountain from George Smith
& Son, Glasgow forms the central focus of the design. Described as
Franco-Italian in character and eight metres high, it is embellished
with dolphins, seahorses, walruses and herons and crowned with a
cluster of aquatic plants. Around the border of the eighteen metre
diameter basin were blocks of rock cast in iron, with shells and small
animals clinging to them. The colour of the cast iron ranged from
sombre tints at the base, interspersed with small bits of brilliant
colouring 'to avoid any feeling of heaviness', with variegated bronzes
above. There were also four other smaller fountains.[7]

Locke Park, formerly Barnsley Park was one of the few parks that
was donated by a woman, Phoebe Locke, and the tower commemorating her gift is one of the few structures dedicated to women,
apart of course from those dedicated to Queen Victoria. Some years
after the gift of Barnsley Park, Phoebe Locke's sister donated an
adjoining piece of land and the tower was erected in 1877 to celebrate
both gifts (see Fig. 69). The inscription on it reads 'To the Memory of
the Donor of the Park, Phoebe, Widow of Joseph Locke, M.P., this

69 The Tower, 1877, Locke Park, Barnsley.

70 Memorial mural drinking fountain to Henry Fawcett, Victoria Embankment Gardens, London (Sculptor Mary Grant)

Tower was erected, and Twenty Acres of Land added to the Park by
her Sister, Sarah McCreery, A.D.1887.' Joseph Locke, the civil
engineer, was a native of Barnsley and its representative in Parliament and his statue stands in the park. The tower consists of three
tiers with balconies on the first and third tiers which gave excellent
views of the surrounding countryside. It is 22 metres high and sur-
mounted by a lantern and weather vane with the gilded initials of the
donor on it.[8] Commemorative structures erected by women were as

71 Ashton Memorial, 1906–9 (J. Belcher and J.J. Joass) Williamson Park,
Lancaster.

rare as those dedicated to them. Figure 70 shows the drinking fountain erected in Victoria Embankment Gardens in 1887, as the plinth
records, by the women of England. This commemorates the efforts of
Henry Fawcett, the blind Postmaster General, to introduce female
labour into the Post Office.

Another commemorative tower, although a much simpler one, was
the Queen's Observatory, also known as Southworth's folly after the
Mayor of Grimsby, in the People's Park, Grimsby (1889). This was
built to mark Queen Victoria's eightieth birthday and it opened in
1900. Constructed of slag, it had a spiral staircase inside, with one step
for each year of the Queen's life, and at the top was an observation
platform. It was demolished in 1949 and some of the 'stones' were
used as a border around the rose beds near the lake.[9]

Of all the commemorative park buildings 'the grandest monument
in England' is the 45 metre high Ashton Memorial in Williamson
Park, Lancaster.[10] This was designed by John Belcher and J. J. Joass,
1906–9 in a flamboyant Edwardian interpretation of the English
Baroque (see Fig. 71). James Williamson, the donor of the park, had

147

72 Sir Joseph Paxton (Sculptor, W.F. Woodington) Crystal Palace Park,
Sydenham, erected 1869.

made his fortune from the manufacture of linoleum. The park
opened to the public in 1896, and Williamson's son, who later became
Lord Ashton, commissioned the building as a memorial to his family;
and it is positioned on a commanding point in the park overlooking
the city and surrounding landscape. The main staircase leading to the
building is of granite, as are the balustrades, and the memorial itself is
of Portland stone. The interior consists of two domed chambers one
above the other. The lower chamber has a geometrically patterned
marble floor, and the dome above has four large frescoes representing
Commerce, History, Art and Science, four smaller frescoes of the
seasons, and the coat of arms of the city of Lancaster. In the upper
chamber there are three stained glass windows, two showing the coat
of arms of the city and the other showing Lord Ashton's coat of arms.
A stone spiral staircase leads to the gallery that runs round this

chamber and to the upper balconies. Although the two chambers contained a few display cases, the primary purpose of the memorial was as a belvedere and it still dominates the landscape for miles around.[11]

The commemoration of royalty and of particular individuals was a feature common to virtually all parks. Park designers, however, were seldom remembered, the portrait head of Sir Joseph Paxton in Crystal Palace Park, Sydenham being a rare exception (see Fig. 72).

It is when one comes to look at what is commemorated that is specific to a locality that one can see more clearly how parks reflected local enterprise, local industry and civic pride. When Victoria Park, Aberdeen was laid out in 1871 a massive granite fountain made of fourteen different granites was positioned at the centre of the park (shown in Fig. 73). The commercial exploitation of the technique of polishing granite developed in Aberdeen in the 1830s, the key figure in its development being Alexander MacDonald, whose firm held the

73 Fountain, Victoria Park, Aberdeen.

monopoly in funerary monuments supplied to London in the 1840s. In the 1850s granites from other parts of the country began to be polished and the following decades saw the increasing use of polished granite in public and commercial architecture.[12] The fountain in Victoria Park was designed, produced and presented to the town by the granite polishers, master builders and companies of Aberdeen. Each contribution was initialled by the donor on the relevant part of the work, and so it represents a rare example of a memorial to, as well as by, local artisans and skilled craftspeople.[13] The more conventional attitude to industry and entrepreneurship can be seen in Lister Park, Bradford, formerly the ancestral home and estate of Samuel Cunliffe Lister, later Lord Masham. Lord Masham's statue stands on a granite pedestal facing the main entrance of the park. On the pedestal are bronze reliefs illustrating hand-woolcombing, the power-loom machine and woolcombing machinery 'in the improvement of which he was intimately concerned'.[14] The celebration of technological feats can also be seen in the memorial to John Fowler, C. E. who gained the first prize of £500 at the Royal Show, Chester in 1858 for his steam cultivator. A monument of the steam plough stands in South Park, Darlington (Fig. 74). Forms of direct advertising also appeared in the parks in the 1870s, for example a 90 metre floral carpet display advertised the name of the Glasgow Herald Newspaper in 1876.[15]

Liverpool's maritime pride could be seen in the figures of James Cook, 'Explorer of Australia'; Henry the Navigator, 'Father of Atlantic exploration'; and Mercator, 'Father of modern cartography', positioned around the octagonal palm house in Sefton Park. They were accompanied by statues of Charles Darwin, John Parkinson 'Apothecary to James I' and André le Nôtre 'The most famous of garden architects', figures of major importance to botanical scientific developments. Local pride was combined with education and the inscriptions on the plinths explained the importance of each of the figures to the park visitors.

GEOGRAPHY AND PREHISTORY

In addition to the achievements of local industry and commerce, local pride showed itself in references to local beauty spots and to prehistoric remains and geological specimens. In Lister Park, Bradford

74 Fowler's Steam Plough, South Park, Darlington.

for example, the well-known Yorkshire waterfall known as Thornton Force was recreated in miniature c.1903,[16] while in Wales miniature standing stone circles with a stone altar at the centre were included in Cathays Park, Cardiff and Victoria Gardens, Neath around the turn of the century (for example, see Fig. 75). Miniature

75 Druid's circle/Gorsedd ring, Victoria Gardens, Neath.

features such as these have a long history, for in 1791 a copy of the first cast-iron bridge at Coalbrookdale was reproduced at one third scale in Wörlitz Park, Magdeburg, Germany and there was also one in a park in Raincy.[17] Miniaturisation offered a means of extending the variety of the park without overwhelming other features and its reintroduction at the turn of the century may perhaps have been inspired by the influence of Japanese gardening.

Among the prehistoric remains there was a fossilised tree trunk and roots, which had been dug up during quarrying in the district, displayed in Horton Park, Bradford,[18] and a grove of ten fossil stems and roots of trees which had been uncovered when Victoria Park, Glasgow (1887) was being laid out by the unemployed from the shipbuilding yards.[19] The most dramatic and largest of all the prehistoric displays was undoubtedly the life-sized range of prehistoric animals gathered on four islands in the lower lake at the Crystal Palace Park (Fig. 76). The islands themselves provided lessons in geology and represented various strata of the earth's crust, although this was obscured by vegetation. Nearby artificial geological cliffs were created with seams including mountain limestone, millstone grit, bands of ironstone, coal and red sandstone (Fig. 77). On the islands pterodactyls, iguanodon, icthyosaurus, plesiosaurus and labyrinthodont were among the ten different prehistoric creatures depicted according to the latest research of the time.[20] They had been commissioned by the Crystal Palace directors and built under the guidance of the senior palaeontologist, Professor Richard Owen. It was Owen who established prehistory as an academic discipline and who first introduced the word 'dinosaur' to the language. The models were constructed by Waterhouse Hawkins from shells of brick, reinforced with iron and faced with stucco, and they represented one of the earliest attempts to portray these creatures three-dimensionally and full-sized. To celebrate the completion of his commission Waterhouse Hawkins organised a grand banquet inside the half-completed body of the iguanodon, on New Year's Eve 1853, with Professor Owen, the guest of honour, seated at the head of the table in the skull and the twenty guests seated on either side of the table in the body.

The models were so strongly constructed that it was more than a century before repairs became necessary. Subsequent research has shown that the mid nineteenth century ideas about the form of these

76 Prehistoric animals, Crystal Palace Park.

77 Artificial cliffs, Crystal Palace Park.

creatures should be modified, but there is no intention of altering or updating them. They are now Grade 1 listed structures and can still be enjoyed in their original environment on the islands in the park.[21]

During the course of the century local authorities gradually acquired the powers necessary to confront some of the major urban problems and the resulting growth in civic pride and consciousness found its expression in the parks from the 1870s onwards. The carpet-bedding displays of local authority coats of arms (Fig. 87), or the mayor's name set out in flowers, illustrate one aspect of that pride, but one of its most dramatic expressions can be found in Kelvingrove Park, Glasgow. In 1872 the Stewart Memorial Fountain was erected by the Water Commissioners, to celebrate the bringing of clean water from Loch Katrine to the people of Glasgow (Fig. 78). Robert Stewart, who had fought for the project 'in the face of the greatest opposition', had been Lord Provost of Glasgow when the Act of Parliament giving the city the necessary powers had been passed in 1854.[22] The Loch Katrine system was completed in 1855–9 and the formal opening ceremony, at the entrance to the tunnel on the loch, was performed by Queen Victoria in 1859. Some years later the question of a memorial to Robert Stewart was raised by the Water Commissioners and a competition was advertised. The winner from among some seventy entries was announced in 1870. James Sellars' winning design was no 'mere garden fountain', indeed it was designed so that water only played an occasional part. Its iconography is based on Sir Walter Scott's poem 'The Lady of the Lake' and the Lady herself, in gilded bronze, crowns the structure. The bust of Lord Provost Stewart is positioned at the base, together with the city arms and the arms of the Stewart family. To the west an allegorical trophy represents the source of the water, while that to the east represents the introduction of the water to the city. Above the twenty metre diameter basin is a crown or lantern of cross ribs which supports the pedestal on which the Lady stands.[23]

78 Stewart Memorial Fountain, 1870 (James Sellars) Kelvingrove Park, Glasgow.

NATIONAL PRIDE

Figures of national and international renown found a place in the parks. Shakespeare's tercentenary, for example, was celebrated by raising a votive altar in Victoria Park, Bath in 1864. The opening ceremony was somewhat marred by the collapse of the platform which the town crier and principle officials in their regalia had just mounted, but no one was hurt and once the audience had got over their surprise they were able to appreciate the scene.[24] In the last two decades of the century the commemoration of well known figures increased. A statue of Robert Burns was erected in Fountain Gardens, Paisley in 1896, and in 1887 bronze statues of Burns, Scott and Watt were installed in Auchmountain Glen. This was a beauty spot which had been transformed in the depression of 1886 into 'a fairy glen', accessible to the residents of Greenock.[25]

Sunderland, with its important naval shipyard, celebrated its pride in those naval traditions in the People's Park (later Mobray Park) with a statue of Britannia holding a shield and a figure holding part of an anchor. Both were installed on the terrace the year after the park opened in 1857. In the following decades other statues were erected and in 1890 the statue of Jack Crawford, a local naval hero and son of a Wear keelman, was installed. Jack Crawford had served on the flagship HMS Venerable in the battle of Camperdown in 1797, when he had climbed up and nailed the colours to the broken mast under heavy fire. For his bravery he was awarded a Government pension and a silver medal was presented by the people of Sunderland. In 1831 he became one of the first victims of the cholera epidemic and was buried in an unmarked grave. His life story was published in 1887 and attention was drawn to the lack of any memorial. The following year a tombstone was unveiled in Sunderland Parish Church and this was followed by the commissioning of a statue.[26] The interesting question here is why his commemoration should strike a chord and be found so appealing in the late 1880s and how it was related to Britain's imperial pre-eminence.

IMPERIALISM

In certain views British imperialism dates from 1877, the year when Queen Victoria was created Empress of India, but a broader view takes a longer timescale and interprets it as the aggrandisement of the State through military conquest, or by more subtle means such as economic strategies, scientific and technological achievements, sport, or other cultural activities. It was in the late 1850s that overt examples of imperialism began to appear in the parks. The Victoria Arch, Peel Park, Salford, designed by Thomas Groom Barker to commemorate the second visit of Queen Victoria and Prince Albert in 1857 is one example (shown in Fig. 67). The arch was opened in 1859 and it featured Indian elements in its horseshoe arches and onion finials. Indian architecture was not new to Britain at that date, but after the completion of Brighton Pavilion in the 1820s it had ceased to play an important role in Britain's architectural development. In the 1850s the main attention of architects was directed towards the development of the High Victorian Gothic and the reasons why this arch was designed as it was may lie elsewhere. One particular event of significance at that time was the transferring of India to the Crown in 1858.

Such arches were not common features, unlike the guns from the Crimean war. From 1857 to the early 1860s a considerable number of municipal parks acquired guns from this war and displayed them with pride. Sometimes the acquisition coincided conveniently with the opening of a new park, sometimes they were added to existing parks, and sometimes they were given to the town and only arrived in the park some years later. The opening of The People's Park, Halifax was marked by a general holiday on 14 August, 1857. The festivities started with a procession to the park from Skircoat Moor and leading the procession were the Sixth West Yorkshire Militia Staff and Band, escorting two Russian guns taken at the fall of Sebastopol. The guns were positioned at the foot of the central steps leading to the terrace, but have since been removed.[27] Vernon Park, Stockport, the gift of Lord Vernon, was opened officially on 20 September, 1858, the fourth anniversary of the battle of Alma, and Lord Panmure, the Secretary of State for War, donated two Russian guns captured in the Crimea.[28] By 1860 Peel Park, Salford had two Russian guns from Sebastopol,[29] and Peel Park, Bradford had received two guns, which flanked a raised platform at one end of the terrace in the park.[30] In Birmingham, two guns which the government had sent were placed near the main entrance of Adderley Park, mounted on their original wooden carriages.[31] Derby Arboretum also received two guns.[32] Some of these guns were in working order, and in 1861 when some 50,000 people gathered in Corporation Park, Blackburn to listen to the playing of eleven brass bands, the occasion was marked by the firing of one of the Russian guns.[33] Usually two guns were given, and Darlington requested two guns but was sent only one. This was placed in what is now South Park (then Bellasses Park) in 1860.[34] In some instances Crimean guns were placed next to figures or objects commemorating other wars. In the People's Park in Sunderland a statue to Sir Henry Havelock was erected by public subscription in 1861, another being erected in Trafalgar Square, London. Sir Henry, the son of a Sunderland shipbuilder, had been sent to relieve Lucknow and Cawnpore in the Indian mutiny of 1857, and had died of dysentery two days after the relief of Lucknow. Two Crimean guns were placed beside the Havelock statue[35] (see Fig. 79).

79 Sir Henry Havelock, Mobray Park, Sunderland.

Some towns such as Middlesbrough received their Sebastopol gun in 1857, but did not place it in a park until more than a decade later. Middlesbrough's gun spent its first years in the Commercial Street Gas Works, and when Albert Park opened in 1868 the gun was placed in it. There it remained until 1949 when it was moved to another park, Stewart Park, and finally, 'when it was falling to pieces', it found a resting place in the Drill Hall, Stockton Road.[36] Unlike most towns which had their Russian guns presented to them free, those in Saltaire Park were purchased by Sir Titus Salt and were British man o' war guns, which had been 'in the Russian war in the Baltic' and 'may have been at the battle of Trafalgar, possibly also at Acre'.[37]

No other war was so widely commemorated as the Crimean War, until the First and Second World Wars. Although the first Nelson's Column was erected on Glasgow Green in 1806, this was exceptional, for the commemoration of the Napoleonic wars occurred in the period before the park movement developed. The 1850s marked a period in which foreign policy was engaging public attention in a way that it had not done since the end of the Napoleonic wars. Britain was waging war on the North West frontier of India and in China, as well as in the Crimea, yet it was the latter that was widely commemorated. Geographically, it would certainly have been easier to bring guns from the Crimea than from the North West frontier, or from China. The questions of why guns were chosen as the means of commemorating the Crimean war and why they were displayed in the municipal parks have no simple answers. It was assumed that all would wish to join in the celebrations associated with the successful conclusion of the Crimean war and would concur in the widespread placing of war trophies associated with it. In that period the technique of rifling was developing and those guns could perhaps be seen as examples of redundant technology, which the War Office had decided to get rid of. Enormous quantities of both guns and ammunition had been captured at Sebastopol, to the value of £26,000, according to a Return made to the House of Commons in 1863.[38] This nevertheless still does not adequately explain why so many guns appeared in so many parks, within such a short time. Another question to consider is the role that the display of such trophies played in stimulating the emotions of pride and patriotism and in so doing, stimulating recruitment to the army and navy. Britain had no standing army or navy, conscription was not compulsory and there was no longer a press gang, yet it was important that recruitment be maintained.

Other wars were commemorated, but not nearly so widely. The 16 ton lion in Forbury Gardens, Reading was erected in 1886 to commemorate the members of the Royal Berkshire Regiment who fell at Maiwand and Khandahar, and during the Afghan campaign (1879–80) (see Fig. 80). There were also Russian guns on Forbury Hill which used to be fired on special occasions.[39] Nottingham Arboretum, which opened in 1852, still features a pagoda flanked by four guns (see Fig. 81). From this pagoda a bell was suspended, which had been taken from a large temple near the east gate of Canton by the Nottinghamshire Regiment of Foot, when that city was captured in 1857. The bell, a mixture of steel and silver, had stood in the principal part of the temple, and was struck during religious ceremonies to call attention to the Joss, or God, or to announce his presence. Two of the guns flanking the pagoda were from Sebastopol and had arrived in 1857 when they were placed outside the Arboretum refreshment room. Subsequently they were placed as seen

80 Lion, 1886, Forbury Gardens, Reading.

here, with two replicas and piles of cannon-balls. The bell was removed in 1956 because the pagoda was unsafe, and it was given to the East Lancashire Regiment, the only other regiment with Canton battle honours on their colours. The balls were removed because the children enjoyed rolling them down the slopes, but the park keepers did not enjoy carrying them back up again! One of the critics of the Opium Wars wrote of the pagoda, 'Is it not a pity that the memory of

81 Pagoda, Nottingham Arboretum, c.1900
The pile of cannon-balls can be seen between the two cannon on the right.

wars that might have been avoided, and which brought us no national credit, should thus be perpetuated', but such criticisms were rare.[40]

Two final examples of imperialism in the parks took very different forms from the war trophies and memorials so far identified. One was a miniature version of the Khyber Pass constructed in artificial stone by E. A. Peak as part of the original layout of East Park, Hull (1887)[41] (shown in Fig. 82). The other was that quintessentially imperial emblem, the Doulton Fountain in Glasgow (see Fig. 83). This red terracotta fountain, designed by E. A. Pearce, was made by Doulton for the International Exhibition of 1888 and placed in Kelvingrove Park. It was moved to Glasgow Green two years later. Its subject is Queen Victoria reigning over her Empire, and at the time that it was made it was the largest terracotta statue in the world, being fourteen metres high. At the top is the Queen wearing the

82 Khyber Pass, East Park, Hull 1887.

Imperial crown and holding an orb and sceptre. Near the centre of the lower 21 metre basin are four groups representing the Dominions: India, South Africa, Canada and Australia. Australia is represented by a gold-digger resting on his spade, and a female figure carrying a sheaf of wheat rests her hand on a sheep; a vine grows beside her and behind is a fan palm. The references are to the main resources of the country. The second basin is six and a half metres in diameter and above it are the figures of a sailor and of Scots, Irish and English soldiers in uniforms of the Black Watch, the Royal Irish Fusiliers and the Grenadier Guards.[42] The imagery in other words is not only that of the 'peaceful' contributions of the Empire, but also of the power of the British army and navy that made such conquests possible.

Few guns remain in the parks today, although many war trophies were added in the period immediately following the First World War when 'public authorities vied with each other in an endeavour to secure captured weapons and disused tanks from the War Office' to set up in their parks.[43] A few years later public opinion changed and when demands were made for the 'reminders of a terrible war' to be removed there were few who protested. The Russian guns tended not to be removed in that period of anti-war feeling, but many of those that remained were melted down for the Second World War munitions. The distribution across the country of the Russian guns and other structures commemorating particular wars seems to have been

83 Doulton Fountain, 1888 (A. E. Pearce).

very general and they were not particularly associated with, say, major naval ports. The emblems were primarily emblems of victory and of the power of the Empire and unlike the memorials to the dead of both the First and Second World Wars, the names of those who died in battle were rarely recorded.

CHAPTER EIGHT

Planting and park maintenance

For many park visitors it was the flowers that were the main attraction and park superintendents at the beginning of the twentieth century strove to satisfy this taste by providing 'vast expanses of colour over as long a period as possible'.[1] Spring bulbs were followed by hardy and half-hardy annuals and other summer flowering plants and these were replaced, as summer drew to a close, by dahlias and chrysanthemums. These floral displays cheered the visitors, as well as holding a deeper significance by providing metaphors about society as a whole. During the course of the park movement the emphasis on flowers varied, as did styles of planting and the types of garden in which flowers were planted. Since so many municipal parks were located in areas of heavy air pollution, this proved a significant influence on the type of planting that was possible.

One of the main differences between the gardening of the eighteenth and the nineteenth centuries had been the prolific growth in the new species available, for many new plants and trees had been brought back to Britain from Australasia, North and South America and Asia. Some of them became acclimatised, while others needed protection from the rigours of the British climate if they were to thrive at all. Gardeners faced the problem of growing an increasing variety of unfamiliar plants and sought ways of incorporating them into an overall theory of landscape design. Repton's principles of landscape gardening advocated variety and contrast, with particular species planted in different types of garden, such as the rock garden, the flower garden, the American garden, rosarium and arboretum. Within these gardens individual plants or species did not tend to be emphasised. The great increase in new and exotic species encouraged the wish to show individual plants and trees to advantage and it was J. C. Loudon's development of the Gardenesque School of landscape gardening which provided the principles for such planting. The aim of the Gardenesque School was to allow individual plants to develop to their full glory and 'to add, to the acknowledged charms of the Repton School, all those [of] which the sciences of gardening and botany in their present advanced state are capable'.[2]

At Derby Arboretum trees and shrubs were planted so that their growth was uninhibited. In addition the trees were planted on small hills so that their surface roots appeared above the ground, for Loudon argued that this was essential for their health. Visitors could admire the form of the trees, their relationship to each other and the effects of the changing seasons. They could also note the variety of the specimens displayed and respond to the associations evoked. One example only of each tree or shrub was displayed and each was labelled, in order to encourage visitors 'to take an interest in the name and history of each species, its uses in this country or other countries'.[3] Pleasure and education were the aims, with botany and geography neatly illustrated on one small label.

Certain of the parks of the 1840s, such as Victoria Park, London, included arboreta among their attractions but although the import-ance of flowers was recognised, they rarely formed the main feature of the parks of this period, as the plans showed. In Birkenhead Park for example Kemp recommended 'showy flowering plants' such as fuchsias for the flower beds near the boundaries.[4] Two years after Major had completed his design of Peel Park, Salford, the flowers were given greater emphasis by the addition of a flower garden of three-quarters of a hectare, featuring a rosarium and two circular mounds, two and a half metres, and three and a half metres high respectively. These mounds were planted with geraniums, roses, fuchsias and climbing plants such as virginia creeper and honeysuckle. The top of one was crowned by a terracotta vase, while the other larger one had a maypole, surrounded by rockwork and four casts of antique heads. Within the flower garden there was also a circular 'secret' garden, surrounded by a privet hedging, with forty-eight beds inside. The privacy of this area was enhanced by the twelve beds surrounding it, which were planted with thorns, acacia, ever-greens, weeping elms, ashes, juniper and yew.[5] While this flower garden offered many attractions it must nevertheless have presented a rather fragmented appearance, for there was no unifying principle linking any of the separate elements.

It became the custom in the early 1850s to grow herbaceous plants and annuals among the trees and shrubs in the Manchester parks, but as the annuals only bloomed for a short period and looked rather 'slovenly' once they had done so, the Public Parks Committee recommended a new technique of planting, perhaps as a result of the publicity given to the Crystal Palace Park. Instead of flowers being grown among the trees, the grass was extended under them, as this was neater and easier to maintain. Flower beds were given the sunniest positions and bedding plants, which 'remain the most blooming during the whole of the Summer and Autumn months', were planted so that they could be viewed from above.[6]

CRYSTAL PALACE PARK, SYDENHAM

The newly erected Crystal Palace was situated at the top of a hill and below it Paxton designed a series of terraces. A flight of steps 36 metres wide led down from the main transept of the building to the upper terrace and from there further grand flights of steps led to the next terrace some four and a half metres below, with flower beds, pools, fountains and statuary on either side (see plan Fig. 22). Below, the gardens and pools were laid out symmetrically, with the design becoming more informal in the more distant parts of the park. Because of the enormous scale and the formal axial layout a unifying principle of planting was essential. Paxton's solution was to lay out the whole flower garden on the promenade system, with flower beds alongside the walks and the shape of the beds kept very simple. The beds were planted with neutral centres and the strongest colours around the outside, so as to enhance their apparent size. Tom Thumb scarlet geraniums were planted around the edges, with either *salvia patens*, ageratums, heliotropes, petunias or verbenas in the centre, and the rhododendron and azalea beds were planted with straight edgings of heath. Throughout the predominant colours were red and yellow.[7] All the major horticultural journals commented on the results, although it was not without its critics. Colour theorists criticised the choice of colours, others the layout and the choice of plants, but because it was so widely reported it proved very influential, particularly in promoting vivid massed displays of bedding plants, first in the royal parks and subsequently in the municipal parks.

THE FLORAL DEBATE

Flower planting in parks became the subject of vigorous debate at various times during the course of the century, and when flowers began to be introduced into the royal parks, where hitherto there had been only grass, trees and water, there was an outcry. The introduction of flowers to the royal parks was an innovation of the Commissioner of the Board of Works in the late 1850s, which was commended by some, on the grounds that it gave that vast majority of people who were without gardens the opportunity to see flowers. Others, particularly professional landscape gardeners, opposed the principle and thought that parks were no place for 'floral prettiness'. It was 'impossible to speak in language too severe' of what was happening in Hyde Park, where upwards of 100,000 plants were bedded out annually, wrote Alexander McKenzie, the designer of Alexandra, Finsbury and Southwark Parks.[8] A moderate display of flowers was all very well, but the attempt 'to convert our parks into tropical gardens . . . cannot be too strongly condemned'.

For the remainder of the century massed displays of flowers continued to be a popular feature of municipal parks, although they too were not without their critics. While Kemp's layout of Stanley Park, Liverpool (1870) (see Fig. 29) was praised, the ornate character of the ornamental grounds and the elaborate and expensive architectural works were criticised. Flowers had a role to play in Stanley Park and there was no reason why the public of Liverpool, to whom the park belonged, 'should not learn, like other communities, to appreciate the beautiful in nature and to take a pride and pleasure in its preservation', but green turf with trees and paths would have given more freedom and enjoyment 'to the toiling multitudes for whom the park was intended'.[9]

In order that these massed displays of bedding plants be seen to advantage they were planted in a variety of differently shaped beds. One solution was to plant ribbon beds along either side of footpaths, using one species for each strand of the ribbon, with the plants graded in height, as if they were in a mixed herbaceous border (for example, see Fig. 35). The limited sight-lines of passers-by meant that large flat beds planted with massed displays of flowers could not be seen properly unless they were viewed from a terrace or other vantage point. Raised and inclined beds were a partial answer to this problem

84 Inclined beds in Victoria Gardens, Neath.

and to complaints about the monotony of flat displays, but inclined beds had the disadvantage that they could only be seen satisfactorily from one position (see Fig. 84).

BATTERSEA PARK AND SUB-TROPICAL GARDENING

Some critics of massed bedding objected to the gaudy glare of colour and to the resulting monotony, which could have equally well been 'spread out by the cotton printer', but while they were doing so John Gibson was developing a form of gardening in Battersea Park based on foliage rather than on vivid flowers.[10] The technique of sub-tropical gardening is generally considered to be Gibson's main contribution to nineteenth-century gardening and as its name implied, it was based on plants indigenous to sub-tropical climates, which featured dramatic foliage and unusual shapes. It represented a move away from the use of flowers, towards an emphasis on leaf shape and colour, and the particular sub-tropical plants used were identified and discussed in great detail by the horticultural journals of the period. In 1870 the East Indian *musa superba* was bedded out at Battersea park for the first time 'with very satisfactory results' and dark foliaged varieties of coleus were planted underneath fine foliaged plants 'to the greatest advantage'. The best bed in the sub-tropical garden at that date was about four and a half metres long by one metre wide, with a half metre high *abutilon Thompsonii* in the centre. Under it the dark foliage of *coleus nigricans* contrasted with the golden mottled leaves of the abutilon. The bed was bordered by a row of silver-edged pelargonium Daybreak, with the outèr margin planted with *alternanthera amoena* and 'a more pleasing combination we have rarely or never seen'[11] (see Fig. 85).

Sub-tropical gardening added to the range of plants available and provided an alternative to massed bedding, although some fears were expressed that it would lead to a lack of flowers. It also exemplified Britain's role as the centre of a far-flung Empire, a point that was clearly recognised at the time.

It is a most important fact for persons of taste to observe that the subtropical (at Battersea) has purely English surroundings, and that the eye ranges from amongst the proper denizens of the place – the giant grasses, the feathery

85 Sub-tropical gardening in Battersea Park. Large specimens of tree ferns and other sub-tropical plants were set out so that their shape and form could be clearly seen, while in the background were examples of carpet-bedding.

Humeas, the gaunt Philodendrons – to belts of beech and birch and elm, and all the rest of the green and homely acompaniments of the purest English style.[12]

CARPET-BEDDING

One of the main objections to the massed bedding system was its lack of subtlety, and various attempts were made in private gardens to break up and remodel the colour masses. One of the most notable of these experiments took place at Cliveden where the chief gardener, John Fleming, had been experimenting with spring planting since the mid 1850s. To break up the masses of colour he planted brightly coloured tulips against a background of white catchfly or white forget-me-nots, and white tulips were planted against a background of blue forget-me-nots.[13] These experiments were reported in the gardening press and became an important influence, as did subtropical gardening, on the carpet system of bedding out, which developed in the later 1860s.

The basis of carpet-bedding was to plant the surface of a bed, which could be flat, concave, convex, or undulating, with a natural cover, or close carpet. Dwarf foliage plants native to Britain, or from South America or elsewhere, provided a ground cover that was even in texture and could, if necessary, be kept close-clipped like grass. Flowering plants such as pelargoniums, or shrubs, could be planted at intervals in this carpet, so that each plant could be seen against the background of the carpet surface. John Gibson's carpet-bed of succulents in Battersea Park, in which a dwarf grey-tinted sedum formed the neutral carpet for *echevaria* and shrubby *sempervivums*, was particularly praised by the *Gardeners' Chronicle* and carpet-bedding soon became a feature of Battersea and other parks.[14] Embossed bedding, tapestry, mosaic and artistic bedding were some of the other names used for this new style of planting, in which the carpeting plants were kept pinched, or clipped to a regular height so that the panels presented an even appearance (see Fig. 86). In the Italian garden in Regent's Park, designed by Markham Nesfield, vivid displays of verbenas, calceolarias and pelargoniums were contrasted with panels of grass, ivy, variegated mint, amaranthus and other plants, and the effect was of a floral frieze with bands and circles of colour. The advantage of carpet-bedding over other systems

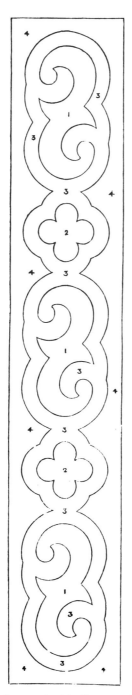

86 Design of carpet-bed in Battersea Park, 1870
1. Pyrethrum Golden Feather; 2. *Santolina incana*; 3. *Alternanthera amoena*;
4. *Alternanthera paronychiodes* and edged with *echevaria secunda glauca*.

of planting was a much longer season, for the plants used lasted longer than the flowers in the massed bedding system.

Carpet-beds were designed in a variety of forms including scrolls and serpentines and the technique lent itself to dramatic effects, such as that achieved by the superintendent of Crystal Palace Park in 1875 when he planted six beds in the shape of butterflies. The wing colours were reproduced as accurately as possible and the idea was soon imitated elsewhere. Many parks established a reputation for their 'magnificent display and management of flowers' and such was Victoria Park's reputation in the 1870s that an address of commendation was sent to the First Commissioner of Works.[15] Carpet-bedding lent itself admirably to commemorative planting, and in Victoria Park in 1871 one commentator particularly noted an 'especially beautiful [bed], in the shape of the Prince of Wales' feathers'.[16] It also provided an opportunity for the display of civic pride and Fig. 87 shows carpet-bedding in the form of Wolverhampton's municipal coat of arms. When Victoria Park, Portsmouth opened in 1878, the beds by each entrance gate were also laid out in the form of the borough coat of arms,[17] while in Middlesbrough municipal pride led to the display of the mayor's name in flowers in 1898.[18] In Bridlington the gardeners took the phrase 'carpet-bed' literally when they used a wire frame to achieve the effect of a roll of carpet with a length unrolled[19] (see Fig. 88).

Towards the end of the century carpet-bedding fell out of favour on private estates, but it remained popular in municipal parks, receiving an added impetus from the development of sculptural planting. In sculptural planting a galvanised wire frame provided the support for three-dimensional designs in which plants were packed into peat or soil and held into position. Such displays were ideal for commemorative planting for they were dramatic, long-lasting and clearly visible. At Cannon Hill Park, Birmingham, the reputation for carpet-bedding was 'increased in later years through the attraction of *Tours de force* such as the Tudor Crown[20] and Fig. 89 shows the bed designed at West Park, Wolverhampton to commemorate the coronation of George V in 1911.[21] This floral piano in Bowling Park, Bradford (Fig. 90) demonstrated municipal pride and the horticultural skills of the Bowling Park keepers. The competition between the keepers of Bowling Park and Wibsey Park was fierce and the latter's answer to the piano was an organ with a large set of pipes.

87 Municipal coat of arms, West Park, Wolverhampton.

88 Floral carpet, Prince's Parade, Bridlington.

89 Tudor crown for the coronation of George V, Cannon Hill Park,
Birmingham, 1911.

90 Floral piano, Bowling Park, Bradford, 1928.

91 Floral clock, Bridlington.

One of the most popular forms of sculptural planting was undoubtedly the floral clock, introduced by J. McHattie, the superintendent of the Edinburgh parks, in 1903. The clock mechanism was set in the ground under the bed, which was then planted as a clock face with moving arms. McHattie may have got the idea from *The Skillful Gardener* published in 1678 where Andrew Marvell described a floral clock or, more probably, from a recent exhibition in Paris where a floral clock had been displayed. Despite the popularity of floral clocks, they were regarded by certain parks departments 'with a distaste almost amounting to abhorrance[22] (one is shown in Fig. 91).

Among the most vociferous critics of the planting practised in municipal parks in general and of carpet-bedding in particular was Gertrude Jekyll, who created some 350 gardens, many of them in conjunction with houses by the architect Edwin Lutyens.[23] Gertrude Jekyll thought that park planting was 'not only unbeautiful' but gave the impression of 'hopeless dreariness'. Instead of bedding plants which were planted before they were due to flower and lifted once their flowering season was over, she advocated plants that were positioned permanently, with the varieties juxtaposed so as to bring out the harmony and contrast of colour, form and foliage at different

175

seasons. This quite different system of planting was more subtle in its effects, but not necessarily less expensive in upkeep. Another major critic of carpet-bedding was William Robinson, who introduced the wild garden to Victorian gardening.[24] In the wild garden foxgloves and other wild plants belonging to particular regions were planted and the result was to increase the range of plants available to the gardener. In Hull Botanic Garden J. C. Niven planted giant hogweed on an island, in order to inhibit its invasive tendencies and the Hull parks became noted for their wild flower collections and served as a model for later parks.[25] The effects of wild gardening could also be seen in the planting of spring bulbs in the grass, in areas where they were not likely to be walked on.

TYPES OF GARDEN

Wild gardens, rose gardens, alpine gardens and Japanese gardens were among particular types of garden that were introduced into the municipal parks. Some of them, such as the rose garden and alpine garden, represented the continuation of a tradition established in the private parks and gardens of the previous century, but with the introduction of a wider range of plants they took on a new form. For park superintendents the problem with these specialised gardens was how to provide an interesting collection and observe the horticultural tenets of the correct types of plants, while at the same time meeting the perceived tastes of the visitors for masses of colour.

In the 1830s Loudon advocated the cultivation of alpine plants in the more appropriate surroundings of the rock garden. Early rock gardens were usually constructed from local stone, but Battersea Park's Alpine Point and the rockworks by the reservoir illustrated the technological ingenuity of the period, for they were constructed by James Pulham & Son of Broxbourne out of artificial stone (1866–72). Pulham's technique for reproducing geological effects and for imitating varieties of stone was so successful that on occasion they were mistaken for the real thing. In Battersea Park Pulham's rockworks rose 'naturally out of their surroundings' and featured meandering streams, rock pools and a cascade that could be seen and heard from afar (see Fig. 92). The alpine garden was designed to represent an alpine scene in miniature, with the slopes planted in ascending zones of vegetation. On the 'low warm plains' were palms

92 Pulham rockworks in Battersea Park, without the cascade, streams or rock-pools. The cascade was in the darkened area in the centre.

and the 'snow-clad' heights were planted with *gnaphalium tomentosum*.[26]

The rock garden illustrated the park superintendent's problem, for in order to produce an interesting effect over a long period, plants had to be introduced 'that no expert would tolerate in a private rock garden'. W. W. Pettigrew, the superintendent of the Manchester parks from 1913, advised his colleagues to exercise their freedom of choice in planting, but not to take this too far 'and risk making the park's rock garden an occasion for derision among alpine lovers'.[27] He also recommended the planting of rarer alpines whenever it was safe to do so, although these were frequently stolen no matter how much they were guarded.

Another innovation was the introduction of the Japanese garden, with its emphasis on rocks, water and features familiar from willow pattern china. A miniature Japanese garden and village had been exhibited at the 1873 Vienna Exhibition and it was afterwards reassembled in the grounds of Alexandra Palace.[28] There was rather a time lag before Japanese gardens were introduced into municipal parks, but early in the twentieth century Battersea Park and Abbey Park, Leicester were among the parks that featured them. Botanical gardens for students of botany were also introduced into certain parks and one was donated in 1886 to Cannon Hill Park, Birmingham and opened the following year.[29] In Lister Park, Bradford a botanical garden was laid out in classified beds and this opened in 1903.[30]

The new styles of planting and these particular types of garden fostered knowledge of new species of plants and how they could be used. By contrast the emphasis of the Shakespeare garden was on the plants of the past and the old-fashioned flowers that had been mentioned in Shakespeare's plays. The Shakespeare garden, like the cottage garden, was part of the vernacular revival in gardening and the counterpart of the vernacular revival in architecture. It had been largely stimulated by the publication of a number of books on Shakespeare's flowers.[31] The Shakespeare garden was introduced into municipal parks by J. J. Sexby, the first officer of the London County Council Parks Department, and the first park to have one was Brockwell Park (1892) in south London (see Fig. 93). This park was created out of an existing estate which included a walled kitchen garden, and this was retained by Sexby, who planted it as an old-fashioned garden with the flowers mentioned in Shakespeare's plays.[32] The result was so popular that he included similar gardens in other parks and in Peckham Rye Park the garden became known as the Sexby garden (shown in Fig. 94).

PARK MAINTENANCE AND THE PROBLEMS OF AIR POLLUTION

From the early days of the park movement the problems of maintenance were met by the appointment of park keepers and attendants. In the 1840s their hours of work were from 6.00 a.m. to dark in the spring, 5.00 a.m. to 9.30 p.m. in the summer, 5.00 a.m. to dark in the autumn and 7.00 a.m. to dark in the winter, and they were responsible for enforcing the regulations as well as for all aspects of maintenance.[33] The numbers employed depended on the size of the park and the complexity of its design; in Derby Arboretum for example, Loudon thought one man would be sufficient for mowing the grass. In the summer an additional labourer would be needed to wipe the seats, weed and maintain the flower garden and urns, but in winter only a head gardener and one labourer would be necessary.[34]

In many parks the grass was let for grazing, which had the advantages not only of keeping it down, but also that the income from the

788   BROCKWELL PARK. — Ye Olde Garden. — LL.

93 Old walled garden, Brockwell Park, c.1910.

THE OLD GARDEN
PECKHAM PARK

1451

94 Sexby Garden, Peckham Rye Park, c.1910.

leases could be set against the running costs of the park. In the summer the grass could also be used for hay-making, which provided another source of income. In view of these uses the question of how much the public should be allowed to use the grass could be a source of debate between the park keepers and the parks' committees. In Whit week in Manchester 'all the Green Sward is appropriated for public recreation' but at other times the public were moved around from one plot to another, but 'all reasonable facility [was] given for their enjoyment'. The acquisition in the late 1850s of two Budding pony-drawn lawnmowers did much to solve these problems.[35]

One of the main problems of park maintenance in industrial cities related to the air pollution and its effects. In Manchester in the mid 1850s plants and trees were carefully selected in order to withstand the atmospheric conditions and the healthy state of the rhododendrons was particularly noted.[36] Twenty years later the effects of pollution had become so severe, particularly in Philips Park, that a special sub-committee was set up to inspect the nearby industrial works and make recommendations. They reported that 'so considerable was the quantity of smoke sent over the Park ... that the atmosphere was perfectly clouded by it, and the smell of the smoke was stifling.'[37] The trees were suffering badly, but all that the committee could recommend was that greater care should be taken in the construction of the chemical and other works. Ten years later the problem had, if anything, become worse and even the plane trees, which thrived in London, could not withstand the Manchester atmosphere. 'In a climate like that of Manchester, where the sun is, for the most part, obscured by rain or smoke-clouds, and where ... every object is thickly coated with the solid matters showering from the atmosphere, the culture of trees and plants generally cannot fail to be a most difficult problem.' Common elder, privet and Japanese knotweed (*Polygonum cuspidatum*) proved to be 'the best of all plants for the centres of great manufacturing towns'.[38] When the Metropolitan Public Gardens Association (see Chapter 10) started converting disused burial grounds and churchyards into open spaces for recreation, they too were concerned with the problem of planting to withstand London's polluted atmosphere and their First Report (1883) listed appropriate plants and trees[39] (Appendix 3).

Further evidence of the effects of air pollution was given by W. W. Pettigrew in a lecture to the Smoke Abatement Society in 1928, when he spoke of how impossible it was to grow pine trees successfully within three miles of the town hall. Philips Park was still the most badly affected of all the Manchester parks, due partly to the prevailing winds which were from the south-west, and partly to the presence of a large gas works on its western boundary and a large electricity works on its southern boundary. Although Queen's Park was only a mile and a half away, not only could four times the varieties of trees, shrubs and plants be grown there, but also they did not need replacing so frequently. The amount of new planting that was necessary to maintain Philips Park in a presentable condition was enormous, – '2,500 Rhododendron bushes, 2,500 Poplar trees, 1,000 Willows, 750 Elders and about 300 different kinds of flowering shrubs' were planted anew *each year*. These were all raised in the Park Department's own nurseries in the country, but although the rhododendrons survived for three years in Philips Park, they only bloomed well in their first year. The only other shrub it was worth attempting to grow, apart from privet and elder, was a shrubby honeysuckle (*Lonicera Ledebourii*, syn. involucrata). Few herbaceous perennials survived the winter other than lupins, funkia (hosta) and the German iris. 'It is therefore well worth noting that many annuals and biennials prove the most satisfactory subjects to cultivate on this account.'[40]

Pettigrew's paper made clear the enormous effort that was required to maintain urban parks in the period before the passing of the Clean Air Act, and it is important to note the design implications of this.[41] Trees normally provide the main structure for any planting, but they were unlikely to survive to maturity and indeed early twentieth-century photographs of Philips Park and other parks of this period show few trees of any size (see Fig. 95). Park superintendents were faced with the problem of creating a landscape in which trees had only a short lifespan of two or three years, instead of providing the basic permanent framework of the design. Bedding plants were a logical solution, for they provided a colourful display at much less cost and physical effort than that involved in replacing a large number of trees, even though some beds in important positions could be changed up to eight times a year.

Another reason for the continued use of bedding plants was the way in which the tastes of the park visitors were perceived. Park designers saw their work in terms of providing an enjoyable environ-

95 Parks Committee visit to Philips Park, Manchester 1913.

ment which offered a wide range of activities for large numbers of
people, while park superintendents were faced with the day-to-day
problems of upkeep and of providing a vivid display of colour.
'Experience goes to prove that the vast majority of visitors are more
impressed by spectacular effects than by the individual beauty or
interest of the plants producing them.'[42] Others thought that lessons
could be learnt from the very ways in which nature was displayed in
the parks. 'Flowers not only charm, they teach',[43] but what lessons did
they teach? The bedding plants were cared for during their useful life
and then discarded, in effect mirroring the experience of working
people, while the emphasis given to individual plants, which were set
against a neutral background, provided a metaphor for the ways in
which society as a whole was organised.

In Macclesfield, where research had indicated the degree to which
drunkenness and other anti-social behaviour had decreased as a result
of the opening of a municipal park, the effects of the way in which the
park was maintained were equally clear.

The other elevating influences of the park must by degrees train and educate
the people to neatness in dress, habit of order, and respectability of conduct
and behaviour. It is remarkable how the very perfection of order and

96 London County Council, commemorative carpet-bed in Victoria Park, planted for the coronation of 1937.

condition in which the park is kept, influences the manner and conduct of those who hitherto had been unaccustomed to the sphere of such examples. It is one secret of its success in training the unruly.[44]

The controlled way in which nature appeared in the parks was quite different from nature in the wild, and reflected the ways in which working people were controlled in life and, generally speaking, the way middle-class people liked things to be (see, for example, Fig. 96). This point was clearly recognised by William Morris. He and others such as the Commons Preservation Society fought to preserve wild places that were near the urban centres, not only because they were open spaces, but because the experience of nature there was so different from that in the parks. 'The official mind ... is seriously setting Dame Nature to rights, and by putting her into an approved Nineteenth Century costume hopes to impress the public mind with the necessity of not being too familiar with natural objects.'[45] That official mind did not include J. J. Sexby, who recognised that 'The Commons have a peculiar charm in their freedom and natural beauty,

183

97 Distribution of plants, Victoria Park, 1891.

as opposed to the restrictions and artificialness of a made park'.[46]

Despite the controlled nature of the floral displays there is no doubt that they were very popular, and this popularity was enhanced by the distribution of large numbers of surplus plants at the end of the season. In the case of the five Glasgow parks, some 15,000 plants were distributed.[47] 'Brightening many poor ... homes' by this means strengthened the links between the community and its local park and was both appealing and possible, whereas the problems of inadequate housing demanded more wide-ranging solutions. Figure 97 shows 'how greatly this boon is appreciated in the East End of London', with people waiting for the plants to be distributed, parents and children involved in bringing 'a ray of consolation' home and the unsuccessful turning away disappointed.[48]

CHAPTER NINE

Permitted pastimes

Parks were places where people could enjoy the open air and the beauty of the flowers and trees, and through a variety of activities become physically, socially and morally improved. Generally these activities tended to be rather sober in comparison with those offered by the pleasure gardens, but there were exceptions to this, particularly on special occasions such as a park opening. Three days of celebrations marked the opening of Derby Arboretum on 16 September 1840. The Corporation's procession to the Arboretum and the official opening ceremonies were followed the next day by a second procession, this time of trades and societies, and the celebrations included a balloon ascent, dancing and a firework display. On the third day, children's day, there were sports, games and more dancing.[1] Subsequently 15 August, the birthday of the donor Joseph Strutt, was celebrated by a general half-holiday, with a procession, massed bands and special attractions in the Arboretum.[2] At the opening of Birkenhead Park on 5 April 1847 the crowd, estimated at 10,000, enjoyed the sports, the bands and the Lancashire bellringers who performed on the upper storey of the boathouse (Fig. 43), but the highlight of the day was the rural sports competition. This included sack, hurdle, foot and blindfold wheelbarrow races, races for women and other competitions such as a grinning match, eating a bowl of 'stirrah' or porridge, and catching the greasy pig. The pigs were prepared for this ordeal by shaving them and soaping their tails.[3] To enable people from the surrounding towns to enjoy the opening of the People's Park, Halifax, ten years later, special excursion trains were laid on. There was a general holiday, a huge procession to the park led by the Sixth West Yorkshire militia followed by nine bands, and thousands came from Huddersfield, Bradford and Leeds to participate in the feasting which lasted into the small hours. 'There never was a more happy day in all our town's history than August 14th, 1857. Gladness beamed in every eye; pleasure ruled in all hearts; happiness filled every mind, joy lighted up every individual's face.'[4]

Parks were places which large numbers of people could use and they did so, on special occasions and on ordinary Sundays. Blondin, the tightrope walker and hero of Niagara Falls, performed at the two fêtes held in the August Wakes week in Queen's Park, Longton, when some 33,000 people attended,[5] but when Glasgow held a census of park use on Sunday 9 July 1883, they recorded 100,000 people entering Glasgow Green and 'a corresponding number every other good day of rest'. The previous Sunday 48,611 people had entered Kelvingrove Park and there was an average attendance of 8,000 for the weekly musical performances.[6]

The best documented uses of parks tend to focus on special events, official openings, or a visit by royalty. The petty misdemeanours and various forms of antisocial behaviour that occurred in parks are also well documented. By contrast, the activities that were part of everyday life, such as meeting friends, walking and playing went largely unrecorded (Fig. 98). The vivid picture painted by Mrs Layton in about 1865 of the need to get everyone out of the house on washday and of the happy time spent by the children in Victoria Park in London, is very much part of that hidden history.

My fourth sister and I always stayed away from school on washday to mind the babies. In the summer it was real sport, because so many people did their washing on the same day, and everyone had large families and generally kept the elder girls, and sometimes boys, at home to mind the little ones. We used to plan to go out all together with our babies and prams into Victoria Park. Very few people had prams of their own, but we could hire them at 1d. an hour to hold one baby, or 1½d. an hour to hold two. Several mothers would pay a few pence for the hire of a pram and the children used to manage between them how they were to be used. I need hardly say that each pram was used to its full seating capacity. The single pram had always to accommodate two and the double pram three or more, and we always kept them the full length of time for which we had paid. We would picnic on bread and treacle under the trees in the Park, and return home in the evening a troop of tired but happy children.[7]

The opportunity for people to use the parks depended in part on their hours and days of work, the opening times of the park and its distance from work or home. The time available for recreation increased only gradually during the century, although the pattern of

98 Summer day in Hyde Park. Oil painting by J. Ritchie, 1868.

holidays changed. The availability and cost of other forms of recreation, such as cheap railway excursions which opened up the opportunities for travel, also affected park use. As the Saturday Half-Holiday Movement progressed, guides were published pointing out places which could be visited by foot, rail or omnibus on a Saturday afternoon. *The Birmingham Saturday Half-Holiday Guide* of 1879 provided information on the surroundings of Birmingham and on where to find sports such as bathing, cricket, athletics and bicycling. In London the summer edition of *The Saturday Half-Holiday Guide*, c.1870, dedicated to the Duchess of Sutherland and the Ladies' Half-Holiday Committee, pointed out particular attractions in London's parks and in the areas surrounding the capital. It also gave details of cricket grounds and the rivers which provided opportunities for rowing, canoeing and angling.

THE PEOPLE'S VOICE

Most parks had a lake and open areas of grass which could be used for a variety of sports, for hay, for grazing sheep, for picnics or meetings, but not for all of these simultaneously. The uses allowed reflected some of the changing attitudes towards recreation, but in the choice of activities the people's voice was rarely heard. Many parks had been created out of commons and open spaces accessible to the community, where fairs, horse races, sports and games, election meetings and radical protests were traditionally held. The Barkerend races and fair held each October on Bradford Moor Common did not continue on that site once the Common had been enclosed by the Council in 1878[8] and there was no counterpart in municipal parks to the racecourse in the Bois de Boulogne in Paris. Alexandra Park in north London, which opened in 1863, included a racecourse among its attractions, but like its rival, the Crystal Palace Park, it was a speculative development and a semi-public park, not a municipal park. Similarly the radical protests and election meetings that had been held on Kennington Common, London came to an end after it became a park. There is, however, evidence of the persistence of some of these traditional activities in certain parks. Windmill Hills, Gateshead, the only open space near the town, had traditionally been used for election meetings and demonstrations, a use which persisted after it became a public park in 1861,[9] and the fair held on Glasgow Green from the beginning of the century continued there until 1870.[10]

Some parks such as Victoria Park acquired a reputation for public debate which could perhaps be seen as continuing an aspect of the working people's rallies that had been held on Bonner's Fields. These meetings were held near the Victoria Fountain and 'on Sunday ... the attractions are not the beautiful scenery or the fresh air, but those of public discussion and debate ... all are engaged in strenuous controversy on social questions, as seen from the religious, political or economic point of view'.[11] Meetings were held on Glasgow Green throughout the century and the authorities saw them in 1898 as 'giving free course and comparatively harmless outlet to sentiment and opinions which otherwise might sometimes attain explosive force. It is a safety valve which should find a place in every great community'.[12] This had also been one of the benefits of parks identified by the early park promoters.

MEETINGS

Religious and political meetings, listening to music, and military drilling, were among the events that could be held in parks, the

189

response of local authorities varying according to the particular circumstances. In the regulations proposed for the Manchester parks in 1846 no mention was made of meetings of any type,[13] but Government anxiety about the use of parks for political meetings was evident in 1848, the peak of Chartist activity, when the Duke of Wellington, who had been given military command of London, recommended the closure of all the parks there.[14]

In Victoria Park, London all preaching was prohibited in 1856 in order to 'prevent the occurrence of the unbecoming scenes which took place in the park last year',[15] while in Birkenhead the Parks Committee decided in 1866 that they could not sanction religious services in the park.[16] That they had been held there until that date was corroborated by a local resident, J. R. Kaighin, who recalled the 'open air meetings and services of any character' of his youth in the 1860s, when he attended Temperance meetings and evangelical services in Birkenhead Park on Sunday evenings.[17] In 1886 a Birkenhead bye-law prohibited the holding of political or religious demonstrations in the park,[18] while in Manchester the 1897 bye-laws prohibited meetings unless application was made to the Corporation, when permission could be granted for holding meetings and demonstrations in specific parks and recreation grounds.[19]

Religious and political meetings were part of urban life, but as parks were seen as peaceful places, such potentially divisive activities were generally prohibited. This did not mean that military events had no place in them. Indeed, in the 1860s fear of invasion by Napoleon III led to the formation of Volunteers in a number of towns and drilling took place in parks up and down the country. In Birkenhead the Rifle Volunteer Battalion was allowed to drill in the park on Saturday afternoons, but drilling was restricted and was not allowed to continue for longer than half an hour after sunset, following complaints about the drill continuing late and the presence of horsemen in the park.[20] Drilling offered a public spectacle and an added attraction for some park visitors, and this use of parks was generally accepted for it was in the national interest, with which, it was assumed, all were in agreement.

Parks could also be used for agricultural and horticultural shows, but the Courts were concerned about the question of admission charges to public open spaces. It was probably for this reason that the Public Health Acts Amendment Act 1890[21] gave Urban and Rural

Councils special powers of charging for entry to parks on a limited number of days, and powers to close any park to the public and grant its use to any public charity or institution. Money could then be charged for admission, but closure was limited to twelve days in the year and for not more than four consecutive days, which could not include Sundays or public holidays. Fairgrounds may have been part of the attractions of these shows for this same Act gave Councils powers to make bye-laws to prevent danger from steam-powered whirligigs and swings.

SPORTS AND OPPORTUNITIES FOR WOMEN

Apart from drilling, meetings, or listening to music, the other main use of the open spaces was for sports. The range of sports allowed expanded gradually, but it was only at the end of the century that opportunities for women to participate became available. When Loudon wrote on the subject of laying out public gardens in 1835 he suggested that 'archery grounds, cricket grounds, bowling greens and grounds for playing golf, skittles, quoits etc. may be considered useful establishments, with a view to the health of citizens who pass the day in sedentary occupations.'[22] Thirteen years after Derby Arboretum opened Andrew Jackson Downing, the American landscape gardener, particularly noticed the '*skittle grounds* – a favorite English game with ball; at which numbers of men and boys were playing while I was there'.[23] Archery, shuttlecock, quoits, skittles and games with local associations were among the sports included in the parks of the 1840s and 1850s. Both men and women participated in archery, but only men can be seen enjoying it in Peel Park c.1850 (Fig. 18). In Glasgow golf was played on Glasgow Green until 1832 and it subsequently became a favourite game in Kelvingrove Park. In Manchester two favourite games were knurr and spell, and the graces. Knurr and spell was similar in some ways to trapball, in which a ball was propelled from a trap and then struck by the players. The spell was a spring fastened to an iron back or wooden board. About five centimetres from the loose end of the spring was a small cup to hold the knurr, a two and a half centimetre diameter boxwood ball. The loose end of the spring was held in a toothed rack and when released the knurr was hurled upwards. The player making the longest drive with the pommel was the winner (Fig. 99). In the graces two players had two small sticks and two small hoops. The aim was to throw and catch the hoops, with either one or both sticks, without allowing them to fall to the ground[24] (Fig. 100).

Another popular activity was skipping, and sites were set aside for this in the Manchester and Salford parks (see Figs. 17a, b, c). Adults and children skipped, but not all parks were prepared to allow it and in Victoria Park, London, those who persisted were liable to be arrested. 'Rope-skipping seems to be a forbidden pleasure in Victoria Park ... On Whit-Monday a company of rope-skippers, having disregarded the notice of the police to desist, one of them was arrested and fined 5/-. His wife, who had interfered with the police by pulling a constable's whiskers, had to pay a penalty of 20/-, or 14 days' imprisonment.'[25]

In general football was among the last sport to be allowed in the parks, although it was permitted in a few of the parks that had been formed on the traditional sites of the game. The site of Calthorpe Park, Birmingham had been an open field and 'a favourite place of resort of cricket and football clubs', and open space was retained for those sports after the park opened in 1857.[26] Football was also played in Norfolk Park, Sheffield from 1841 when the park opened; but these were exceptions. In Victoria Park, London the cricket grounds dated from 1849[27] and archery and trapball were introduced in the early years, but football was not allowed until 1888,[28] while in Scotland, Glasgow Green was the birthplace of the Rangers (1873) and the Celtic (1888) football clubs.[29] This period also saw the introduction of new sports such as tennis and the redefinition of old sports such as football. Football clubs had been in existence before the 1840s, but it was not until 1863 that the Football Association was established and a unified code of play adopted.[30] Before that there were few rules, referees, or limits to the size of the teams and the 'ground' could embrace the whole of a parish with the goals several miles apart.[31] Park keepers and parks committees were understandably reluctant to open the gates to the game in that form.

As the century progressed, an increasing range of sports was introduced in the parks and by 1898 Battersea Park offered, according to the season, cricket, football, skating, tennis, riding, gymnasia, quoits, bowling and cycling. Battersea Park became the place for cycling, and this soon became established as a fashionable pastime (Fig. 101). Victoria Park, London at that date contained thirty cricket pitches,

99 Knurr and Spell.

100 The Graces.

101 Cycling in Battersea Park.

thirty-seven free tennis courts, four gymnasia and a swimming pool.[32] A summary of the sports provided in London's municipal parks showed that in 1906 there were 452 cricket pitches and 231 football pitches and provision for athletic training, lacrosse, hurling and roller-skating in certain parks. There were men's gymnasia at Battersea, Southwark, Finsbury and Victoria Parks and separate gymnasia for children at fifteen places. There were also gymnasia for girls 'to which women are also admitted as far as practicable, at 10 places'.[33]

As in other areas of recreation, class and gender in sport reflected contemporary power relationships and middle-class males became the arbiters of the new sporting culture.[34] With the gradual shortening of the working day, opportunities for recreation increased and the emphasis on sport changed from suppression to control. Rules were standardised, the sports bureaucracy increased and the new sporting controls reinforced class identity and gender distinctions. At the beginning of the century, middle-class women's sports had been limited to croquet and archery, but gradually the range increased until by the end of the century it included tennis, cycling, hockey, golf and climbing. The limited number of sports that became available to women were strictly segregated from male sports and were based on the myth that middle-class women and girls were physically unfit for sport. It was not until the Royal Commission on School Education (Taunton Commission) of 1868 that official concern began to be voiced about the physical and mental aspects of middle-class girls' education. While middle-class women were deemed not to be strong enough for sport, working-class women were assumed to be quite able to work a ten-hour day or longer, and a six-day week, on the land, in the factory and elsewhere, as well as running a home and bringing up their children.

Although there was no official campaign promoting women's sport, the question became part of the movement for emancipation. Sport was active, so whether playing tennis, or riding a bicycle, it challenged the view that women were passive and was one of the many factors that helped to undermine the constraints imposed on them, which had prevented them taking control of their own bodies and lives. One specific example of this was the influence of the bicycle on women's dress and the activities of the Rational Dress Society.[35]

PLAYGROUNDS AND GYMNASIA

Playgrounds and gymnasia were included in the Manchester/Salford parks from the beginning and the question of boys and girls playing together was confronted at an early stage by the Manchester Public Parks Committee. They recommended that the girls' swings in Queen's Park be positioned far from those used by the boys, 'it having already been found that where boys and girls are mixed together, the former exclude the latter from the use of the swings'.[36] By 1848 the boys' playground in Queen's Park, Manchester contained 'eight swings, a "giant strides" post, and the gymnastic apparatus'.[37] Figure 102 shows part of this apparatus which could be swung from, or 'walked' along using the hands. Other gymnastic apparatus included

102 Gymnastic apparatus (left) Queen's Park, Manchester, c.1852.

103 Giant stride.

pole and rope climbing, and climbing up an inclined plank. Only males were allowed to use this apparatus, but pillars were available for female exercise.[38] For safety the Committee recommended that tanner's bark or spent dyewood should be laid down in the gymnasia, to prevent injuries from falls.

Playground equipment included ordinary and circular swings, and seesaws, but the equipment most frequently referred to was the giant stride, which consisted of a pole with an iron top and revolving iron cap. Hooks with ropes on them were attached to the cap and the last three feet or so of the ropes could be knotted every few inches in order to improve the grip, or could have a cross-stick through a loop at the end (see Fig. 103). The aim was to hold on to the rope and leap in giant strides around the pole. This equipment seems to have been an innovation in the 1840s for the superintendent of Victoria Park requested instructions on how it should be used and how to prevent the ropes being stolen.[39] Evidently there was sufficient demand for a company, B. Hirst & Sons Ltd. of Halifax, to be set up in 1846 specifically to manufacture playground and gymnastic apparatus[40] (see, for example, Fig. 104).

Just as the variety of sports increased towards the end of the century, so too did the other facilities for children. André had included a bird park and a deer park in his design for Sefton Park, Liverpool in 1872, and by 1898 Victoria Park, London combined education with entertainment with an aviary, guinea pigs, goats on a rockery and a deer enclosure. The introduction at the turn of the century of sand-pits, paddling pools and goat-cart rides extended park facilities to the needs of very young children. The use of playgrounds was generally supervised, but the children were not directed in their play. Birmingham Parks Committee, however, decided in the early years of the twentieth century that as the poorer children of the slums and some of those of the artisan districts knew nothing of the children's games common in country districts, they should be taught how to play organised games in parks and recreation grounds. This, they argued, would bring cheer to the lives of those whose days were spent in the crowded districts 'where joy is for the most part an infrequent visitor' for it would bring back 'something of the brightness and gaiety of "merrie England" '.[41]

At the other end of the age range were the Seven Days Rest Associations, or Brotherhoods, for retired men. At the turn of the

104 Playground, Victoria Park, London c.1900.

century the pavilions in the Bradford parks were designated 'Arbours of Refuge' where the men could play chess or draughts and chat in comfort all the year round, as they were heated during the winter.[42]

THE USES OF WATER

A sheet of water in the form of a lake contributed to the tranquillity of the park and this atmosphere could be retained if certain activities such as fishing were allowed, but not if large numbers were allowed to swim. From virtually the beginning, bathing became the activity associated with Victoria Park, London. By 1849 it was estimated that in about three hours 3,000 bathed in the eastern lake and if the facilities were improved the number would more than double. Pennethorne, the park's first designer, thought that bathing would entirely destroy 'the value of the Park as a place of residence', for the bathing costume was not used.[43] Only males swam and the absence of local bath-houses meant that open waters such as the canals, lakes and rivers had to serve instead. This practice had been well established for many years and witnesses to the SCPW in 1833 had reported the absence of bathing places 'to which the Humbler classes can resort'.[44] Nude bathing was against the law and people did so 'at their own peril, sometimes being taken into custody for it'. Bathing in the eastern lake was only allowed at specified times but:

Persons are seen to undress and plunge into the water before the appointed time, and when the police attempt to take possession of their clothes, as a means of securing their persons, the garments are carried off to a distance by friends – sometimes by women, – and the bather is next seen running about in a state of nudity while other persons availing themselves of the absence of the police, commit the offence of the pursued.[45]

Bathing took place both summer and winter and a request was made in 1858 for shelter for winter bathers. This was not granted, on the grounds that if it were solely for their use, it would have to be locked at other times, to prevent it becoming 'the resort of bad characters'. Also 'as the Park and its benefits are intended for the many, the locking up would perhaps be considered too exclusive' and such socially divisive actions should be avoided. Two years later permission was sought for a wooden structure by the eastern lake 'for the reception of persons apparently drowned, which as the skating season is approaching, is an important consideration', but this also was not allowed.[46]

The lakes were also used for dog-washing but in 1873 the western lake, which was known as the ornamental lake, was cleaned and a new concrete wall with granite coping erected around it. The unprotected portions of the lake had wire netting placed around them to 'prevent dog-washing and swimming, a nuisance which has for several years been considered a great source of annoyance',[47] and officially only boating was allowed. By 1898 the swimming facilities in the eastern lake had been improved and it had a concrete bottom, diving boards and shelters 'and all the accessories to make it a perfect out-door swimming bath ... the finest in the world'. Its popularity may be judged by the fact that on a summer morning, before 8 a.m. more than 25,000 bathers were counted.[48]

In Birkenhead, by contrast, no swimming or boating was allowed on either lake. 'One or two gentlemen' had in 1849 sought permission to bathe but this was refused. Skating was allowed and Kemp, the superintendent, was authorised to provide ropes and poles to prevent accidents; he also suggested that the ice should be swept after each day's skating and this was acted upon.[49] In 1855 angling was allowed in both lakes, at places fixed by the Committee. No fishing was allowed between 9.00 a.m. and 4.00 p.m. or after 9.00 p.m. Annual tickets cost 21/- each with additional tickets at 10/6d for members of the same family.[50] The lakes were stocked with waterfowl and attracted wild birds to them, and the practice of shooting birds in the afternoons was reported in 1848. It was agreed that the shooting of rabbits only should be allowed, and then only in the early mornings.[51] Despite this a member of the Committee recalled that the policemen in charge of the park had instructions from the Committee to shoot one or two of the wild ducks that reared their young in the park and 'send them to each member of the Committee by turn'.[52] This was not a facility that the Committee was prepared to extend beyond its members, but it was apparently not an uncommon practice. In Alexandra Park, Hastings, the ducks and geese had become so numerous by 1871 that two were sent to each member of the Council.[53] The use of the lakes illustrated the conflict between the ideals of tranquil nature, in which the park was seen as a place of retreat, and the ideal of the park as a place for sport and exercise. The conflict was largely unresolvable and Victoria Park and Birkenhead Park illustrated two different approaches to the problem.

MUSIC AND SUNDAYS IN THE PARK

Sunday was the day when most people had the opportunity of visiting parks, but it was also the day when use was restricted by religious concerns. Many parks were closed on Sunday mornings in order to encourage people to attend church services. Derby Arboretum, for example, was closed between 10.00 a.m. and 1.00 p.m., Peel Park, Macclesfield was closed between 9.00 a.m. and 12.00 noon and Saltaire Park opened at noon. Sunday was also the day when people could most easily take part in sports or use the gymnasia, but on that day no games were allowed and the gymnasia were closed. The Manchester Public Parks Committee forbad such use in 1846[54] and the bye-laws of parks across the country show that this practice was widely applied not only during the 1840s but throughout the century. Under the influence of the Sabbatarians these restrictions increased in the 1850s.

The Sabbatarians believed that amusements should be limited to weekdays and that it was a sin to take recreation on Sundays, for the day should be reserved for spiritual exercise only. Servants' labour could, however, be enjoyed by their employers on Sundays. At the same time the Sabbatarians successfully claimed to be acting on working people's behalf by protecting their right to a day of rest. They told those who had little opportunity for recreation during the week, that if they used Sundays for recreation, the religious nature of the day would be broken and with it the embargo on Sunday labour. They would then lose their day of rest and be made to work seven days a week. The Sabbatarians distinguished between private and public control and so justified the use of horse carriages on Sundays but not of railways, and the use of semi-public parks and gardens by keyholders but not the use of public parks by the general public. Their attitude to parks was that it was better 'that a man should be feeble and sickly, . . . than that he should be strong and healthy through disobeying God'.[55] The Sabbatarians argued that if all places of recreation were closed on Sunday, then all classes would be equally affected. They were unwilling to see that superior resources could overcome many restrictions and that their policies consequently placed greater burdens on the poor than on the rich. Through the Lord's Day Observance Society they attempted to close Regent's Park Zoo on Sundays, to prevent Sunday trading and to ban Sunday travelling by canal, rail and omnibus. Among their successes were the closure of the Crystal Palace on Sundays in 1851, the closure of the British Museum on Sundays in 1855 and the banning of Sunday concerts in the parks.[56] Their attack on Sunday newspapers and Sunday recreations such as visiting museums, attending lectures or listening to music in the parks related directly to political power and authority and to the question of how individual freedom in the area of recreation should be regulated and controlled.

In Manchester bands played on Sundays in both Queen's Park and Philips Park, but in the mid 1850s they came under threat from the Sabbatarian influence. In June 1856 a broadsheet, *Sunday Music for the People*, announced the formation of a committee to counter that influence and promote musical performances on Sundays 'in places of public resort, in accordance with the plan pursued in London . . . and in Leeds'. The proposal was that bands should play in the parks from either 4.00 to 7.00 p.m. or 5.00 to 8.00 p.m. 'avoiding all dancing music' and including works by Haydn, Mozart and Mendelssohn. The numbers present at the concert on 22 June far exceeded normal attendance with not less than 9,500 people entering Philips Park during the afternoon. They were 'chiefly respectable working classes [with] a considerable number of children . . . [and] a numerous class of loose rough characters', and only four drunken people were seen. The success of this committee was short-lived and in August that year Sunday music in the Manchester parks was banned.[57] In Eastbourne and Birmingham Sunday bands were also withdrawn at this time, but in Nottingham and Accrington they continued to play during the summer months, although some concession was made in Accrington, for the band played without a drum 'which we do not consider to be a Sunday instrument'.[58]

The efforts of the Sabbatarians were countered by the National Sunday League founded in 1855, which argued that museums, the relocated Crystal Palace and similar institutions should be open on Sunday afternoons and that music should be provided 'in the open air in a beautiful park'. The League also supported the Society for Securing the Performance of Sunday Music in the Parks, which set up private bands to replace military ones, and after about 1856 Sabbatarian influence on music in the parks tended to decline.

Military and works bands were a very popular form of entertainment in the latter half of the century and concerts were held on weekday evenings and on Sundays in the summer. Large numbers of people would listen to bands such as the Gas Band which played in Alexandra Park, Hastings in the 1880s, or the Hawks, the Crawshay Works Band which played on Windmill Hills, Gateshead on summer evenings throughout the 1850s.[59] Works bands were one way in which working people could take an active role in park events, and when eleven brass bands with a total of 149 players marched through Blackburn in 1861 to the upper terrace of Corporation Park, more than 50,000 people gathered to listen to them. The concert included works by Haydn and Handel and the event ended with the Hallelujah chorus and the national anthem. To mark the occasion one of the Russian guns was fired.[60]

A wide range of classical music was performed at these events, and more people became familiar with it in this way than perhaps at any time hitherto. Music was seen as an important influence '[for] what makes the people vulgar, but the total want of means to render them refined . . . There is hardly any other Method [of social reform] . . . to which greater importance should be attributed, than to the providing of good moral public amusements, especially musical entertainment.'

On the Continent, orchestras gave concerts in the public parks and squares daily, but when the suggestion was put forward for an evening military concert in Trafalgar Square or on the Embankment in London, there were fears of 'a horrid crowd of roughs and pickpockets etc'. In the 1880s it was thought impossible to open a public garden in the centre of London 'so great are the fears of collecting the residuum there'.[61] Nevertheless many bands played in the parks, large numbers of people attended and few misdemeanours were reported.

ENFORCING ORDER

Parks were places of innocent amusement where people could mix and enjoy the beauty of the flowers and trees and in so doing become virtuous and happy. Despite this, a variety of offences was committed within them and the problem of enforcing control was confronted from the inception of each park. Regulations and bye-laws formed an important feature of park management and provided the means of bringing people before a magistrate on a definite charge and of imposing a fine. Without them any nuisance, or breach of order, would be subject to criminal law, which was inappropriate for trivial offences, or to civil action for damages, which was impracticable. The Recreation Grounds Act 1859[62] gave managers of parks and recreation grounds powers to make and enforce bye-laws but did not impose penalties for breach of these. Without penalties the bye-laws could only be enforced by removing the offender from the ground under the ordinary laws of trespass, or by putting into force the laws for preventing a breach of the peace. Subsequently Charity Commissioners approved bye-laws under this Act and inserted the provision for maximum penalties of 40/- or 20/- per day for continuing offences.[63] Under the Public Improvements Act 1860[64] the powers of making bye-laws were those conferred by the Baths and Washhouses Act 1846.[65] These permitted a penalty not exceeding £5 for any breach of the bye-law. Local authorities did not immediately avail themselves of these powers, preferring instead to draw up regulations to preserve order in the parks. In the case of the Manchester parks bye-laws were passed in 1868, some twenty years after the parks opened.

The enforcement of park regulations was the duty of the police and of the park keepers and labourers who were sworn in as special constables (see, for example, Fig. 105). The swearing-in of park

105 Park keepers and police, Bostall Woods c.1890. The strong similarities
between the uniforms reinforced the keepers' role of policing the park.

labourers as special constables was adopted in the Manchester/Salford
parks from 1846 and this seems to have been the general solution to
the problem of maintaining order. In Birkenhead the park police
came under the control of the Head of the Township force, but after
complaints of insufficient time spent policing the park, park labourers
were sworn in in 1849 as special constables for Sunday afternoons,
and the number of park police reduced from three to one.[66] The
offences reported tended to be of a trivial nature; picking flowers
plucking a tail feather from a peacock, bad language, drunkenness by
the visitors, keepers, or labourers and attempted theft. Among his
other duties the first park constable in Alexandra Park, Hastings had
to control skipping, leap-frog, kiss-in-the-ring and persons walking
on the grass edging.[67] In some parks no dogs at all were allowed,
while others permitted 'dogs on a string'.

Local authorities or park benefactors determined the regulations
and these varied widely. Some were strict about unsupervised children; in Saltaire Park, for example, no child under the age of eight
was allowed unless in the care of an adult.[68] Other prohibitions
included vendors, shooting, games, dancing, washing or drying
clothes, beating carpets, and the sale or consumption of intoxicating

liquor. The image of working-class people as unruly and undisciplined before exposure to civilising influences, and neat, docile and orderly afterwards, comes over clearly. The predominant impression from official reports of the use of parks by park keepers, the police or Parks Committees was the expectation of anti-social behaviour by working people, an expectation that was not dimmed by experience to the contrary. Time and time again there are reports of 'very few cases of drunkenness', of peaceful crowds and of no damage to the park, and the tone of these reports seemed to indicate that people were not behaving as it had been assumed that they would.

The dual role of park worker and special constable did little to enhance relations with the public and park keepers acquired a reputation for officiousness from an early date:

there is much insolence displayed by the green men who keep the gates, towards decent poor people ... Do these fellows recollect that themselves and their masters, the ground they are appointed to protect, and the green coats they wear, are bought, fed, maintained, and paid for by the taxation, direct and indirect, contributed from the sweat of the brow of that very poor fellow, among others, this moment repulsed from the gate ...

When children crowded round to get a better view of the ducks in St James's Park 'we observe the verdant-coated verderers of the Office of Woods and Forests, cutting away with ratans at poor little nursery girls and their helpless charges ...'[69]

The park keeper's view is vividly recorded in a long report on the difficulties of maintaining control, sent in 1865 by Mr Harrison, the superintendent of Philips Park, to the Manchester Public Parks Committee. He describes how in fine weather the park was visited by 'a number of exceedingly ill behaved young men whose dress, language and conduct were both disgusting and filthy'. Because of them, respectable people were deterred from visiting the park. If he or the other staff tried to remonstrate with them they were greeted with laughs and sneers against which they could take no action 'for fear of being complained against in the newspapers and accused either of drunkenness or despotism ...' Harrison thought that the reasons for this reaction to the park staff stemmed from the fact that the working people of Manchester had contributed to the costs of acquiring the parks. Consequently they thought they should be privileged to use them as their own private property and they interpreted any restraint on their actions as an act of oppression. A notice displayed at the time of the opening of the park stated that 'This park was Purchased by the People, was made for the People and is given to the People for their protection.' Harrison wrote that when he or the other staff attempted to carry out the regulations 'this placard has been produced and the Park-keeper and his assistants have been told to mind their work, that their masters had entrusted the Park to the People and they were exceeding their duty by interfering with them'. It was very difficult for the park staff to look after the visitors during the day, as they were fully employed on work in the park, generally working close together, so large areas of the park were left unsupervised. When the men started their duties as watchers after working hours, they were not in a fit state 'to run after the young fellows who infest the Park and who feel that they can in most cases, even if detected, evade capture'. This was partly because of the age of the men employed. Out of eight employees, including Harrison, three were aged 59, 61 and 66 respectively, and the 'young' Thomas Williams aged 51 'appeared to be as old and infirm as any of them'. The picture conjured up by Harrison is of elderly and exhausted park workers being taunted and teased by lively young men and women, and trying ineffectually to chase them across the park. The real reason behind the saga seems to have been Harrison's wish to replace his older workers by younger ones.[70]

Parks 'solved the problem' of working-class recreation through the sports that could be played (but not on Sundays), the types of meetings allowed, the choice of refreshments and the almost total ban on alcohol. Events that were assumed to be uncontroversial and non-divisive such as Volunteer drilling were allowed, but political and religious meetings in general were not. The overall lack of activities available for women mirrored the position of women in society as a whole. Some saw parks as places where the classes could mix, but on middle- and ruling-class terms – 'gentility mongering places'.[71] It was customary for park visitors to put on their 'best' clothes, if they possessed any, and this, together with regulations which gave the keepers power to 'exclude any person from the park who is offensively dirty, or not dressed in decent clothes', would appear to reinforce this view.[72] Despite this, parks provided enormous enjoyment and were used by large numbers of people, especially on Sundays and special holidays. Over a period of years many established a reputation for particular activities, such as the bathing and open air meetings in Victoria Park, or the cricket in Birkenhead Park. Peel Park, Bradford became the venue of the Great West Riding Galas[73] and at Avenham Park, Preston thousands of children gathered each Easter Monday to roll their eggs and oranges down the slopes.[74]

CHAPTER TEN

Recreation grounds, parks and the urban environment

In 1878 when the opportunity of acquiring a seven-hectare site for a park occurred in Liverpool, there was fierce discussion on the merits of the proposal. The *Liverpool Argus* was adamant that 'We do not want ornamental waters and dirty swans. We want open spaces where our little ragamuffins can exercise their limbs and fashion themselves into healthy Englishmen.'[1] Most of the major urban centres had, by the end of the 1870s, acquired parks, but if the area of open space was compared with the population figures the achievement seemed less significant. Birmingham had a chain of seven parks on its outskirts, Liverpool had its ring of five parks, Manchester had three parks, but in terms of hectares of open space per head of population Bradford with its five large parks 'is our model city'. Bradford had 'one acre of open space for every 755 of its inhabitants', whereas in Liverpool the figure was 'one acre per 1,011 people, in Birmingham it was 1,665, in Sheffield 3,665 and Wolverhampton had no open space at all' (see also Table 2, p. 73). A comparison with American parks seemed to indicate that achievement there was more substantial. Philadelphia's Fairmont Park was seven miles long and Central Park, New York was larger than both Regent's Park and Hyde Park together[2].

The open spaces movements of the last quarter of the nineteenth century had two main aims: the creation of open space in densely populated districts, and the preservation of the countryside. Although geographically distinct, these targets were interlinked by the organisations and the individuals involved in them. These additional pressures for open space occurred at that time when the park movement itself had received enormous impetus from the passing of the Public Health Act 1875 and the question of accessibility was beginning to be confronted. From virtually the beginning of the park movement it had been recognised that the most densely populated districts had most need of open space for recreation, but large parks could not fulfill that need. Victoria Park in London had only been in use for a couple of years when, in 1847, *The Builder* criticised it, for not being near enough to meet the needs of the poor. A two- or three-mile walk was involved if a woman wanted to take her children there and a better solution would have been a number of small railed-off areas of one or two hectares each, with grass and a few seats, situated in working-class districts. Perhaps because it had little experience in these matters the magazine then went on to suggest that a woman could leave her children in the charge of the gatekeeper while she went to work and the children could play cricket and other games in safety.[3] One large park was inevitably less accessible than a number of smaller ones, particularly if it was located on the outskirts of a town as so many of them were.

Ten years later, when Slaney was presenting his Recreation Grounds Bill in Parliament, *The Builder* again identified the problem in similar terms. 'What seems . . . to be wanted . . . are little plots of ground for public playgrounds, at convenient intervals, in the midst of our densest populations'.[4] The Recreation Grounds Act 1859 and the Public Improvements Act 1860 would, it was hoped, help to solve this problem, but very few such spaces were created until the 1880s.

To expect mothers to carry their children one or more miles from their own homes for the purpose of play, or to suppose that boys and young men are likely after a hard day's work, to undertake a fatiguing walk to a place of recreation, when the time consumed in the walk should have been devoted to the game, is simply absurd. They will not do it. If the children and youth of the working classes are to have recreation, suitable places must be provided near at hand. To facilitate the procuring of such places two Acts of Parliament have recently been passed . . .[5]

These Acts stimulated the generosity of benefactors and the efforts of local authorities, but as their main results were large scale projects the problem of local inner-city open space remained. The terms park and recreation ground were interchangeable in the 1860s, as the title of the Recreation Grounds Act implied, and recreation grounds were not necessarily solely devoted to playgrounds, gymnasia and sports, nor were they of any particular size. They ranged from the quarter-hectare Lemon Street Playground (1864) in Leeds and the one-hectare Derbyshire Recreation Ground (1869) in Bolton, to the seven-hectare Bank Lodge Recreation Ground (1869) in Leeds (see Appendix 2).

An indication of how many small local open spaces existed in large towns can be seen from the replies sent to Manchester's Parks and Cemeteries Committee in 1876. The Council had instructed that Committee to report on available vacant plots of land in Manchester and its suburbs, with a view to acquiring these for use as parks and recreation grounds, and the Committee decided to find out what the position was in other towns. Liverpool, Leeds and the City of London had provided no such spaces. Glasgow was doing so in connection with other city improvements, but intended using them 'for securing air space in densely inhabited localities' rather than for recreation. Bristol sent irrelevant information and Birmingham replied that they were well supplied with parks, but that they were all in outlying areas. 'The great want felt here, is open spaces of land situated in the centre of the most thickly populated parts of the borough, and easily accessible to the people'. Birmingham had recently received a gift of land situated in a densely populated district (Burbury Street Recreation Ground, one and a half hectares, 1877) and had also purchased three and a half hectares in another densely populated part of the town (Highgate Park).[6]

A twelve-month experiment in using a school playground in Manchester as a recreation ground was carried out in 1877–8 at the Domestic Mission School in Embden Street, Greenheys. The school lent its ground (1500 square metres) as a public playground and the Council supervised it, provided seats, swings, poles and other apparatus, and planted shrubs. At first everything went well, but this did not last and the school wrote that 'lending out the ground has practically meant inviting and submitting to the roughest and idlest rascals of the district', children 'are driven off and deterred by these invaders'. Part of the problem was that as the ground did not fall within the jurisdiction of the police they took no action, though they did insist on closing the gates just when they needed to be open for evening classes! If the playground was properly supervised it could be a success, but the Domestic Mission thought that it should not be used by young men, who could go further afield to one of the parks. Finally they put up a notice 'playground closed' and allowed only local children to use it when it was convenient for the Mission to open it. They also asked the Queen's Park head gardener to remove the unwanted benches, which 'only challenge the mob of ruffians to violence and damage'.[7]

After this discouraging experience it was some four years before there was further action on the question of opening school playgrounds. The Manchester School Board suggested opening certain playgrounds for two hours on three evenings a week in 1882, but the Council refused to bear the cost of police supervision. The following year the Manchester and Salford Sanitary Association took up the question. This was followed by a conference held in Manchester in 1884 on recreation in towns, when Lord Brabazon, President of the Metropolitan Public Gardens Association, promised the Corporation £10,000 towards the cost of providing playgrounds. Subsequently meetings in London took place to persuade the Government to look into the question of physical training for the young, and a pamphlet entitled *Parks and Playgrounds for the People* was circulated to Members of Parliament. This pamphlet referred to the terms of the 1845 Enclosure Act, in which land should be set aside for recreation in proportion to the size of the population of a town, and proposed that this principle be applied to all new urban and suburban developments, so that no one would be further than one mile from a recreation ground. Unfortunately the interest of Parliament could not be aroused.[8]

A number of school playgrounds were opened in Manchester in 1885, and the Parks and Cemeteries Committee did manage to acquire open spaces for recreation in densely populated areas, by advertising for offers of plots of land. Fifty sites were offered, out of which five were selected, three of them being presented by the Improvement, Watch and Waterworks Committees and the other two purchased. They ranged in size from 500 to 5,600 square metres and were equipped with seats by the Committee. Only one, the Prussia Street site (3,000 square metres) which had been purchased for £12,000, was provided with playground equipment and a ball court (see Fig. 106). Purchases were restricted as the Committee did not think that this was a suitable time for increasing the burden of the rates. Wistfully they compared the present situation 'when the only donors are the departments of the Corporation itself' with that at the time of the original purchase of Queen's and Philips Parks. The

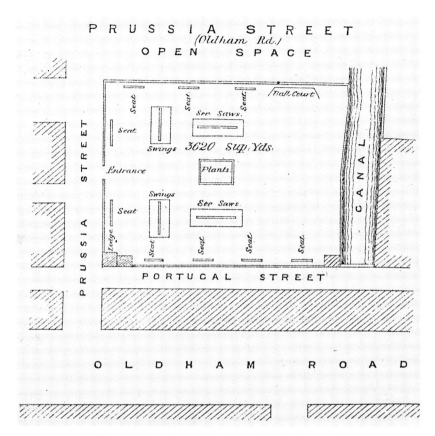

106 Prussia Street Recreation Ground, Manchester, 1884.

Council's attitude was similar to that of the Committee. The Councillors were fully aware of the need for open space and were 'unceasing in their efforts . . . having due regard to cost', but their main duty was to see that public money was used so that it provided as large a yield as possible.[9] Despite this concern for expenditure the acquisition of these sites marked the beginning of a more intensive phase of park acquisition and five parks were acquired and opened in the following decade (Birch Fields and Cheetham Park, 1885; Gorton Park, 1893; Crumpsall Park and Boggart Hole Clough, 1894).

THE OPEN SPACES SOCIETIES

The successful development of small parks and recreation grounds was largely due to the efforts of reforming organisations and to the movement to convert disused burial grounds and churchyards into open spaces for recreation. These organisations included the open spaces societies that were set up in many cities, the Manchester and Salford Sanitary Association (MSSA)[10] set up in 1852, the Commons Preservation Society set up in 1865, the Kyrle Society[11] set up in 1875 and the Metropolitan Public Garden, Boulevard, and Playground Association set up in 1882. The latter changed its name to the less unwieldy Metropolitan Public Gardens Association (MPGA) in 1885. The emphasis of the MSSA was initially on sanitation, but gradually its interests broadened to include housing and open spaces, and in 1880 a separate organisation called the Committee for Securing Open Spaces was set up, which was closely associated with the MSSA. At its first meeting this committee agreed 'to bring the question of Open Spaces ... before the public, giving the movement, in the first instance, the direction of the provision of playgrounds for districts of the city thickly populated or likely soon to be so'.[12] Among the most active members of this committee was Thomas Coglan Horsfall, who was attracting attention for his writings on German methods of town planning. From his experience of the problems of Manchester, Horsfall had become convinced that high housing density was a greater problem than overcrowded houses and that open spaces had an important part to play in any attempt to solve that problem.[13]

The Commons Preservation Society (CPS), the Kyrle Society and the Metropolitan Public Gardens Association worked closely together. The Kyrle Society was founded by Miranda Hill in 1875 as a society 'for the diffusion of beauty' and Octavia Hill, the pioneer of the National Trust, was its treasurer. Its aim was to bring beauty into the lives of working people by planting trees, establishing choirs, controlling smoke and collecting flowers for poor households.[14] In 1879 the Kyrle Society set up a sub-committee to work for the increased provision of open space and to preserve those spaces that were threatened, by working with the local authorities in London and with the Commons Preservation Society. Subsequently Kyrle Societies were set up in many urban centres.[15] William Morris was an active supporter of the open spaces societies in the early 1880s and lectured to both the Kyrle Society and the CPS. Since both societies were committed to working for open spaces within the existing capitalist framework it was inevitable that Morris's enthusiasm for them would wane.[16] The park and open spaces movements also found support from the reforming socialism of the Fabian Society, which advocated the expansion of municipal activities. The Public Health Act 1875 seemed to presage this, for it gave a strong impetus to the development of parks and recreation grounds. The Fabian Society also supported the preservation of footpaths and commons and saw this as a step towards the nationalisation of land.[17]

The Metropolitan Public Garden, Boulevard and Playground Association was set up in 1882 by Lord Brabazon, who was particularly concerned with the question of the physical condition of the urban population and the role that parks and playgrounds could play in improving it. When he was considering setting up the MPGA, he proposed that the open spaces committees of the Kyrle Society and of the National Health Society should combine. The National Health Society agreed, its chairman Ernest Hart becoming the first vice-chairman of the new Association, but Octavia Hill would not consent to the proposal. Meanwhile the Commons Preservation Society was increasingly directing its attention towards the provision and protection of open space outside towns. Transport was improving, working hours were being reduced and the newly introduced Bank Holidays meant increased opportunities for longer journeys. In 1894 the CPS merged with the National Footpaths Association.[18] Although the CPS had been effective in protecting open space and directing attention to the need to do so, it had no powers to acquire land. It was in 1884 that Sir Robert Hunter, the solicitor for the CPS, proposed the creation of an incorporated body to buy and hold land for the nation, arguing that it should be a statutory body, rather than a voluntary organisation.[19] Octavia Hill proposed that a Trust should be formed and in 1895, as the need to protect historic sites and the countryside was assuming increasing urgency, the National Trust for Historic Sites and Natural Scenery was set up.[20] Its link with the CPS was a direct one for Sir Robert Hunter became the National Trust's first chairman and of the nine signatories to the Trust's articles of Association six were CPS committee members.

BURIAL GROUNDS

While these open spaces societies were directing their attention to the wider landscape, local organisations continued to press for open space in inner-city locations, by transforming disused burial grounds into public gardens and recreation grounds, but this was a slow process both physically and legally. Churchyards and burial grounds had become increasingly overcrowded with the growth of urban populations and the 1830s and 1840s saw a growing trend to establish new cemeteries outside city boundaries. These were run on a commercial basis which proved to be less than satisfactory. During the early 1850s a number of Acts of Parliament gave local authorities powers to set up and run cemeteries and local authorities also passed local Acts. Coventry opened a municipal cemetery in 1847 which was designed by Paxton.[21] The Burial Act 1853[22] provided powers for churchyards to be closed and for the prohibition of new grounds if these would constitute a danger to health, and as a result 541 consecrated grounds were closed during 1854–5.[23] One of the earliest municipal burial grounds to be formed as a result of this legislation was Rochdale Cemetery in 1853.[24]

A return made to Parliament in 1874 of the situation regarding churchyards showed that 794 had closed since 1853, and 9,989 remained open in England and Wales. A further return made the following year broke the figures down into towns and showed that in Manchester twenty-one churchyards had closed completely, fourteen of them in 1854–5, and five had closed partially. There were no closures in Liverpool but nine in Birmingham.[25] As no provisions were made for the maintenance of these closed grounds they gradually fell into disrepair and decay and the nuisance arising led in 1876 to proceedings in the Ecclesiastical Courts. One of the results was the conversion of the churchyard of St George's-in-the-East in London into a garden.[26] In the centre of the garden was an obelisk to a benefactress of the parish, Mrs Raine, who had died in 1725. Some tombstones were placed against the walls and some were left standing, and by 1906 the garden contained a nature study museum and a special plot which was looked after by schoolchildren.[27] In the 1880s general Acts were passed which made provision for the future of closed burial grounds and their conversion into public open spaces and gardens. The Open Spaces Act 1881[28] made it possible to transfer the grounds to local authorities for use as public gardens, and the Disused Burial Grounds Act 1884[29] prohibited all building on such places.

In Manchester the MSSA pressed for the conversion of disused burial grounds into open space for recreation. By 1884 the Manchester

Parks and Cemeteries Committee had visited most of the sites in the city, but concluded that they were unsuitable for public use and that 'the position of London is more favourable as regards this conversion than that of Manchester', though they gave no reasons. They expressed willingness to plant trees in burial grounds if application was made, and they did spend £5,000 out of the poor rate to convert a disused burial ground at Angel Meadow into an open space, but generally they showed little interest in taking the initiative.[30]

The Metropolitan Public Gardens Association, like the MSSA before it, aimed to open school playgrounds outside school hours, provide gymnasia in Board schools and acquire disused burial grounds, waste places and enclosed squares for 'breathing and resting places for the old and playgrounds for the young, in the midst of densely populated localities; especially in the East and South of London'. These it planned to lay out either as gardens for adults, with benches, grass and flowers, as playgrounds, or as a combination of the two. Once established, they would be handed over to the local authority, but the Association thought they should be watched over by 'an intelligent man' who could give the children instruction in simple gymnastics. They also proposed to plant trees, place seats in the wider streets and erect baths, washhouses and swimming baths.

The Association lost no time in putting its ideas into practice and its first report summarised the achievements of its first year: tree planting in Mile End Road, gymnasia in a Board school, opening a further three hectares in Regent's Park to the public, and the transformation of disused burial grounds and churchyards into public gardens, forty-two of which had been or were about to be laid out. The sites ranged from the 25 by 30 metre site of the Chapel Royal (Savoy) Churchyard, to the three hectares of St Pancras Burial Ground, but most were between a half and one hectare. The St Pancras site had been opened not by the MPGA but by special Act of Parliament; but it was the Association that levelled the ground, removed some tombstones and placed the headstones in rows along the wall or on rocky mounds. Straight asphalt walks were laid out and a monumental tablet recorded the opening of the gardens.[31] The report also included comments about the new users of these sites. At St Leonard's Shoreditch 'The conduct of children [was] very bad at first, now improved, not yet perfect', clearly implying that these improvements were the result of this site. Others stressed their appreciation: '. . . a pleasant sight, this well-kept garden, in a monotonous area of bricks and mortar', 'A real boon: the visitors quiet, and deserving to be quiet, enjoy the repose they can get here'. In the half-hectare site of St John's, Waterloo Road, there was a swing, a giant stride that had been given by Lord Brabazon, parallel bars, and a seesaw given by the Association. The comment on these facilities was succinct: 'This keeps the rest of the ground quiet for adults'[32] (see Fig. 107).

The cemeteries in the worst condition were the private uncon-secrated ones which were initially untouched by the legislation, such as the nine-acre Victoria Park Cemetery in the East End of London. This was laid out and opened as Meath Gardens by the MPGA in 1894, with a garden, facilities for cricket, football and tennis, and two large playgrounds, one for boys and one for girls, containing seesaws, swings and gymnastic apparatus. The girls' gymnasium also con-tained a sandpit.[33] The sites were kept in order by caretakers,

107 Part of the former disused burial ground of St John's Church, Waterloo Road with a Metropolitan Drinking Fountain Association granite fountain.

gardeners or the police and were generally open during the hours of daylight.

The landscape gardeners for the MPGA were Fanny R. Wilkinson and J. Forsyth Johnson. Myatt's Fields, (1889), which was acquired largely through the efforts of the Society, was among the parks and recreation grounds probably laid out by Fanny Wilkinson. It still contains a games area, a children's playground, some large chestnut trees and its original bandstand[34] (see Fig. 58).

Other organisations were also involved in laying out disused burial grounds. The London Parochial Charities contributed part of the purchase cost and assisted in the upkeep of Postman's Park in the East End of London, so called because it was much used by General Post Office workers. This park adjoining St Botolph's Church, Aldersgate was formed out of three disused burial grounds and the GPO, which had the right of light over the whole space, also contributed to its upkeep. One of its features was a sheltered gallery along one side, with forty-eight tablets set in the wall of the church, commemorating the actions of heroic men and women of London who had lost their lives saving others. It was the painter G. F. Watts who suggested that the first jubilee of Queen Victoria should be marked by the erection of these tablets.[35] A road now passes over the site of Postman's Park.

In other cities open spaces societies continued working to acquire small open spaces, and to justify the formation of the Birmingham Open Spaces Society the Medical Officer of Health published a pamphlet which related the area of large towns to the number of persons per acre of open space. In his statistics, Birmingham came bottom of the list. From about 1907, the Birmingham Parks Committee began forming recreation grounds on sites created for the most part by slum clearance. They also experimented with lighting a recreation ground at night (Callow Fields Recreation Ground, two hectares), and keeping it open during the winter until 9.00 p.m. This proved very popular and 'served to withdraw many of the young people from the streets and afford them recreation under more desirable conditions'.[36] In Glasgow, St David's was the first disused churchyard (0.5 hectare) to be opened to the public in 1879. This churchyard and subsequent ones were laid out in a similar way with walks, trees and shrubs, and with the formerly upright monuments generally laid flat. They were open from 10 a.m. to 8.00 p.m. in the

108 St Luke's Gardens, Chelsea
Headstones from the disused burial ground surround the garden, but many are
overgrown.

summer and until dusk in the winter. Unlike London where
philanthropy had secured the transformation, in Glasgow this was the
achievement of the local authorities.[37]

The transformation of churchyards and cemeteries into gardens
did not add a very significant area to the open space available for
recreation, but amenity value cannot be assessed in terms of area
alone. The burial grounds that had been closed tended to be in
districts surrounded by densely populated streets and the value of
even a small open space to the people living nearby was of enormous
significance, particularly to the aged and the very young. Despite the
fact that many of these burial grounds had been grossly overfilled and
since closure had been quite neglected, there was a difference between
how they were treated and what people felt for them. Most people
regarded such places with awe and reverence and for some the
inclusion of playgrounds in what had formerly been burial grounds
was too much to contemplate. The idea of 'children romping about in
the churchyards and turning somersaults on the graves, was too
revolting and disagreeable to be entertained'[38] (see Fig. 108). Despite
such feelings the creation of gardens and open spaces out of church-

yards and burial grounds grew, as the importance of accessible open space was increasingly recognised.

DISTRIBUTION OF OPEN SPACE

Parks, gardens, recreation grounds and playgrounds had all been introduced into the urban environment by the turn of the century, but the question of distribution and accessibility remained. Each development occurred according to particular circumstances rather than according to any general strategy, and effective distribution could not be achieved until a general strategy was agreed upon. The need for accessibility had been recognised from the earliest days of the park movement. The comparison between the merits of large-scale parks and more widely dispersed small open spaces indicated that this problem was being confronted. From the earliest days of the park movement the effect of park creation on the value of the surrounding land had been well understood, although financial success was not always assured. Regent's Park, Prince's Park (Liverpool) and Birkenhead Park were some of the earliest examples of the successful application of this principle. The increase in the value of the surrounding land promoted the building of substantial houses and parks consequently became a focus for middle- and upper-class suburban development. The creation of small open spaces, by contrast, did not result in significant changes in the value of the surrounding residential land. These spaces were introduced where the opportunity occurred and they were not designed in conjunction with housing (see, for example, Fig. 109). Parks were therefore among the many complex factors contributing to the suburbanisation process and to the loosening of the texture of cities which culminated in the development of the Garden City.

The link between parks and physical health had been stressed by the early park promoters and during the course of the nineteenth century the concept of health expanded to include social and moral health. Parks, museums and libraries became a focus for civic pride, providing evidence that local authorities were assuming the role of guardians of cultural ideals. The last decades of the century saw municipal effectiveness being judged statistically, with mortality rates being compared with population densities and the area of parks. This 'evidence' gave local authorities additional justification for municipal

109 Wapping Recreation Ground, 1891
The bandstand is the main focus and the few beds with grass and shrubs are surrounded by a gravelled area. The playground, in which a giant stride can just be seen is top left. The back yards of the terraced housing are screened by trees and in the distance sailing barges on the river Thames can be seen.

expenditure on parks and recreation grounds, even though it could not and did not differentiate between the contribution of parks to improved health as opposed to the introduction of clean water, effective sewage systems or improved standards of housing. This concern with fresh air, physical health and mortality rates was reinforced by concern with the physique of young people and the need for active recreation facilities. The publication of the Report on Physical Deterioration[39] in 1904 marked official recognition of the problem and further evidence came from the medical reports on the prospective army recruits for the Boer War and the First World War. The resulting pressure led to the setting up of such organisations as the National Playing Fields Association. The Report on Physical Deterioration recommended that building bye-laws should include the provision of open space by local authorities, in proportion to the density of the population, and it has a familiar ring. It was the Town Planning Act 1909[40] which for the first time gave local authorities the powers to plan for the future, instead of reacting to the problems of

221

the past and trying to ameliorate them. This then marks the date when the park and open spaces movements became absorbed into town planning.

Parks were created out of commons, private estates and a variety of types of marginal land that presented constructional difficulties, such as gravel pits, quarries, brickfields or city dumps. Similar sites were used for park development in the major European cities, but in addition there was one major source of land for public parks that had little counterpart in Britain and that was ex-military land. Hamburg's fortifications were demolished 1804–21 and the Wallringpark, a central ring of parks, created in its stead. In Copenhagen, after the creation of the Tivoli Gardens in the 1840s, public parks were created out of the city's ring of fortifications. In Vienna the Ringstrasse was created when the city walls were demolished in the 1850s but what had previously been large open areas of recreational space was divided up and sold for development. Land was set aside for public parks but this represented a reduction in comparison with what had hitherto been available.[41] Paris also failed to take advantage of the open land surrounding the city and this too was built on, while the Field of Mars became the site for successive world fairs from 1878 to 1937.[42]

Parks were one manifestation of the rise of modern institutions to control the physical and social processes of urbanisation. The use of urban space was realigned and with it came increased organisation and control. Streets were no longer the playground of the poor, street football was criminalised and recreation was increasingly controlled by commercial or local authorities. In this process parks 'solved the recreation problem' through the types of activities allowed, the choice of refreshments, the music, the meetings, the sports, the planting and the facilities available to women.

Over the whole period in which the municipal park developed, the need for access to open space for recreation was generally agreed upon, but the priority given to it underwent a major change. The transformation of disused burial grounds into open space for recreation provides the most direct evidence of the change in public opinion that had taken place. The feeling that the commemoration of the dead was a normal and indeed an important duty of the living, gave way to a feeling that public health and social welfare were considerations of greater weight. This change in priorities and in public

110 Original entrance gates and railings to Myatt's Fields, London.

opinion was, by nineteenth-century religious standards, a very notable change indeed.

Municipal parks were brought into being by a variety of means in which social conscience, philanthropy, skilful entrepreneurship, politics and municipal enterprise all played a part. They had literally to be sold to society and they were, most successfully. Although the facilities that they offered were rather sober in comparison with those of the pleasure gardens, there is no doubt that parks provided enormous enjoyment. Gated and railed, they were literally and symbolically a world apart, providing oases of green in areas of brick and stone, contact with nature and the joy of walking on grass and under the trees (Fig. 110). Although nature in the parks appeared in well-disciplined forms, it was still refreshing and the flowers were bright and colourful. There was space in which to run freely and safely, or just to sit and dream, and at certain points in the larger parks it was quite possible to imagine oneself in the depths of the countryside, rather than in the centre of a city. The smaller recreation grounds had the advantage of accessibility, which was so important for both young and old, and whatever their size, parks and recreation grounds made a major contribution to the nineteenth-century urban environment.

223

APPENDIX ONE

Summary of Main Legislation promoting Park Development

1836 ENCLOSURE ACT

6 & 7 Will. IV, c.115

Common fields exempted from enclosure if they lay within

10 miles of London	
3 miles of towns of	100,000 population
$2\frac{1}{2}$	70,000
2	30,000
$1\frac{1}{2}$	15,000
1	5,000

1845 GENERAL ENCLOSURE ACT

8 & 9 Vict. c.118, s.15, s.30

Consent of those representing one third in value of interests in the land necessary for an application of enclosure.

Approval of two thirds necessary for sanction of enclosure.

Special reports to be made to Parliament where commons were within

15 miles of London	
4 miles of towns of	100,000 population
$3\frac{1}{2}$	70,000
3	30,000
2	10,000

Where common or wasteland was enclosed, land to be set aside for recreation according to size of population:

10 acres above 10,000 population
8 acres for population 5–10,000
5 acres for population of 2–5,000
4 acres for population under 2,000

1847 TOWNS IMPROVEMENT CLAUSES ACT

10 & 11 Vict. c.34

Urban authorities could purchase, rent or otherwise provide land for recreation provided it was not more than three miles from the principal market or the site was approved by the Inspector.

Local authorities were not empowered to maintain a park out of public funds if it was a gift.

1848 PUBLIC HEALTH ACT

11 & 12 Vict. c.63, s.74

Local Boards of Health empowered to provide, maintain and improve land for municipal parks and to support and contribute towards such land provided by any person whomsoever.

1859 THE RECREATION GROUNDS ACT

22 Vict. c.27

Land not exceeding £1,000 could be bequeathed for the purpose of providing public recreation grounds and playgrounds.

Managers of any recreation ground given powers to make and enforce byelaws. Penalties not specified.

1860 PUBLIC IMPROVEMENTS ACT

23 & 24 Vict. c.30, s.1, s.6, s.7

Adoptive Act applicable to any borough or parish with a population of five hundred or more.

Local authorities could acquire, hold and manage land for public walks, parks and playgrounds and could levy rates for maintaining and improving them, to the maximum of 6d in the £, provided two thirds of the ratepayers of any borough or parish of five hundred inhabitants agreed.

But before this rate could be levied, half the estimated cost had to be raised by private subscription, donations, or other means. Local authorities could not borrow money in order to carry out the purposes of the Act.

Penalties not exceeding £5 for any and every breach of any byelaw.

225

1863 TOWN GARDENS PROTECTION ACT

26 & 27 Vict. c.13, s.4
26 & 27 Vict. c.27, s.5

Protection of neglected town gardens could be vested in the local authority of cities or boroughs, or the Metropolitan Board of Works in the case of London.

1863 PUBLIC WORKS (MANUFACTURING DISTRICTS) ACT

26 & 27 Vict. c.70

Local authorities in certain manufacturing districts empowered to borrow money to improve or provide public works, including parks and recreation grounds.

1866 METROPOLITAN COMMONS ACT

29 & 30 Vict. c.122

All commons within 15 miles of the centre of London protected and regulated.

1871 PUBLIC PARKS, SCHOOLS AND MUSEUMS ACT

34 & 35 Vict. c.13

Extended the provisions of the Recreation Grounds Act 1859. Land up to twenty acres could be donated for the purposes of a public park.

1875 PUBLIC HEALTH ACT

38 & 39 Vict. c.55

Local authorities empowered to raise central government loans for the purpose of acquiring or improving land for recreation. County Councils and Metropolitan Boroughs not empowered. This omission was made good in the Open Spaces Act 1906 (6 Edw. VII, c.25).

Land acquired by an urban authority as open space for recreation could not be used for other and inconsistent purposes. Museums, conservatories and libraries could be built, but not municipal offices.

1876 COMMONS ACT

39 & 40 Vict. c.56

Extended the provisions of the 1866 Metropolitan Commons Act outside the metropolitan area.

1877 METROPOLITAN OPEN SPACES ACT

40 & 41 Vict. c.55

Gave Metropolitan Board of Works power to convert churchyards and make them available to the public.

1881 OPEN SPACES ACT

44 & 45 Vict. c.34

Neglected town gardens could be transferred to local authority.

Provision for closed burial grounds to be converted into public open spaces and gardens.

Chronology of main municipal and public park developments 1800-1885, and map

Opening Date is the date of official opening, if there was one.

Park Name is the name at the opening. Subsequent changes are noted. †By the park name indicates restrictions on public entry.

Size is the size on opening. No attempt has been made to record additions unless they resulted in the creation of a new park, or a change of name.

Designer: (C) indicates that the designer was selected by competition.

Mode of Acquisition:

LA	park acquired by action of local authority
subs	funds raised by subscription
royal	royal park
leased	park not the property of local authority until the date noted
gift	donation of land, or funds for acquisition
spec dev	speculative development by an individual or group

Date of Local Authority Acquisition is the date that the Local Authority acquired the site, or the park. Unless otherwise indicated this was also the date for unrestricted, free entry.

Main Municipal and Public Parks 1800-1885

Opening date	Town	Park	Size (hectares)	Designer	Mode of acquisition	Date of local authority acquisition
1826	London	Regent's Park	142.0	J. Nash	royal	
1830	Bath	Royal Victoria Park	4.0		leased	
1833	Preston	Moor Park	74.0	E. Milner (1864)	LA	1833
1836	Gravesend	Terrace Garden	1.2	J. C. Loudon	Private development	sold for building 1875
1839	Luton	Pope's Meadow			Winch Trust	1894

Appendix 2 Continued

Opening date	Town	Park	Size (hectares)	Designer	Mode of acquisition	Date of local authority acquisition
1840	Derby	The Arboretum†	4.5	J. C. Loudon	gift	1882
1841	Sheffield	Norfolk Park	25.0		gift	1909
1842	London	Primrose Hill			royal	
1842	Liverpool	Prince's Park	16.0	J. Paxton/ E. Milner	spec. dev.	1908
1844	Edinburgh	East Prince's Street Gardens			LA	
1844	Southampton	The Common and The Parks			LA	
1845	London	Victoria Park	78.0	J. Pennethorne/ J. Gibson	royal	1887
1846	Bradford	Woolsorter's Baths and Pleasure Gardens†	3.2	W. Barratt	leased	
1846	Manchester	Philips Park	12.5	J. Major (C)	subs	1846
		Queen's Park	12.0	J. Major (C)	subs	1846
	Salford	Peel Park	12.0	J. Major (C)	subs	1846
1847	Birkenhead	Birkenhead Park	50.0	J. Paxton	LA	1844
	Preston	Avenham Park	10.5	E. Milner (1864)	LA	1847
1849	Darlington	Bellasses Park (later The People's Park, then South Park)	8.3		leased	1877
1850	Bradford	Peel Park	22.6		subs	1863
1852	London	Kennington Park	8.0		royal	1887
	Nottingham	The Arboretum†	7.7	S. Curtis	LA	Free entry 1875
1853	Ipswich	Lower Arboretum†	2.0	W. Pontey		1903
		Upper Arboretum†	3.2	W. Pontey		1928
	Torquay	Torwood Gardens	0.12			1853
1854	Bolton	Bradford Park	8.3		loan	still not municipally owned
	Glasgow	Kelvingrove Park	26.0	J. Paxton	LA	1852
	Macclesfield	Peel Park (later West Park)†	8.3	W. Barron & Sons	LA	1854
1856	Birmingham	Adderley Park	4.0		leased	1871
	Liverpool	Wavertree Park	12.0		LA	1843
	London	Battersea Park	80.0	J. Pennethorne/ J. Gibson	royal	1887
		Crystal Palace Park†	81.0	J. Paxton/ E. Milner	spec. dev.	1952
	Reading	Forbury Gardens	1.6	J. B. Clacy	LA	1854
1857	Birmingham	Calthorpe Park	12.0		leased	1871
	Blackburn	Corporation Park	20.0		LA	1855
	Glasgow	Glasgow Green	55.0	James Clelland (1815-26)	LA	1450 (tolls applied until 1857)

Opening date	Town	Park	Size (hectares)	Designer	Mode of acquisition	Date of local authority acquisition
	Halifax	People's Park	5.0	J. Paxton/ E. Milner	gift	1857
	Leeds	Woodhouse Moor	25.0		LA	1857
	Sunderland	People's Park (later Mobray Park)	5.6	Mr Lawson/ J. Smith	LA	1855
1858	Birmingham	Aston Hall Park†	20.0		Shareholders	1864
	Stockport	Vernon Park	8.5		gift	1851
1859	Devonport	Devonport Park	15.0	R. Veitch & Son (1895)	LA/subs	1858
	Worcester	Arboretum Gardens†	10.0	W. Barron	spec. dev.	land sold for building 1866
1860	Hull	Pearson Park	11.0	J. C. Niven	LA	1860
	Peterborough	Stanley Recreation Ground			gift	
1861	Gateshead	Windmill Hills	4.0		LA	1861
1862	Abingdon	Albert Park	5.6	Mr Chapman of Dulwich (C)	spec. dev.	Still privately owned
	Barnsley	Barnsley Park (later Locke Park)	6.0	Mr Fox	gift	1869
	Glasgow	Queen's Park	23.0	J. Paxton	LA	1857
	Liverpool	Shiel Park	6.0		LA	1847
1863	Dundee	Baxter Park	15.4	J. Paxton	gift	
	London	Alexandra Park	81.0	A. McKenzie	spec. dev.	
1864	Farnworth	Farnworth Park	5.0		gift and lease	1864
	Hastings	St Andrew's Gardens (later part of Alexandra Park)			LA	1864
	Leeds	Lemon Street Playground	0.2		LA	1864
	Preston	Miller Park	4.5	E. Milner	gift	
1865	Bingley	Prince of Wales' Park	7.3		LA and subs	1860
	Croydon	Duppas Hill	14.0		LA	1865
	Warrington	Recreation Ground			rented	
1866	Bolton	Bolton Park (later Queen's Park)	18.6		LA	1864
		Heywood Recreation Ground	3.6	Henderson	part gift, part lease	1862
	Dunfermline	The Public Park	16.0	J. Paxton	gift	1863
	Great Yarmouth	St George's Park	2.0		LA	
	Sunderland	Mobray Extension Park	5.0	J. Lindsay (C)	LA	
1867	Chester	Grosvenor Park	8.3	E. Kemp	gift and subs	
	London	Poplar Recreation Ground	0.75		LA	1867
	Weymouth	Alexandra Gardens			gift	1880
1868	Glasgow	Alexandra Park	20.0	D. M'Lellan	LA	1866

Appendix 2 Continued

Opening date	Town	Park	Size (hectares)	Designer	Mode of acquisition	Date of local authority acquisition
	Liverpool	Newsham Park	46.0	M. Tyerman	LA	1847
	London	Peckham Rye Park	20.0		LA	1868
	Luton	People's Park (incl. Pope's Meadow)			Trustees	1894
	Oldham	Alexandra Park	26.0		LA	1865
	Middlesbrough	Albert Park	30.0	W. Barratt	gift	1866
	Paisley	Fountain Gardens		J. C. Niven	gift	
	Southport	Hesketh Park	12.0	E. Kemp	gift	1865
1869	Bolton	Darbishire Recreation Ground	0.8		gift	1868
	Leeds	Bank Lodge Recreation Ground	7.3		LA	1869
	London	Albert Embankment Gdns		A. McKenzie	LA	
		Finsbury Park	46.5	A. McKenzie	LA	1857
		Southwark Park	25.5	A. McKenzie	LA	1864
1870	Bradford	Lister Park	22.2		LA+gift	1870
	Leeds	Bramley Recreation Ground	4.0		LA	1870
	Liverpool	Stanley Park	40.5	E. Kemp	LA	1866
1871	Aberdeen	Victoria Park (formerly Glennie's Park)	5.6	J. Robertson	LA	1871
	Saltaire	Saltaire Park	5.6	W. Gay	gift	
1872	Ilfracombe	Ropery Meadow			LA	1872
	Leeds	Roundhay Park	175.0	G. Corson	LA	1870
	Lincoln	Lincoln Arboretum	5.2	E. Milner	LA	1870
	Liverpool	Sefton Park	109.0	E. André (C)	LA	1865
1873	Birmingham	Cannon Hill Park	25.0		gift	1873
	Newcastle-upon-Tyne	Leazes Park	4.0		LA	1873
	Stalybridge/ Ashton-under-Lyme	Stamford Park	27.0		gift and subs	1891
	Warrington	Bank Park	7.0		LA	1872
1874	London	Chelsea Embankment Gdns			LA	
		West Ham Park	32.5		LA	
	Rochdale	Broadfield Park	7.7	Stansfield & Son	leased	1894
	Sheffield	Weston Park	5.0	R. Marnock	LA	1873
	Swansea	Brynmill Park			LA	
	Walsall	The Arboretum[†]	2.8		spec. dev.	1881
1875	London	Victoria Embankment Gdns	4.0	A. McKenzie	LA	
	Sheffield	Firth Park	14.0		gift	
	South Shields	North Park Recreation Ground	1.6		gift	
1876	Birmingham	Highgate Park	3.6		LA	1875

Opening date	Town	Park	Size (hectares)	Designer	Mode of acquisition	Date of local authority acquisition
		Summerfield Park	5.0		LA	1876
	Edinburgh	Inverleith Park			LA	1876
	Ilfracombe	Capstone Hill			LA	1876
	Leeds	Woodhouse Ridge	6.5		LA	1876
	Rotherham	Boston Park	9.6	Mr Albiston	leased	1873
	Salford	Seedley Park		H. Moore		
	Swansea	Cwmdonkin Park			LA	
1877	Barnsley	Locke Park (adjoining Barnsley Park)	8.3	W. Barron	gift	1877
	Birmingham	Burbury Street Recreation Ground	1.6		gift	1876
	Gateshead	Saltwell Park	19.0	E. Kemp	LA	1876
	Leeds	Holbeck Intake	1.2		LA	1877
	Paisley	Brodie Park	9.0		gift	1877
	Rochdale	Cronkeyshaw Common	20.6		LA	1877
	Salford	Albert Park	6.0	H. Moore		
1878	Bradford	Horton Park	24.0	W. Gay	LA	1873
	Liverpool	St Martin's Recreation Ground	0.7		LA	
	Llanelli	People's Park	6.5	W. Barron (of Sketty, Swansea)	LA	1878
	Portsmouth	Victoria Park	5.0	A. McKenzie	LA	
	West Bromwich	Dartmouth Park	22.6	C. Turner	leased	1919
	Wigan	Mesnes Park	5.7	J. McClean (C)	gift	1874
1879	Birmingham	Small Heath Park (later Victoria Park)	15.0		gift	1876
	Bristol	Cotham Gardens	1.0		leased	
	Kilmarnock	Kay Park	16.5	D. M'Lellan	gift	
	Leeds	Hunslet Moor	25.5		LA	1879
		Oak Road Recreation Ground	1.8		LA	1879
	London	Silver Street Playground	0.3			
	Manchester	Heywood Park	8.3		LA	1878
	Salford	Ordsal Park		H. Moore	LA	
1880	Accrington	Higher Antley Recreation Ground	6.0		LA	
		Milnshaw Park	2.4		LA	1879
	Altrincham	Stamford Park	6.5	J. Shaw	gift	
	Bradford	Bowling Park	20.0	Kershaw & Hepworth	LA	1878
	Coventry	Swanswell Recreation Ground			LA	

Appendix 2 Continued

Opening date	Town	Park	Size (hectares)	Designer	Mode of acquisition	Date of local authority acquisition
	Leicester	Victoria Park	29.0		LA	1880
	London	St Luke's Parish Playground Whitechapel	0.1		rented	
	Newcastle-upon-Tyne	Armstrong Park	20.0	Mr Fowler	LA+gift	
	Norwich	Chapel Field Gardens	3.0		LA	1866
1881	Edinburgh	West Prince's St Gardens			LA	1876
	Halifax	Shrogg's Park	9.7		LA	
	Lancaster	Williamson Park	14.0	J. McClean	gift	
	Wolverhampton	West Park	20.0	R. H. Vertegans (C)	leased	
	Worthing	People's Park (later Holmfield Park)			gift	
1882	Birmingham	St Mary's Gardens	0.8			
	Hastings	Alexandra Park (including St Andrew's Gardens)	41.0	R.Marnock	LA	1872
	Leicester	Abbey Park	26.7	W. Barron & Sons	LA	1878
	Liverpool	Aubrey Street Recreation Ground	0.6			
	London	Wanstead Park	53.4		LA	
1883	Aberdeen	Duthie Park	17.8			
	Bristol	Bedminster Pleasure Park	10.0		gift	1883
	Ealing	Lammas Park			LA	1881
	Grimsby	People's Park	9.7	W. Barron & Sons (C)	gift	
	Huddersfield	Beaumont Park	10.0		gift	1879
	Southend-on-Sea	Prittlewell Square	0.4			
	West Hartlepool	Ward-Jackson Memorial Park	6.9	Matthew Scott	LA	1883
1884	Brighton	Preston Park	27.0		LA	1883
	Bristol	St Agnes Gardens	1.0		LA	1884
	Leeds	New Wortley Recreation Ground	12.5		LA	1884
	Liverpool	Brow Street Recreation Ground	0.2		LA	
		Kensington Gardens	7.4		LA	
	London	Newington Recreation Ground	0.6		LA	
	Manchester	Mount Street Recreation Ground	0.4		LA	1884
		Churnett Street Recreation Ground	0.6		LA	1884

Opening date	Town	Park	Size (hectares)	Designer	Mode of acquisition	Date of local authority acquisition
		Butler Street Recreation Ground	0.1		LA	1884
		Prussia Street Recreation Ground	0.3		LA	1884
		Queen Street Recreation Ground	0.05		LA	1884
	Newcastle-upon-Tyne	Jesmond Dene	30.0		gift	
1885	Colchester	Recreation Ground	0.25		leased	
	Leicester	Spinney Hill Park	14.5		LA	
	Liverpool	St Luke's Garden	0.4			
		St Michael's Garden	0.5			
		St Thomas's Garden	0.1			
	London	Carlton Square Gdns, Mile End	0.3			
		St Bartholomew's Church-yard, Bethnell Green	0.4			
		St Paul's Churchyard, Rotherhithe				
		Highbury Fields	11.0		LA	
	Manchester	Birchfields Park			LA	
		Cheetham Park			LA	
	Tynemouth	Northumberland Park	4.0		gift	
	Walsall	Redwood Park			LA	
		Palfrey Park			LA	

Map of Great Britain showing main municipal and public park
developments 1800–1880.

235

Trees and plants suitable for London (1883)

TREES

Acacias (Robinia)

Tree of Heaven (Ailanthus Glandulosa)

Pyrus

Catalpa

Maiden Hair Tree (Salisburnia adianifolia)

Tulip Trees (Liriodendron tulipfera)

Willows (Salix)

Poplars (populus)

Almonds (Amygdalus)

Birch (Betula)

Maples (acer)

Plane (Platanus)

Walnut Trees (Juglans Regis)

Oak (Quercus)

SHRUBS

Azalea Pontica, hardy varieties

St John's wort (Hypericum)

Deutzia

Elder (Sambucus)

Guêlder Rose (Viburnum opulus sterilis)

Lilacs (Syringa)

Flowering currants (Ribes)

Snowdrop Trees (Halesia tetraptera)

Cytisus

Genista

Sumach (Rhus)

Conchorus Japonica

Dogwood (cornus)

Forsythia

Meadow sweet (spirea)

Hawthorn (crataegus)

Weigela

Fig Tree (Fiens)

Cotoneaster

CLIMBING PLANTS

Honeysuckle (Lonicera)

Hardy vines (vitis)

Clematis

Crataegus Pyracanthus

Bramble (Rubus)

Trumpet flower (Tecoma radicaus major)

Jasmine (Jasminum)

Virginia creepers (ampelopsis)

EVERGREEN SHRUBS

Griselinia

Holly (Ilex)

Skinimia Japonica

Spindle Tree (Euonymus Europaeus), and other varieties

Ligustrum

Box (Buxus)

Artemesia

Hardy Fuchsias

Rucus

Euonymus radicaus variegata

Vincas

Willow Herb (Epilobium augustifolium)

Ancuba Japonica [sic]

Rhododendrons

Escallonia

Tucea

Cotoneaster microphylla

Iberis

Hesperus

Arundo conspicua

Pernettya

Dianthus

Arabis Albida

Metropolitan Public Garden, Boulevard, and Playgrounds Association, *First Report*, 1883, Appendix E.

Notes

I PUBLIC PARKS AND MUNICIPAL PARKS

1 G. F. Chadwick, *The Park and the Town*, London, 1966, p. 19

2 J. C. Loudon, 'Remarks on laying out public gardens and promenades', *Gardeners' Magazine*, vol. 2, 1835, p. 646

3 38 & 39 Vict. c.55

4 34 & 35 Vict. c.13

5 J. Summerson, *Architecture in Britain, 1530–1830*, London, 6th edition, 1977, p. 385

6 P. Zucker, *Town and Square: from the Agora to the Village Green*, New York, 1959

7 J. Summerson, *The Life and Work of John Nash, Architect*, London, 1980. See also T. Longstaffe-Gowan, 'Georgian Town Gardens', Ph.D. Thesis, University College, London, 1989

8 Second Report of the Commissioners of Woods, Forests and Land Revenues, Appendix 20, p. 113. Quoted in Summerson, *The Life and Work of John Nash*, pp. 116–17

9 Anon. *A Picturesque Guide to the Regent's Park*, London, 1829, pp. 8 and 17

10 J. C. Loudon, *The Gardeners' Magazine*, vol. 1, 1826. Loudon reprinted extracts from an article by Lenné entitled 'General Remarks on British Parks and Gardens', which had appeared in *Transactions of the Prussian Gardening Society*, vol. 1, adding his own comments

11 A. Saunders, *Regent's Park. A Study of the Development of the Area from 1086 to the Present Day*, Newton Abbot, 1969, pp. 53, 146–7

12 'The Struggling Classes, Public Playgrounds', *Builder*, vol. 16, no. 800, 5 June 1858, p. 385

13 S. Lang, 'St James's Park', *Architectural Review*, vol. 110, November 1951, p. 295

14 Anon. *History of the Royal Victoria Park, Bath*, Bath, c.1872, pp. 2–4

15 15 & 16 Will. IV, c.76

16 R. Izack, *Remarkable Antiquities of the City of Exeter*, Exeter, 1681, p. 145

17 J. W. Heath, 'The Quarry, Shrewsbury', paper read to the Caradoc Field Club, 15 November 1912. Burgesses had allotments in The Quarry,

which they could not plough or cultivate without the consent of the town, nor could they graze cattle without paying a fee. In 1879 the Corporation planted trees and erected a bandstand.

18 Chadwick, *The Park and the Town*, p. 44
19 E. P. Hennock, *Fit and Proper Persons*, London, 1973, p. 17. Their government was by Court Leet and Street Commission
20 C. Gill, *History of Birmingham*, vol. 1, London, 1952, p. 410
21 *Preston Chronicle*, 28 September 1833. The effective date for the enclosure was an Order in Council of Preston Borough Council, dated 29 November 1833
22 Chadwick, *The Park and the Town*, pp. 106–7

2 THE NEED FOR PARKS

1 *Select Committee on Public Walks*, (SCPW), BPP, vol. XV, 1833, Cmnd 448
2 22 Vict. c.27
3 R. A. Slaney, *An Essay on the Beneficial Direction of Rural Expenditure*, London, 1824
4 B. R. Mitchell and P. Deane, *Abstract of British Historical Statistics*, Cambridge, 1962
5 W. Ashworth, *The Genesis of Modern British Town Planning*, London, 1954, Ch. 1
6 Anon. *History of Liverpool*, Liverpool, 1785, p. 84. Quoted in E. H. Roberts, 'A Study of the Growth of the Provision of Public Facilities for Leisure Occupation by Local Authorities of the Merseyside', unpublished MA Thesis, University of Liverpool, 1933, p. 62
7 A. Prentice, *Historical Sketches and Personal Recollections of Manchester*, London, 1851, 3rd edition, 1970, p. 114
8 W. A. West, 'Provision of open spaces in urban development', *J. Planning and Environmental Law*, January 1973, pp. 23–6
9 R. Cheyney, *Industrial and Social History of England*, New York, 1901, p. 221
10 Report of the Proceedings of a Public Meeting held at the Town Hall, Manchester, 8 August 1844, p. 16. Manchester Parks Committee Scrapbook (MPCS) MS 352–7
11 J. D. Chambers, *A Century of Nottingham History*, Nottingham, 1954
12 GLC Record Office: Office of Works Papers on Parks. Quoted in M. P. G. Draper, *Lambeth's Open Spaces*, London, 1979, p. 22
13 D. Thompson, *The Chartists*, London, 1984, p. 325
14 Draper, *Lambeth's Open Spaces*, p. 22
15 *Royal Commission on Common Land*, BPP, 1955–8, Cmnd 462, p. 162.

Between 1750 and 1850 Acts relating to wasteland, which could be the subject of commons rights, dealt with the enclosure of 850,000 hectares. In addition about 1.82 million hectares were enclosed of which an unknown proportion represented common pasture.

16 W. Cobbett, *The Progress of a Ploughboy to a Seat in Parliament*, Quoted in *Royal Commission on Common Land*, op. cit., p. 164

17 *SCPW*, pp. 5, 66

18 W. E. A. Axon, *The Annals of Manchester*, London, 1886, p. 182

19 H. Heartwell, 'Characteristics of Manchester', *North of England Magazine*, vol. 1, 1842, p. 164

20 *SCPW*, p. 44

21 A. Pope, 'The walks and avenues of Dorchester', *Dorset Natural History and Antiquarian Field Club Proceedings*, vol. 38, May 1916–May 1917, 1918, pp. 23–33

22 G. Andela, 'The Public Park in the Netherlands', *J. Garden History*, vol. 1, no. 4, October–December 1981, p. 369

23 *SCPW*, p. 21

24 Report of the Proceedings of a Public Meeting held at the Town Hall, Manchester, 8 August 1844, p. 14

25 S. Smiles, 'What is doing for the People in Public Amusement and Recreation', *The People's Journal*, vol. 2, 1847, p. 13

26 J. A. Roebuck, Speeches on the motion 'That this House views with concern the present state of industrial towns', 1828. Quoted in F. E. Hyde, 'Utilitarian Town Planning', *Town Planning Review*, Summer 1947, pp. 153–9

27 A. Delves, 'Popular Recreation and Social Conflict in Derby, 1800–1850'. In E. Yeo and S. Yeo, *Popular Culture and Class Conflict 1590–1914*, Brighton, 1980, pp. 89–129

28 5 & 6 Will. IV, c.50, c.72

29 A. Lewis, 'Recreation a Religious Duty', *Dark Blue*, vol. 1, 1871, pp. 348–9

30 H. Cunningham, *Leisure and the Industrial Revolution*, London, 1980
A. P. Donajgrodski (ed.), *Social Control in Nineteenth Century Britain*, London, 1977
J. Walvin, *Leisure and Society 1830–1950*, London, 1978

31 M. Arnold, *Culture and Anarchy*, London, 1969 edition, p. 102

32 B. Harrison, 'Religion and Recreation in Nineteenth-Century England', *Past and Present*, no. 38, Dec. 1967, pp. 116–18

33 R. W. Malcolmson, *Popular Recreations in English Society 1700–1850*, Cambridge, 1973

34 F. Tillyard, 'English Town Development in the Nineteenth Century', *Economic Journal*, vol. 23, p. 554

35 S. P. Bill (ed.), *Victorian Lancashire*, Newton Abbot, 1974, p. 173
36 *Select Committee on Public Houses*, BPP, vol. XXXVII, 1853, p. 218
37 L. Faucher, *Manchester in 1844: its present condition and future prospects*, London, 1844 (1969 edn), p. 542
38 *Select Committee on Drunkenness*, BPP, vol. VIII, 1834, p. 328
39 *Select Committee on the Sale of Beer*, BPP, vol. VIII, 1834, p. 328
40 J. A. Roebuck, 'On the Amusements of the Aristocracy and of the People', *Pamphlets for the People*, vol. 1, 1835, p. 3
41 J. G. Southworth, *Vauxhall Gardens. A Chapter in the Social History of England*, New York, 1941
42 W. Wroth, *The London Pleasure Gardens of the Eighteenth Century*, London, 1896
  W. Wroth, *Cremorne and the Later London Pleasure Gardens*, London, 1907

Vauxhall	opened 1661	closed 1859
Ranelagh	opened 1742	closed 1803
Eagle Tavern Gardens	opened 1822	closed 1882
Royal Surrey Gardens	opened 1831	closed 1877
Cremorne	opened 1843	closed 1877

43 Axon, *The Annals of Manchester*, p. 319
44 H. W. Gwilliam, *Old Worcester, People and Places*, Worcester, undated, pp. 35–6
45 Anon. *The Strangers' Guide Through Birkenhead*, Birkenhead, 1847, p. 35
46 *Select Committee on Arts and Manufactures*, 1836, pp. 173, 175
47 *SCPW*, p. 66
48 Report of the Proceedings of a Public Meeting, p. 11
49 *Second Report*, Appendix Part II, p. 127
50 *SCPW*, pp. 5–8
51 F. Place to J. C. Hobhouse, 5 December 1830. B.M. MS 35148 f.75. Quoted in A. Fein, 'Victoria Park: its Origins and History', *East London Papers*, vol. 5, October 1962, p. 74
52 Report of the Proceedings of a Public Meeting, p. 17
53 B. W. Richardson, *The Health of Nations: a Review of the Works of Edwin Chadwick*, vol. 2, 1887, p. 128
54 *SCPW*, pp. 8–9, 350
55 *Select Committee on Public Houses*, p. 455
56 *SCPW*, p. 10
57 Ibid., p. 18

3 PIONEERING PARK DEVELOPMENT

1 Sheffield City Library, plan

2 Roebuck, MSS. Roebuck to Henrietta Falconer, 1833. Quoted in F. E. Hyde, 'Utilitarian Town Planning, 1825–45', *Town Planning Review*, Summer, 1947, p. 157

3 6 & 7 Will. IV, c.115

4 *Hansard*, 9 April 1839. Quoted in Hyde, 'Utilitarian Town Planning', p. 158

5 Lord Eversley, *Commons, Forests and Footpaths*, London, 1910, p. 16. In 1841 a return made to Parliament of land enclosed since 1837, showed that 222 acres had been set aside for recreation out of 41,420 acres enclosed, i.e. 1 acre in 186

6 PRO. Payments out of the Sum of £10,000 Granted by Parliament in 1841. Office of Works and Public Buildings Act and Papers, vol. XLVIII 1857–8, 27 August 1857

7 5 & 6 Vict. c.78. There had been some intention of forming a cemetery on this site, which belonged to Eton College and Lord Southampton. Nearly 60 acres were bought for £300 per acre

8 4 & 5 Vict. c.27 and 5 & 6 Vict. c.20

9 The other sites were Copenhagen Fields and Hackney Downs. *SCPW*, p. 18

10 J. J. Sexby, *The Municipal Parks, Gardens and Open Spaces of London*, London, 1898, p. 11

11 C. Poulsen, *Victoria Park: a Study in the History of East London*, London, 1976, pp. 16–20

12 14 & 15 Vict. c.46. This Act amended the two previous Acts relating to Victoria Park

13 VPP, vol. 1, 1841–5. W. Tyler and W. Herring to the Chief Commissioners of Woods and Forests, 28 July 1841. Quoted in A. Fein, 'Victoria Park: its Origins and History', *East London Papers*, vol. 5, October 1962, p. 75

14 VPP, vol. 1, 1840. Letter from G. Offer to F. Young, 15 January 1840. Quoted in Fein, 'Victoria Park', p. 76

15 VPP, vol. 2, 4 June 1845, Minutes of Evidence of Victoria Park Approaches

16 VPP, vol. 1, 1841–5. Quoted in Fein, 'Victoria Park', p. 75

17 VPP, vol. 2, 1846

18 *Builder*, vol. 5, No. 210, 9 January 1847, p. 11

19 *Builder*, vol. 13, No. 638, 28 April 1855, p. 203

20 50 & 51 Vict. c.34

21 J. J. Sexby was in charge of the LCC Parks Department. His book lists

all the open spaces administered by the LCC in and outside the County of London in 1898

22 J. Strutt, *Address to the Town Council of Derby*. Quoted in J. C. Loudon, *The Derby Arboretum*, London, 1840, p. 83

23 M. Simo, 'John Claudius Loudon: on planning and design for the garden metropolis', *J. Garden History*, vol. 9, part 2, 1891, pp. 184–201. For a full discussion of Loudon see M. L. Simo, *Loudon and the Landscape: From Country Seat to Metropolis*, New Haven and London, 1988

24 *Encyclopaedia of Gardening*, London, 1822, p. 1186

25 *Gardeners' Magazine*, 1829, pp. 686–90

26 *Gardeners' Magazine*, 1836, pp. 13–26

27 T. H. D. Thomas, 'John Claudius Loudon and the Inception of the Public Park', *Landscape Design*, no. 140, November 1982, pp. 33–5
See also R. P. Cruden, *The History of the Town of Gravesend*, London, 1843, p. 517

28 According to Robert Chambers writing in *Chamber's Edinburgh Journal*, 4 May, 1844, p. 285

29 'Opening of Derby Arboretum', *Derby and Chesterfield Reporter*, 16 September 1840. Quoted in *Westminster Review*, vol. 35, no. 2, 1841, pp. 423–30

30 J. E. Heath, 'The First Public Park in England', *Derbyshire Life and Countryside Magazine*, October 1975, p. 68

31 W. H. Phillips, 'Liverpool's Public Parks and Recreation Grounds', University of Liverpool, typescript, 1949, p. 20

32 Chadwick, *The Park and the Town*, p. 35
For a discussion of suburban development see Ashworth, *The Genesis of Modern British Town Planning*, Chapter 6; M. J. Daunton, *House and Home in the Victorian City*, London, 1983
For later suburban development in Manchester see M. Harrison, 'Housing and Town Planning in Manchester before 1914', in A. Sutcliffe (ed.), *British Town Planning: the formative years*, Leicester, 1981

33 *Second Report of the State of Large Towns and Populous Districts*, Vol. 38, 1845, p. 86

34 G. F. Chadwick, *The Works of Sir Joseph Paxton*, London, 1961, pp. 49–50

35 6 & 7 Vict. c.13, s.10

36 Chadwick, *The Works of Sir Joseph Paxton*, pp. 50–52

37 Ashworth, *The Genesis of Modern British Town Planning*, p. 40

38 W. W. Mortimer, *The History of the Hundred of Wirral*, Didsbury, Manchester, 1947, pp. 368, 370

39 MBC Proceedings, 10 May 1843, pp. 92–3

40 Edinburgh, Dublin, York, Glasgow, Canterbury, Derby and Devonport

were contacted. No reasons were given for selecting these particular towns and only Glasgow would seem to have shared a similar scale of problems to Manchester. 'The Public Parks, their Progress, Completion and Opening', MPCS, MS 352–7

41 Report of the Proceedings of a Public Meeting, p. 9

42 Notice, Public Walks, Parks, Gardens and Play-Grounds, 22 August 1844, MPCS, MS 352–7

43 Address adopted at an Aggregate Meeting of the Operatives of both Towns, 10 September 1844, MPCS, MS 352–7

44 Report of the Proceedings of a Public Meeting, p. 22. For full details of the subscriptions and the development of the Manchester/Salford parks see H. Conway, *J. Garden History*, vol. 5, no. 3, 1985, pp. 231–60

45 Faucher, *Manchester in 1844*, p. 55, footnote 24

46 *Builder*, vol. 3, no. 116, 26 April 1845, p. 200

47 MBC Proceedings, 6 August 1845, p. 30

48 MBC Proceedings, 18 September 1846, p. 195

49 F. Engels, *The Condition of the Working Class in England*, London, Pelican 1968 edn, pp. 78–80

50 W. Farr, *Vital Statistics*, London, 1885

51 E. Chadwick, *The Practice of Interment in Towns*, Supplementary Report in *The Sanitary Condition of the Labouring Population of Great Britain*, 1843

52 'Recreations for the People', *Penny Magazine*, no. 435, 12 January 1839, p. 10

53 *Bradford Observer*, 21 May 1846, p. 8

54 W. Cudworth, *Manningham, Heaton and Allerton, treated historically and topographically*, Bradford, 1896, pp. 220–1

55 *Second Report of the State of Large Towns and Populous Districts*, 1845, pp. 30, 86

56 'The Lungs of London', *Blackwood's Magazine*, vol. 46, August 1839, pp. 213–14

57 'Parks and Pleasure Grounds', *Westminster Review*, January 1841, p. 418

4 THE PARK MOVEMENT

1 H. J. Laski, W. I. Jennings and W. A. Robson, *A Century of Municipal Progress, 1835–1935*, London, 1935, Chapter 2

2 8 & 9 Vict. c.118, s.15, s.30

3 Between 1845 and 1869, 614,800 acres of common land were enclosed, out of which 4,000 acres were set aside for public purposes: 1,742 for recreation grounds and 2,200 for allotments, i.e. 1 in 154 acres, compared

with 1 in 186 acres between 1837 and 1841 (Eversley, *Commons, Forests and Footpaths*, pp. 16–17)

4 10 & 11 Vict. c.34

5 11 & 12 Vict. c.63, s.74
   The Public Health Act was an adoptive Act which could be used by local authorities if they chose to do so. Adoptive Acts simplified and cheapened the legislative procedure, but if the general legislation did not suit particular problems towns could and did draft local Bills, especially when a general Act carried with it some form of supervision by central government, as was the case with the Public Health Act

6 J. Bentley, *Illustrated Handbook of the Bradford City Parks, Recreation Grounds and Open Spaces*, Bradford, 1926, p. 19. The trustees spent an additional £6,000 on the development of the park and they successfully applied for a grant of £1,500 from the Government fund

7 PRO. Office of Works and Public Buildings Act and Papers, Vol. 48, 1857–8. Payments out of the sum of £10,000 granted in 1841 were made to: Dundee and Arbroath (1842), Manchester (1845), Portsmouth (1848), Preston and Inverness (1849), Inverness (1850), Sunderland (1854), Bradford and Macclesfield (1855), and Waterford (1856). With the exception of Bradford (£1,500) and Manchester (£3,000), no grant exceeded £750

8 D. M'Lellan, *Glasgow Public Parks*, Glasgow, 1894, p. 88

9 Chadwick, *The Works of Sir Joseph Paxton*, pp. 56–65. Glasgow Green had probably belonged to the people of Glasgow since 1450 (King, *The People's Palace*, p. 20)

10 *The Liverpool Health of Towns Advocate*, 1846, pp. 85–96. Cited by Ashworth, *The Genesis of Modern British Town Planning*, p. 63

11 *Builder*, vol. 8, no. 405, 9 November 1850, p. 532. Quoted in Ashworth, *The Genesis of Modern British Town Planning*, p. 63

12 B. D. White, *A History of the Corporation of Liverpool 1835–1914*, Liverpool, 1951, p. 84

13 28 Vict. c.20, s.114

14 10 & 11 Vict. c.24

15 B. Harrison, *Drink and the Victorians*, London, 1971

16 J. C. Scholes, *History of Bolton*, Bolton, 1892, p. 500

17 *Halifax Guardian*, 7 February 1847

18 *Royal Commission on Employment of Children*, 1842

19 3 & 4 Will. IV, c.103

20 34 & 35 Vict. c.17

21 'People's Parks and People's Holidays', *Illustrated London News*, vol. 43, no. 1222, 19 September 1863, p. 278

22 M. C. Hodgson, 'The Working Day and the Working Week in Victorian Britain', M.Phil. Thesis, Birkbeck College, London, 1974

23 J. Dennis, *The Pioneer of Progress*, London, 1860, p. 112. Quoted in Hodgson, 'The Working Day', p. 151

24 *National Sunday League Record*, no. 5, September 1856, p. 34

25 22 Vict. c.27. Its provisions were extended in the Public Parks, Schools and Museums Act 1871 (34 & 35 Vict. c.13) to include gifts of land for schools and museums

26 23 & 24 Vict. c.30

27 Memorandum of Proposed Gift, 24 December 1844. Quoted in H. Heginbotham, *Stockport: Ancient and Modern*, vol. 2, London, 1892, p. 414

28 *Builder*, vol. 26, no. 1332, 15 August 1868, p. 607

29 Chadwick, *The Park and the Town*, p. 110

30 *Liverpool Review*, 28 June 1890, p. 9

31 J. T. Bunce, *History of the Corporation of Birmingham*, Birmingham, 1878, vol. 2, p. 194

32 R. K. Dent, *City of Birmingham: History and Description of the Public Parks, Gardens and Recreation Grounds*, Birmingham 1916, p. 14. According to Dent, Adderley Park, Saltley was Birmingham's first park, but he does not distinguish between leased parks and those that were the property of the local authority

33 J. Cox, *City of Birmingham: Public Parks and Pleasure Grounds*, Birmingham, 1892, p. 45

34 J. A. Langford, 'Parks and Public Places of Recreation for the People', *Trans. National Association for the Promotion of Social Science, 1857*, London, 1857, p. 447

35 D. Cannadine, *Lords and Landlords*, Leicester, 1980, pp. 188–9

36 D. J. O'Neill, *The Saving of Aston Hall*, Birmingham, 1909, p. 4

37 Langford, 'Parks and Public Places', p. 448

38 *Builder*, vol. 16, no. 830, 1 January 1853, p. 15

39 T. R. Tholfsen, 'The Artisan and the Culture of Early Victorian Birmingham', *University of Birmingham Historical Journal*, vol. 4, 1954, pp. 146–66

40 C. J. Holyoake, *Sixty Years of an Agitator's Life*, 1906 edition, p. 17. Quoted in Thompson, *The Chartists*, pp. 252–3

41 R. A. Arnold, *The History of the Cotton Famine*, London, 1864, pp. 204–6, 297

42 Union Aid Relief Act 1862. 25 & 26 Vict. c.110
   Union Aid Relief Act Continuance 1863. 26 & 27 Vict. c.91
   Public Works (Manufacturing Districts) Act 1863. 26 & 27 Vict. c.90

43 Arnold, *The History of the Cotton Famine*, p. 454

Sums loaned under the 1863 Act:

Roads	£555,082 2s 6d
Water	£230,718
Sewage	£229,558 17s 6d
Parks	£29,050
Cemeteries	£28,500
Land Drainage	£14,493
Gas Works	£10,332
Public Baths	£5,000

Arnold, Table 1

44 It was estimated that the land, building and labour would cost £27,000 and that a rate of 1d in the pound would repay the interest and capital in 30 years. *Builder*, vol. 22, 5 March 1864, p. 174

45 H. Hamer, *Bolton 1838–1938. A centenary record of municipal progress*, Bolton, 1938, p. 57

46 W. A. Abram, *A History of Blackburn*, Blackburn, 1877, p. 378

47 Arnold, *The History of the Cotton Famine*, p. 561

48 T. Aspden, *Preston Guide*, Preston, 1868, p. 36

49 A. Hewitson, *A History of Preston*, Preston, 1883, p. 328
The cost of forming the Avenham and Miller Parks was £20,207 7s 9d. This sum included £4,000 for the purchase of land for Avenham Park. The laying out of Moor Park cost £10,826 7s 9d

50 E. King, *The People's Palace and Glasgow Green*, Glasgow, 1988, pp. 21–2

51 Lord Eversley, *Commons, Forests and Footpaths*, London, 1910

52 P. C. Gould, ' "Back to Nature" and "Back to the Land" and the Socialist Revival 1880–1900', M.Phil. thesis, University of Sheffield, 1982, p. 183

53 38 & 39 Vict. c.55

54 PRO. Reports from the Commissioners of Local Government Boards, 1874–90

55 Keighley requested four loans of 10, 20, 30 and 50 years in 1890

56 Attorney General v Corporation of Sunderland, 1876. L.R. 2 Ch. Div. 634. Quoted in Sir R. Hunter and P. Birkett, *Gardens in Towns, being a statement of the law relating to the acquisition and maintenance of land for the purposes of recreation*, London, 1916, p. 19

57 Lambeth Overseers v LCC, 1897, A.C. 625; 36 Digest 247, 12. R. J. Roddis, *The Law of Parks and Recreation Grounds*, London, 1974, p. 112. Brockwell Park was bought by Lambeth and the LCC in 1891

58 Hennock, *Fit and Proper Persons*, p. 174

59 Hennock, *Fit and Proper Persons*, p. 143

60 *Leeds Mercury*, 30 September 1871. Quoted in B. J. Barber, 'Leeds

Corporation 1835–1905: a history of its environmental, social and administrative services', Ph.D. Thesis, Leeds University, 1974–5, p. 292

61 *Leeds Mercury*, 12 August 1845. Quoted in Barber, 'Leeds Corporation', p. 116

62 *Leeds Mercury*, 5 October 1850. Quoted in Barber, 'Leeds Corporation', p. 116

63 19 & 20 Vict. c.65

64 *Leeds Mercury*, 30 September, 1871. Quoted in Barber, 'Leeds Corporation', p. 292

65 *Leeds Mercury*, 14 October 1871. Quoted in Barber, 'Leeds Corporation', p. 294

66 Barber, 'Leeds Corporation', p. 297

67 F. Dolman, *Municipalities at Work. Social Questions of Today*, London, 1895, p. 139

68 *Brighton Herald*, 9 September 1876

69 J. W. R. Whitehead, 'Fluctuations in the land-use composition of urban development', *Erdkunde*, vol. 35, 1981, p. 138

70 A. J. Downing, *Rural Essays*, New York, 1853, pp. 515–16

71 Chadwick, *The Park and the Town*, explores the park movement internationally

5 DESIGN AND DESIGNERS

1 J. C. Loudon, *The Landscape Gardening and Landscape Architecture of the Late Humphry Repton Esq.*, London, 1840

2 J. C. Loudon, 'Remarks on laying out Public Gardens and Promenades', *Gardeners' Magazine*, vol. 2, 1835, p. 650

3 Loudon, *The Derby Arboretum*, pp. 71–2. Pleasure grounds were the areas away from the house and were distinct from the ornamental grounds adjacent to the house

4 Loudon, *The Derby Arboretum*, p. 76

5 BRIC, Minutes, 1853–8, 5 October 1857

6 *Gardeners' Magazine*, vol. 2, 1835, p. 650

7 Memorandum, Public Parks, Walks, Playgrounds, etc. 21 November 1844, *MPCS*, MS 352–7

8 Instructions to Competitors, 18 August 1845. *MPCS*, MS352–7

9 'Designs for laying out the public parks at Manchester', *Builder*, vol. 3, no. 144, 8 November 1845, p. 541

10 The nine entries were from James Pringle, York; H. Bigland & Co., Manchester; Richard Forrest, London; Thomas Diggles, Singleton, W. Manchester; P. & H. Richardson, Nr Ardwick, W. Manchester;

N. Niven, Dublin; Robert Rea, Cirencester; George Towers, Rose Hill; Joshua Major & Son, Knowstrop, Nr. Leeds

11 Memorandum of Agreement between the Public Parks Committee and Joshua Major & Son. *MPCS*, MS 352–7

12 Manchester Public Parks Committee, 5 December 1845. *MPCS*, MS 352–7 M5

13 Anon, *A Few Pages About Manchester*, Manchester, c.1849, p. 32

14 Major set out his ideas on landscape gardening in *The Theory and Practice of Landscape Gardening*, London, 1852

15 The danger of these archery grounds was noted in the Manchester Public Parks Committee (MPPC) Minute Books, 1847

16 These are summarised in *A Few Pages About Manchester*, which provides a description of each park on the occasion of the official opening ceremony, followed by a description of the alterations, abridged from the *Manchester Courier*, 2 and 9 May 1849

17 *Gardeners' Chronicle*, 15 May 1847, p. 325; 11 December 1847, p. 817

18 B. Elliott, 'The Manchester/Salford Parks: two additional notes', *J. Garden History*, vol. 6, no. 2, 1986, pp. 141–5 provides an excellent summary of this controversy

19 *Illustrated London News*, vol. 43, no. 1222, 19 September 1863, pp. 277–8

20 Pennethorne's plan of 1841 is reproduced in Chadwick, *The Park and the Town*, p. 113

21 *Illustrated London News*, vol. 2, no. 59, 17 June 1843, p. 426

22 VPP, vol. 2, 1845–6, 25 November 1845

23 *Illustrated London News*, vol. 8, no. 209, 2 May 1846, p. 285

24 VPP, vol. 2, 1845–6, 18 May 1846

25 VPP, vol. 3, 1847–52, 17 September 1847

26 VPP, vol. 4, 1853–60, 12 December 1854

27 F. L. Olmsted, *Walks and Talks of an American Farmer in England*, London, 1852, p. 79

28 Birkenhead Road and Improvement Committee (BRIC) Minutes, 1845–7, pp. 118–19. Letter from Mr Paxton to Commissioners, 27 August 1845

29 BRIC Minutes, 1847–50, 29 March 1848, p. 135

30 BRIC Minutes, 1845–7, 13 August 1845, p. 111

31 BRIC Minutes, 1845–7, 6 May 1846, p. 229

32 *The Strangers' Guide Through Birkenhead*, Birkenhead, 1847, p. 34

33 BRIC Minutes, 1850–3, 27 June 1850, p. 41

34 BRIC Minutes, 1853–7, 3 April 1854, p. 67

35 BRIC Minutes, 1853–7, 5 October 1857

36 BRIC Minutes, 1858–63, 20 November 1861, p. 262. Pasture land was set aside for football from 1 October to 31 March inclusive

37 Prospectus of Crystal Palace Co. 17 May 1852. Quoted in Chadwick, *The Works of Sir Joseph Paxton*, p. 154

38 'The Crystal Palace – June 18th', *The Cottage Gardener and Country Gentleman's Companion*, 24 June 1856, p. 217

39 T. Tiffany, *The People's Park Halifax. Jubilee of Opening, 1857–1907*, Halifax, 1907

40 Bentley, *Illustrated History of the Bradford City Parks*, p. 23–5

41 M'Lellan, *Glasgow Public Parks*, p. 75. A plan of Queen's Park showing the design of the winter gardens is reproduced in Chadwick, *The Works of Sir Joseph Paxton*, p. 64

42 In 1854 a grant of £750 was made to Sunderland from the government fund and a Mr Lawson, gardener to Lord Londonderry, and Joseph Smith, who had worked at Chatsworth, levelled the ground and laid out the walks.

43 Plans of these parks are published in J. C. A. Alphand, *Les Promenades de Paris*, Paris, 1867–73

44 LC, Proceedings, 1868–9, Report on Sefton Park, April 1867, p. 637

45 *Builder*, vol. 25, no. 1281, 24 August 1867, p. 625

46 *Hampshire Telegraph & Sussex Chronicle*, 29 May 1878, p. 3

47 'Opening of Bolton Park and the "Heywood" Recreation Ground', *Bolton Guardian*, May 1866, p. 13

48 A. Holroyd, *Saltaire and its Founder, Sir Titus Salt, Bart*, Bradford, 1873, pp. 62–4

49 'The Park', *Rochdale Household Almanack*, Rochdale, 1871

50 Bentley, *Illustrated Handbook of the Bradford City Parks*, p. 19

51 W. Lillie, *The History of Middlesbrough*, Middlesbrough, 1968, p. 229

52 *Builder*, vol. 37, no. 1903, 26 July 1879, p. 836; vol. 40, no. 2001, 11 June 1881, p. 744

53 Sexby, *The Municipal Parks*, p. 556

54 *Builder*, vol. 35, no. 1853, 10 August 1878, p. 844

6 LODGES, BANDSTANDS AND THE CULTIVATION OF VIRTUE

1 VPP, vol. 2, 1845–6, 17 February 1845

2 *Builder*, vol. 5, no. 210, 9 January 1847, p. 11

3 VPP, vol. 4, 1853–60, 17 September 1857

4 C. H. J. Smith, *Parks and Pleasure-Grounds: practical notes on country residences, public parks and gardens*, London, 1852, p. 161

5 LC Proceedings, 1868–9, Report on Sefton Park, April 1867, p. 637

6 *Builder*, vol. 23, no. 1281, 24 August 1867, p. 627

7 J. S. Curl, *The Life and Work of Henry Roberts 1803–1876*, Chichester, 1983

8 M. P. G. Draper, *Lambeth's Open Spaces*, London, 1979, p. 23

9 Metropolitan Drinking Fountain and Cattle Trough Association, *A Century of Fountain: Centenary Report 1859–1959*, London, 1959. See also P. Davies, *Troughs and Drinking Fountains*, London, 1989

10 B. Cherry and N. Pevsner, *The Buildings of England: London : South*, London, 1983, p. 384

11 Downing, *Rural Essays*, p. 515

12 Loudon, *The Derby Arboretum*, p. 71

13 MPPC Proceedings, 18 September 1846, p. 222

14 MPPC Minutes, vol. 1, 11 September 1846, p. 12

15 *A Few Pages About Manchester*, p. 28

16 'Peel Park, and the Museum', *Guide to the Collections*, Salford, 23 May 1860

17 Smith, *Parks and Pleasure Grounds*, p. 159

18 MPPC Minute Book, vol. 3, 1855, 26 October 1855, p. 157

19 MBC Proceedings, 5 February 1864, p. 146; 14 May 1865, p. 168

20 Hennock, *Fit and Proper Persons*, p. 215

21 MPPC Minute Books, vol. 1, 11 September 1846

22 F. Fuller, 'On our Paramount Duty to Provide Wholesome Recreation and Amusement for the People, and the Dire Results which attend our Neglect of it', *Trans. National Association for the Promotion of Social Science*, 1874, p. 748

23 J. May, 'Sanitary Measures in a Provincial Town, and their Results', *Trans. National Association for the Promotion of Social Science*, 1857, p. 407

24 *Gardeners' Chronicle*, 26 August 1871, p. 1106

25 W. & J. Halfpenny, *Rural Architecture in the Chinese Taste*, London, 1750, 1752, 1755

26 W. Chambers, *Plans, Elevations, Sketches and Perspective Views of the Gardens and Buildings at Kew in Surry* [sic], London, 1763, plates 22–35

27 H. Honour, 'Pagodas for the Park', *Country Life*, vol. 125, 29 January 1959, pp. 192–4. See also E. Von Erdberg, *The Chinese Influence on European Garden Structures*, Harvard, 1936

28 J. C. Loudon, *Encyclopaedia of Cottage, Farm and Villa Architecture*, London, 1836. Figures 1429 and 1431

29 VPP, vol. 3, 1847–52, 2 February 1849

30 Olmsted, *Walks and Talks of an American Farmer in England*, p. 80

31 G. Goreham, *The Parks and Open Spaces of Norwich*, Norwich, 1961, p. 32

32 T. J. Edelstein, *Vauxhall Gardens*, New Haven, 1983, Ill.15, The Vauxhall Fan, 1837

33 W. Wroth, *Cremorne and the Later London Pleasure Gardens*, London, 1907

34 *Builder*, vol. 19, no. 978, 2 November 1861, p. 754
35 *Illustrated London News*, 2 June 1855, p. 533
36 *Dictionary of National Biography*, vol. 20, London, 1889, pp. 79–81
37 *Hampshire Telegraph and Sussex Chronicle*, 29 May 1878, p. 3
38 London County Council, *London Parks and Open Spaces*, London, 1906, p. 73
39 G. Jekyll, *Public Parks and Gardens*, Bromley, 1918, p. 9
40 E. Cecil, *London Parks and Gardens*, London, 1907, p. 123
41 W. S. Jevons, *Methods of Social Reform*, London, 1883, p. 2
42 Walter Macfarlane & Co., *Architectural Ironwork*, Glasgow, c.1920
43 R. Blomfield, 'Of Public Space, Parks and Gardens', in T. J. Cobden-Sanderson, W.R. Lethaby *et al.*, *Art and Life and the Building and Decoration of Cities*, Lectures delivered at the fifth exhibition of the Arts and Crafts Exhibition Society, London, 1897, pp. 203–4 and reprinted by the Civic Arts Association
44 *Trans. Horticultural Society*, vol. 2, 1817, pp. 171–7
45 J. C. Loudon, *Sketches of Curvilinear Hothouses*, London, 1918, unpaginated. Quoted in Simo, *Loudon and the Landscape*, pp. 113–14
46 M. Girouard, *The Victorian Country House*, New Haven, 1979, p. 43
47 R. Millington, *The House in the Park*, Corporation of the City of Liverpool, 1957, p. 74
48 *Reporter*, 5 October 1907. Quoted in *The John Neild Conservatory, Stamford Park*, Official Opening, 3 April 1985, Tameside Metropolitan Borough Council
49 H. Forrester, *Twopence to Cross the Mersey*, Fontana, London, 7th edn, 1986, p. 121
50 Sir J. Bell and J. Paton, *Glasgow: its Municipal Organization and Administration*, Glasgow, 1896, pp. 345–6
51 H. Roberts, *Proposed People's Palace and Gardens for the Northern and Midland Counties to Employ Factory Operatives*, London, 1863
52 King, *The People's Palace*, Chapter 1
53 *Derbyshire Life and Countryside Magazine*, October 1975, p. 68
54 Sunderland Central Library, *Mobray Park: History*, 1978
55 W. W. Pettigrew, *Municipal Parks*, London, 1937, p. 206

7 LOCAL PRIDE AND PATRIOTISM

1 'Peel Park and the Museum', *Guide to the Collection*, Salford, 23 May 1860
2 J. W. Mayfield, *History of the Springfield Waterworks and how the Pearson Park was obtained for the People*, Hull, 1909, pp. 64–5
3 Dent, *City of Birmingham*, pp. 24–5

4   E. S. Darby, 'Statues of Queen Victoria and of Prince Albert. A Study in Commemorative and Portrait Statuary 1837–1924', Ph.D. Thesis, University of London, 1983

5   'Peel Park and the Museum', 1860

6   J. A. Picton, *City of Liverpool: Municipal Archives and Records*, Liverpool, 1886, p. 478

7   'Inaugural ceremonies in honour of the opening of Fountain Gardens, Paisley', Paisley, 1868

8   *Builder*, vol. 35, no. 1801, 11 Aug. 1877, p. 807

9   *People's Park Centenary Brochure, 1883–1983*, Grimsby, 1983

10   N. Pevsner (ed.), *The Buildings of England, North Lancashire*, 1969

11   *Ashton Memorial Booklet*, Lancaster District Library, c.1960

12   M. Kerney, 'Polished granite in Victorian architecture', *Victorian Society Annual*, 1987–8, pp. 20–32. Deane and Woodward's Oxford University Museum (1855–60) features shafts of a variety of marbles and granites from all over the country, clearly labelled with their geographical origin

13   C. Graham, '100 Years of Aberdeen Parks', *Aberdeen Press and Journal*, 8 May 1971

14   Bentley, *Bradford City Parks*, p. 25

15   *Gardeners' Magazine*, vol. 19, 1876, p. 197

16   Bentley, *Bradford City Parks*, p. 28

17   I am indebted to Dr Barry Trinder, Ironbridge Gorge Museum Trust for drawing my attention to these examples

18   Bentley, *Bradford City Parks*, p. 37

19   I am indebted to Elspeth King, People's Palace, Glasgow for this information

20   The display included: dicynodonts (2), labyrinthodont (1), plesiosaurus (3), icthyosaurus (3), teleosaurus (1), hylaeosaurus (1), megalosaurus (1), iguanodon (2), pterodactyls (2), mosasaurus (1)

21   P. K. Phillips, *Crystal Palace Park: Draft Landscape Plan*, Bromley, 1986

22   M'Lellan, *Glasgow Public Parks*, p. 49

23   *Building News*, 23 August 1882

24   *History of the Royal Victoria Park*, Bath, pp. 6–7

25   S. Smith, *History of Greenock*, Greenock, 1921, p. 328

26   *Mobray Park: History*, 1978

27   Tiffany, *The People's Park, Halifax*, p. 26

28   H. Heginbotham, *Stockport: Ancient and Modern*, vol. 2, London, 1892, p. 414

29   'Peel Park and the Museum', 23 May 1860

30   Bentley, *Bradford City Parks*, p. 23

31   Dent, *City of Birmingham*, p. 17

32   *Countryside Magazine*, Oct. 1975, p. 68

33 W. A. Abram, *Blackburn Characters of a Past Generation*, Blackburn, 1894, p. 60

34 R. Scar, *History of South Park*, Darlington, 1954

35 *Mobray Park: History*, 1978

36 Lillie, *The History of Middlesbrough*, p. 233

37 Holroyd, *Saltaire and its Founder*, p. 643

38 Return of Captures at Sebastopol, *Army Accounts and Papers* Session 5 Feb. – 28 July 1863, vol. 33
Among the artillery captured were: 720 guns, 920 percussion muskets, 37,629 × 42 pounder solid shot, 30,850 × 24 pounder solid shot, 18 mortars, 1 howitzer, 324 carronades

39 *Berkshire Mercury*, 11 Feb. 1971

40 R. Mellors, *The Gardens, Parks and Walks of Nottingham and District*, Nottingham, 1926, pp. 47–51

41 Elliott, *Victorian Gardens*, p. 190

42 F. Worsdall, *Victorian City*, Glasgow, 1982, p. 129

43 Pettigrew, *Handbook of the Manchester Parks*, p. 211

8 PLANTING AND PARK MAINTENANCE

1 Pettigrew, *Handbook of the Manchester Parks*, p. 171

2 J. C. Loudon, *The Landscape Gardening and Landscape Architecture of the Late Humphry Repton Esq*, London, 1840, p. ix

3 *Westminster Review*, vol. 35, no. 2, January 1841, p. 431

4 BRIC, Minutes, 1845–7, 14 May 1846, p. 268

5 *A Few Pages About Manchester*, pp. 32–3

6 MPPC Minutes, vol. 3, 26 October 1855, p. 222

7 *Cottage Gardener*, vol. 13, 1855, pp. 38–40

8 A. McKenzie, *The Parks, Open Spaces and Thoroughfares of London*, London, 1869

9 Picton, *City of Liverpool*, p. 412

10 *Gardeners' Chronicle*, 3 September 1864, p. 843

11 *Gardeners' Chronicle*, 27 August 1870, p. 1157

12 *Saturday Half-Holiday Guide*, Summer, 1870, p. 6

13 *Gardeners' Chronicle*, 9 May 1868, p. 487

14 *Gardeners' Chronicle*, 15 September 1866, p. 487

15 VPP, vol. 6, 1870–91, 1 June 1876

16 *Gardeners' Chronicle*, 26 August 1871, p. 1106

17 *Hampshire Telegraph and Sussex Chronicle*, 29 May 1878, p. 3

18 Lillie, *The History of Middlesbrough*, p. 232

19 B. Elliott, *Victorian Gardens*, London, 1986, p. 156. This provides a detailed analysis of the theory and practice of Victorian gardening

20 Dent, *City of Birmingham*, p. 232

21 Wolverhampton Borough Council, *Wolverhampton West Park, 1881–1981*, 1981

22 Pettigrew, *Handbook of the Manchester Parks*, p. 173

23 Jekyll, *Public Parks and Gardens*, p. 9

24 W. Robinson, *The Parks, Promenades and Gardens of Paris*, London, 1869, p. xx. Robinson's writings were very influential, particularly *The Wild Garden*, London, 1870 and *The English Flower Garden*, London, 1898

25 *Gardeners' Magazine*, vol. 48, 1905, p. 574

26 *Saturday Half-Holiday Guide*, p. 6

27 Pettigrew, *Handbook of the Manchester Parks*, p. 172

28 R. C. Carrington, *Alexandra Park and Palace*, London, 1975

29 Dent, *City of Birmingham*, p. 19

30 Bentley, *Bradford City Parks*, p. 28

31 H. N. Ellacombe, *The Plant-lore and Garden-Craft of Shakespeare*, London, 1878 and later editions; W. Crane, *Flowers from Shakespeare's Garden: a posy from the plays*, London, 1906

32 Cecil, *London Parks and Gardens*, pp. 170–4

33 MBC Proceedings, 18 September 1846, p. 223

34 Loudon, *The Derby Arboretum*, p. 77

35 MPPC, Minute Books, vol. 3, 26 October 1855, 26 September 1856, 2 May 1857, 28 March 1858

36 MPPC, Minute Books, vol. 3, 26 September 1855, p. 211

37 MCC Proceedings, Parks and Cemeteries Committee, Sub-Committee Report, 6 August 1873, p. 377

38 MCC Proceedings, Parks and Cemeteries Committee Report, 6 February 1884, pp. 136–7

39 Metropolitan Public Garden, Boulevard, and Playgrounds Association, *First Report*, 1883, Appendix E, p. 62

40 W. W. Pettigrew, 'The influence of air pollution on vegetation', *Gardeners' Chronicle*, vol. 2, 1928, p. 308. See also B. Elliott, *J. Garden History*, vol. 6, no. 2, 1986, pp. 141–5

41 M'Lellan makes similar points in *Glasgow Public Parks*

42 Pettigrew, *Municipal Parks*, p. 171

43 N. Cole, *The Royal Parks and Gardens of London*, London, 1877

44 J. May, 'Sanitary Measures in a Provincial Town, and their Results', *Trans. National Association for the Promotion of Social Science*, vol. 1, 1857, pp. 467–8

45 *Freedom*, May 1885, p. 11

46 Sexby, *The Municipal Parks*, p. xvii

47 M'Lellan, *Glasgow Public Parks*, p. 157

48 *The Penny Illustrated Paper*, 24 October 1891, p. 268

9 PERMITTED PASTIMES

1 *Westminster Review*, vol. 35, no. 2, January 1841, pp. 422–30
2 *Derbyshire Life and Countryside Magazine*, October 1975, p. 67
3 *Liverpool Mercury*, 8 April, 1847. Quoted in C. E. Thornton, *The People's Garden*, Birkenhead, undated, p. 10
4 Tiffany, *The People's Park, Halifax*, pp. 13–14
5 *Farmers' New Borough Almanack*, 1890, pp. 3–4
6 *Gardeners' Chronicle*, 12 April 1884, p. 477
7 Mrs Layton was born on 9 April 1855. 'Memories of Seventy Years', in M. H. Davies (ed.), *Life as We Have Known It*, London, 1931, pp. 1–3
8 D. Russell, 'The Pursuit of Leisure', p. 206. In D. G. Wright and J. A. Jowett (eds), *Victorian Bradford*, Bradford, 1981
9 F. W. D. Manders, *History of Gateshead*, Gateshead, 1973, pp. 241–2
10 King, *The People's Palace*, p. 86
11 Sexby, *The Municipal Parks*, p. 564
12 King, *The People's Palace*, p. 28
13 MPPC Minute Book, vol. 1, 31 August 1846; MBC Proceedings, 18 September 1846, p. 223
14 Thompson, *The Chartists*, p. 839
15 VPP vol. 4, 1853–60, Notice, 1856
16 BRIC Minutes, 1863–7, 7 June 1866, p. 318
17 J. R. Kaighin, *Bygone Birkenhead, Sketches Round and About the Sixties*, Birkenhead, 1925, p. 251
18 Bye-law No. 26, 1886
19 MPPC Minutes, 6 January 1897, Bye-law No. 4, p. 247
20 BRIC Minutes, 1858–63, 21 March 1861, p. 199
21 53 & 54 Vict. c.59, s.38, s.44(1), s.44(2)
22 *Gardeners' Magazine*, vol. 2, 1835, p. 516
23 Downing, *Rural Essays*, p. 516
24 *Cassell's Complete Book of Sports and Pastimes*, London, 1903, pp. 126–7, 281
25 *East London Advertiser*, 7 June 1873. Quoted in Poulsen, *Victoria Park*, p. 54
26 Bunce, *History of the Corporation of Birmingham*, p. 196
27 VPP, vol. 3, 1847–52, 1 March 1850
28 Poulsen, *Victoria Park*, p. 53
29 King, *The People's Palace*, p. 90
30 A. Mason, *Association Football and English Society, 1880–1939*, Brighton, 1980
31 A. Delves, 'Popular Recreation and Social Conflict in Derby 1800–1850'. In E. Yeo and S. Yeo, *Popular Culture*, pp. 89–129

32 Sexby, *The Municipal Parks*, pp. 15, 556
33 London County Council, *London's Parks and Open Spaces*, London, 1906, p. 82
34 K. E. McCrone, *Sport and the Physical Emancipation of Women*, London, 1988
35 S. M. Newton, *Health, Art and Reason*, London, 1974
36 MBC Proceedings, 1845–6, pp. 221–2
37 *A Few Pages About Manchester*, p. 30
38 MPPC Letter Book M9/58/3/1/, 30 August 1862
39 VPP, vol. 3, 1847–52, 14 May 1847
40 Pettigrew, *Handbook of the Manchester Parks*, advertisement p. vi. Unfortunately all company records relating to this period were destroyed in a fire. According to A. Saint, 'Safety First', *New Statesman*, 22 Feb. 1980, p. 291 playground equipment had only been expressly manufactured since the First World War, but the discovery of this company operating in 1846, indicates a much longer history.
41 Dent, *City of Birmingham*, p. 59
42 Bentley, *Handbook of the Bradford City Parks*, p. 98
43 VPP, vol. 3, 1847–52, 20 August 1849; 21 June 1847
44 SCPW Report, p. 355
45 VPP, vol. 2, 1845–6, 16 June 1846
46 VPP, vol. 4, 1853–60, 12 October 1858, 30 October 1860
47 *Builder*, vol. 31, no. 1579, 10 May 1873, p. 371
48 Sexby, *The Municipal Parks*, p. 556
49 BRIC Minutes, 1847–50, 28 January 1846, p. 280
50 BRIC Minutes, 1853–8, 28 June 1855
51 BRIC Minutes, 1847–50, 29 November 1848, p. 216
52 H. K. Aspinall, *Birkenhead and its Surroundings*, Liverpool, 1903, p. 245
53 *Alexandra Park*, Hastings Borough Council, 1982
54 MPPC Minute Book, 31 August 1846
55 Lord's Day Observance Society, *Quarterly Publication*, July 1852, pp. 306–7. Quoted in J. Wigley, 'Nineteenth-Century Sabbatarianism. A Study of Religious, Political and Social Phenomena', Ph.D. Thesis, University of Sheffield, 1972, p. 351
56 J. Wigley, 'Nineteenth-Century Sabbatarianism', p. 48
57 MPPC Letter Book, MG/68/3/1/, 12 June, 1856; 20 June 1856; MPPC Minute Book, 2 July 1856, p. 194
58 *National Sunday League Record*, No. 5, September 1856, pp. 35, 37
59 Manders, *History of Gateshead*, p. 241
60 Abram, *A History of Blackburn*, p. 60
61 Jevons, *Methods of Social Reform*, pp. 2–12
62 22 Vict. c.27

63 Hunter and Birkett, *Gardens in Towns*
64 23 & 24 Vict. c.30
65 9 & 10 Vict. c.74
66 BRIC Minutes, 1845–7, 27 March 1845, p. 39; 20 March 1849, p. 154
67 *Alexandra Park*, Hastings Borough Council, 1982
68 Holroyd, *Saltaire and its Founder*, p. 63
69 *Blackwood's Magazine*, vol. 46, August 1839, p. 220
70 MPPC, Minute Books, vol. 3, 22 December 1865, pp. 150–3
71 *Blackwood's Magazine*, vol. 46, August 1839, p. 227
72 MCC Minutes, 4 March 1868. Park Bye-law No. 4
73 Bentley, *Handbook of the Bradford City Parks*, p. 24
74 Hewitson, *A History of Preston*, p. 323

10 RECREATION GROUNDS, PARKS AND THE URBAN ENVIRONMENT

1 *Liverpool Argus*, May 1878. Quoted in Roberts, p. 69
2 M. J. Vernon, 'On Public Parks and Gardens', *Trans. National Association for the Promotion of Social Science*, 1878, pp. 512–13
3 *Builder*, vol. 5, no. 210, 9 January 1847, p. 11
4 *Builder*, vol. 16, no. 800, 5 June 1858, p. 385
5 W. T. Marriott, 'On the Necessity of Open Spaces in Large Towns', *Manchester and Salford Sanitary Association Report*, 13 December 1861. Quoted in W. G. Jackson, 'An Historical Study of the Provision of Facilities for Play and Recreation in Manchester', M.Ed. Thesis, University of Manchester, 1940, p. 52
6 MCC Proceedings, 6 February 1884, 125–6, 139
7 MCC Proceedings, 6 February 1884, pp. 141–3
8 Jackson, 'The Provision of Facilities for Play', pp. 67–9
9 MCC Proceedings, 6 February 1884, pp. 125–32
10 A. Ransome, *The History of the Manchester and Salford Sanitary Association, or Half-a-Century's Progress in Sanitary Reform*, Manchester, 1902. The full title of the MSSA was the Manchester and Salford Association for Diffusing Knowledge of the Laws of Health among the Inhabitants of Two Boroughs and Neighbourhoods
11 E. M. Bell, *Octavia Hill: a Biography*, London, 1965 edn
12 Open Spaces Committee, 14 July 1880. Quoted in Jackson, 'The Provision of Facilities for Play', p. 64
13 T. C. Horsfall, *An Ideal Life in Manchester Realisable If . . .*', Manchester 1900
14 O. Hill, 'Colour, Space, and Music for the People', *Nineteenth Century*, May 1884, pp. 741–52
15 W. T. Hill, *Octavia Hill, Pioneer of the National Trust and Housing Reformer*, London, 1956, p. 107

16 E. D. Le Mire, *The Unpublished Lectures of William Morris*, Detroit, 1969, p. 51. Quoted in P. Thompson, *The Work of William Morris*, London, 1977, p. 72

17 *Practicable Land Nationalisation*, Fabian Tract 12, 1894. Cited in Gould, ' "Back to Nature" ', p. 191

18 Eversley, *Commons, Forests and Footpaths*, p. x

19 R. Fedden, *The Continuing Purpose: a History of the National Trust, its Aims and Work*, London, 1968, p. 6

20 Bell, *Octavia Hill: A Biography*, p. 232
   G. Darley, *Octavia Hill*, London, 1990

21 Chadwick, *The Works of Sir Joseph Paxton*, p. 260

22 16 & 17 Vict. c.134

23 C. Brooks, *Mortal Remains*, Exeter, 1989
   J. S. Curl, *The Victorian Celebration of Death*, Newton Abbot, 1972
   A Celebration of Death, London, 1980

24 I am grateful to the Local Studies Librarian, Rochdale for this information

25 PRO, *Return as to Population and Number of Burial Places in England and Wales Open and Closed by Order in Council*, 1874

26 Hunter and Birkett, *Gardens in Towns*, p. 51

27 Cecil, *London Parks*, p. 247

28 44 & 45 Vict. v.34

29 47 & 48 Vict. c.72

30 MCC Proceedings, 6 February 1884, p. 145

31 Cecil, *London Parks*, p. 244

32 Metropolitan Public Garden, Boulevard, and Playground Association, *First Report*, 1883

33 Sexby, *The Municipal Parks*, p. 574

34 Draper, *Lambeth's Open Spaces*, p. 54

35 London County Council (LCC), *Return of Outdoor Memorials in London*, London, 1910, p. 12

36 Dent, *City of Birmingham*, pp. 46–7

37 M'Lellan, *Glasgow Public Parks*, pp. 131–4

38 W. Hardwicke, 'House accommodation and open space', *Trans. National Association for the Promotion of Social Science*, 1877, p. 513

39 *Inter-Departmental Committee on Physical Deterioration*, BPP, vol. XXXII, 1904, pp. 85, 91

40 9 Edw. VII, c.44

41 R. Wagner-Reiger, *Der Wiener Ringstrasse: Bild einer Epoch*, Vienna, 1969–81

42 F. Baltazavec and R. Schedivy, 'The economic origins of Europe's largest city parks', *Parks and Recreation*, July and August 1981, pp. 15–20, 35–42

Bibliography

PARLIAMENTARY PAPERS

Select Committee on Public Walks, 1833
Select Committee on the Sale of Beer, 1833
Select Committee on Drunkenness, 1834
First Report of the Royal Commission on Municipal Corporations of England and Wales, 1835
Select Committee on Arts and Manufactures, 1836
Select Committee on the Health of Towns, 1840
Royal Commission on Employment of Children, 1842
Report on the Sanitary Condition of the Labouring Population of Great Britain: Supplementary Report on the Practice of Interment in Towns, by Edwin Chadwick, 1843
Select Committee on Enclosure, 1844
First Report of the Commissioners for Inquiring into the State of Large Towns and Populous Districts, 1844
Second Report of the Commissioners for Inquiring into the State of Large Towns and Populous Districts, 1845
Fifth Report of the Commissioners on Improving the Metropolis, 1846
Report of the House of Lords Committee on the Sale of Beer, 1849–50
Select Committee on Public Houses, 1853
First and Second Reports from the Select Committee on Open Spaces (Metropolis), 1865
First Report of the Royal Sanitary Commission, 1868–9
Second Report of the Royal Sanitary Commission, 1871 and 1874
Royal Commission on Child Employment, 1862 and 1866
Select Committee on the Bank Holiday Bill, 1868
Report of the Royal Commission on Municipal Corporations, 1880
Inter-Departmental Committee on Physical Deterioration, 1904
Report of the Royal Commission on Common Land, 1955–8
Report of the Minister of Housing and Local Government on Allotments, 1969

THESES

Baldwin, D. 'The Establishment of Public Parks in Manchester', MA Thesis, Manchester University, 1981

Balmer, K. R. 'Open Space Planning in England and Wales', Ph.D. Thesis, University of Liverpool, 1972

Barber, B. J. 'Leeds Corporation 1835–1902: a History of its Environmental, Social and Administrative Services', Ph.D. Thesis, Leeds University, 1974–5

Bather, L. 'A History of Manchester and Salford Trades Council', Ph.D. Thesis, University of Manchester, 1956

Branston, G. 'The Development of Public Open Spaces in Leeds during the Nineteenth Century', M.Phil. Thesis, Leeds University, 1972

Brooke Smith, M. 'The Growth and Development of Popular Entertainment and Pastimes in the Lancashire Cotton Towns', D.Litt. Thesis, Lancaster University, 1970

Calhoun, C. J. 'Community, Class and Collective Action: Popular Protest in Industrial England', D.Phil. Thesis, Oxford University, 1979

Daniels, S. 'Moral Order and the Industrial Environment in the Woollen Textile Districts of West Yorkshire, 1750–1880', Ph.D. Thesis, University of London, 1980

Darby, E. 'Statues of Queen Victoria and Prince Albert. A Study in Commemorative Statuary, 1837–1924', Ph.D. Thesis, Courtauld Institute, University of London, 1983

Foster, W. H. 'Factors in the Development of the Public Park in the West Midlands', M.Soc.Sc.Thesis, Birmingham University, 1974

Gill, R. ' "Till we have built Jerusalem". A Study of the Correlation between Social Thought and Physical Planning in Britain during the Nineteenth and Twentieth Centuries', Ph.D. Thesis, University of Sheffield, 1959–60

Gould, P. C. ' "Back to Nature" and "Back to the Land" and the Socialist Revival, 1880–1900', M.Phil. Thesis, University of Sheffield, 1982

Hodgson, M. C. 'The Working Day and the Working Week in Victorian Britain, 1840–1900', M.Phil. Thesis, Birkbeck College, University of London, 1974

Jackson, W. G. 'An Historical Study of the Provision of Facilities for Play and Recreation in Manchester', M.Ed. Thesis, University of Manchester, 1940

Longstaffe-Gowan, T. 'Georgian Town Gardens', Ph.D. Thesis, University College, London, 1989

Metcalf, S. 'The Establishment of Provincial Public Parks in Victorian England', M.Phil. Thesis, University of London, 1988

Naslas, M. 'The Effect of Technological, Socio-economic, Political and Cultural Transformations upon the Origins and Development of the Industrial Town in England from 1760–1880, with special Reference to Bolton, Preston, Halifax, Dudley and Worcester', Ph.D. Thesis, Reading University, 1974

Pemble, R. 'The National Association for the Promotion of Social Science, 1857–1886. Some Sociological Aspects', M.A. Thesis, University of Nottingham, 1968

Phillips, W. H. 'Liverpool's Public Parks and Recreation Grounds', Typescript, University of Liverpool, 1949

Roberts, E. H. 'A Study of the Growth of the Provision of Public Facilities for Leisure Occupation by Local Authorities', M.A. Thesis, University of Liverpool, 1933

Wigley, J. 'Sabbatarianism. A Study of Religious, Political and Social Phenomena', Ph.D. Thesis, University of Liverpool, 1972

BOOKS

Abram, W. A. *A History of Blackburn*, Blackburn, 1877
  Blackburn Characters of a Past Generation, Blackburn, 1894
Aitken, W. C. *Official Guide to Aston Hall and Park*, Birmingham, 1858
Alison, A. *Essays on the Nature and Principles of Taste*, London, 1790
Alphand, J. C. A. *Les Promenades de Paris*, Paris, 1867–73
André, E. *L'art des Jardins: Traité Général de la Composition des Parcs et Jardins*, Paris, 1879
Anon. *Alexandra Park*, Hastings, 1982
  Cassell's Complete Book of Sports and Pastimes, London, 1903
  A Few Pages About Manchester, Manchester, c. 1849
  History of the Royal Victoria Park, Bath, Bath, c. 1872
  People's Park Centenary 1883–1983, Grimsby, 1983
  A Picturesque Guide to the Regent's Park, London, 1829
  The Strangers' Guide Through Birkenhead, Birkenhead, 1847
  Wolverhampton West Park, 1881–1981, Wolverhampton, 1981
Arnold, M. *Culture and Anarchy*, London, 1869. Reprinted 1969
Arnold, R. A. *The History of the Cotton Famine*, London, 1864
Ashworth, W. *The Genesis of Modern British Town Planning*, London, 1954
Aslet, C. *The Last Country Houses*, London, 1982
Aspden, T. *Preston Guide*, Preston, 1868
Aspinall, H. K. *Birkenhead and its Surroundings*, Liverpool, 1903
Axon, W. E. A. *The Annals of Manchester*, London, 1886
Bailey, F. A. *A History of Southport*, Southport, 1955
Bailey, P. *Leisure and Class in Victorian England: Rational Recreation and the Contest for Control, 1830–1885*, London, 1978

Baines, T. *Liverpool in 1859*, London, 1859

Baker, R. *The Present Condition of the Working Classes*, London, 1851

Balgarnie, R. *Sir Titus Salt: his Life and its Lessons*, London, 1877

Barry, A. *The Life and Work of Sir Charles Barry*, London, 1867

Beattie, S. *A Revolution in London Housing*, London, 1980

Bell, E. M. *Octavia Hill: A Biography*, London, 1942. Reprinted 1965

Bell, Sir J. and Paton, J. *Glasgow: Its Municipal Organization and Administration*, Glasgow, 1896

Benevolo, L. *The Origins of Modern Town Planning*, London, 1967

Bentley, J. *Illustrated Handbook of the Bradford City Parks, Recreation Grounds and Open Spaces*, Bradford, 1926

Bill, S. P. *Victorian Lancashire*, Newton Abbot, 1974

Blomfield, R. 'Public Spaces, Parks and Gardens', in Cobden-Sanderson, T. J. *et al. Art and Life and the Building and Decoration of Cities*, London, 1897

Blount, T. *Tenures of Land and Customs of Manors*, London, 1874. Revised edition 1915

Blunt, W. *The Ark in the Park: The Zoo in the Nineteenth Century*, London, 1976

Boulton, W. B. *The Amusements of Old London*, London, 1901

Bowler, I. R. and Strachen, A. J. *Parks and Gardens in Leicester*, Leicester, 1976

Bradshaw, G. *Handbook for Tourists of Great Britain and Ireland*, Section IV, Manufacturing Districts of Lancashire and Yorkshire, c.1868

Briggs, A. *The Age of Improvement*, London, 1959
  Victorian Cities, London, 1963. Penguin edn 1968

Brooks, C. *Mortal Remains*, London, 1989

Brown, J. *The Art and Architecture of English Gardens*, London, 1989

Bruce, J. C. *A Handbook to Newcastle-on-Tyne*, London, 1863

Brunton, J. *Prince's Street Gardens: an Historical Guide*, Edinburgh, 1956

Bunce, J. T. *History of the Corporation of Birmingham*, Birmingham, 2 vols, 1878

Burnap, G. *Parks, their Design, Equipment and Use*, Philadelphia, 1916

Burnett, J. *A Social History of Housing*, Newton Abbot, 1978

Burnett, J. (ed.) *Useful Toil. Autobiographies of Working People from the 1820s to 1920s*, London, 1974

Cannadine, D. *Lords and Landlords*, Leicester, 1980

Carrington, R. *Alexandra Park and Palace. A History*, London, 1975

Carter, G., Goode, P. and Laurie, K. *Humphry Repton, Landscape Gardener 1752–1818*, Norwich, 1982

Cecil, E. *London Parks and Gardens*, London, 1907

Chadwick, G. F. *The Works of Sir Joseph Paxton, 1803–1865*, London, 1961
  The Park and the Town, London, 1966
Chambers, J. D. *A Century of Nottingham History*, Nottingham, 1954
  A History of Working Class Housing, Exeter, 1971
Chambers, W. *Plans, Elevations, Sketches and Perspective Views of the Gardens and Buildings at Kew in Surry* [sic], London, 1763
Chapman, J. M. and Chapman, B. *The Life and Times of Baron Haussmann*, London, 1957
Cherry, G. E. *Urban Change and Planning*, Henley-on-Thames, 1972
Clark, Sir J. *The Sanative Influence of Climate*, London, 1841
Clarke, J. *et al. Working-Class Culture: Studies in History and Theory*, London, 1979
Clifford, D. *A History of Garden Design*, London, 1962
Clifford, F. *A History of Private Bill Legislation*, London, 1887
Clunn, H. P. *Famous South Coast Pleasure Resorts Past and Present*, London, 1929
Cobden-Sanderson, T. J. *et al. Art and Life and the Building and Decoration of Cities*, London, 1897
Cole, N. *The Royal Parks and Gardens of London*, London, 1877
Coleman, B. I. *The Idea of the City in Nineteenth Century Britain*, London, 1978
Colman, H. *European Life and Manners*, Boston, 1850
Cook, C. C. *A Description to New York Central Park*, New York, 1869
Cox, J. *City of Birmingham Public Parks and Pleasure Grounds*, Birmingham, 1892
Crane, W. *Flowers from Shakespeare's Garden, a Posy from the Plays*, London, 1906
Cranz, G. *The Politics of Park Design*, Cambridge, Massachusetts, 1982
Creese, W. L. *The Search for Environment: The Garden City Before and After*, New Haven, 1966
Cruden, R. P. *The History of the Town of Gravesend*, London, 1843
Cudworth, W. *Manningham, Heaton and Allerton, treated Historically and Topographically*, Bradford, 1896
Cunningham, C. *Victorian and Edwardian Town Halls*, London, 1981
Cunningham, H. *Leisure and the Industrial Revolution*, London, 1980
Curl, J. S. *The Victorian Celebration of Death*, Newton Abbot, 1972
  A Celebration of Death, London, 1980
  The Life and Work of Henry Roberts, Chichester, 1983
Dancy, E. *Hyde Park*, London, 1937
Darley, G. *Villages of Vision*, London, 1975
  Octavia Hill, London, 1990

Daunton, M. J. *House and Home in the Victorian City*, London, 1983

Davey, P. *Arts and Crafts Architecture: The Search for Earthly Paradise*, London, 1980

Davies, M. H. (ed.) *Life as We Have Known It*, London, 1931

Davies, P. *Troughs and Drinking Fountains*, London, 1989

Davies, V. L. and Hyde, H. *Dudley and the Black Country, 1760–1860*, Dudley, 1970

Dawson, W. H. *Municipal Life and Government in Germany*, London, 1914

Delgado, A. *The Annual Outing*, London, 1977

Dennis, J. *The Pioneer of Progress: or the Early Closing Movement in relation to the Saturday half-holiday and the early payment of wages*, London, 1861

Dent, R. K. *City of Birmingham. History and Description of the Public Parks, Gardens and Recreation Grounds*, Birmingham, 1916

Dixon, R. and Muthesius, S. *Victorian Architecture*, London, 1978

Dobson, M. J. *Memoir of John Dobson, of Newcastle-upon-Tyne*, London, 1885

Dolman, F. *Municipalities at Work. Social Questions of Today*, London, 1895

Donajgrodzki, A. P. (ed.) *Social Control in Nineteenth Century Britain*, London, 1977

Downing, A. J. *Rural Essays*, New York, 1853

   Cottage Residences, New York, 1842

   A Treatise on the Theory and Practice of Landscape Gardening, New York, 1841

Draper, M. P. G. *Lambeth's Open Spaces*, London, 1979

Duff, Hon. E. G. *The Life-Work of Lord Avebury, 1834–1913*, London, 1924

Duffield, H. G. *The pocket companion or strangers' guide to Manchester and Salford*, Manchester, c.1860

Edelstein, T. J. *Vauxhall Gardens*, New Haven, 1983

Edlein, H. L. *The Public Park*, London, 1971

Edwards, E. 'Commons, Parks, and Open Spaces, near London; their History and Treatment', London, 1867. Guildhall Library, MS 547

Ellacombe, H. N. *The Plant-lore and Garden-craft of Shakespeare*, London, 1878

Elliott, B. *Victorian Gardens*, London, 1986

Eversley, Lord *Commons, Forests and Footpaths*, London, 1910

Farr, W. *First Annual Report of the Registrar-General of Births, Deaths and Marriages in England, 1837–9*, London, 1839

   Second Annual Report, 1839–41, London, 1841

Faucher, L. *Manchester in 1844*, London, 1844

Fedden, R. *The Continuing Purpose: a History of the National Trust, its Aims and Work*, London, 1968

Fleetwood, W. L. *History of Hyde Park*, London, 1909

Foster, J. *Class Struggle and the Industrial Revolution*, London, 1974

Fraser, D. (ed.) *Municipal Reform and the Industrial City*, Leicester, 1982

Gardener Wilkinson, Sir J. *On Colour and the Necessity for General Diffusion of Taste among all classes, with Remarks on Laying out Dressed or Geometrical Gardens*, London, 1858

Garrard, J. *Leadership and Power in Victorian Industrial Towns, 1830–1880*, Manchester, 1983

Geddes, P. *City Development: a Study of Parks, Gardens and Culture Institutes*, Edinburgh and Westminster, 1904

Gill, C. *History of Birmingham*, Vol. 1, London, 1952

Gilpin, W. *Three Essays on Picturesque Beauty*, London, 1792

Girardin, R-L. *An Essay on Landscape*, translated by D. Malthus, London, 1783

Gloag, J. *Mr Loudon's England*, London, 1970

Goodall, C. *Illustrated Royal Handbook to Roundhay Park*, Leeds, 1872

Goode, P. and Lancaster, M. (eds) *The Oxford Companion to Gardens*, Oxford, 1986

Goreham, G. *The Parks and Open Spaces of Norwich*, Norwich, 1961

Gothein, M. L. *A History of Garden Art*. Translated by Mrs Archer-Hind, London, 1928

Hadfield, M. *A History of British Gardening*, London, 1960

Hamer, H. *Bolton 1838–1938. A Centenary Record of Municipal Progress*, Bolton, 1938

Harland, J. *Collectanea Relating to Manchester and its Neighbourhood*, Manchester, 1867

Harrison, B. *Drink and the Victorians*, London, 1971

Harrison, R. J. *Before the Socialists. Studies in Labour and Politics, 1861–1881*, London, 1965

Heginbotham, H. *Stockport: Ancient and Modern*, Vol. 2, London, 1892

Henard, R. *Richesse d'Art de la Ville de Paris, Les Jardins et les Squares*, Paris, 1911

Hennebo, D. and Schmidt, E. *Geschichte des Stadtgrüns*, Vols I–III, Hannover, Berlin and Sarstedt, 1972

Hennock, E. P. *Fit and Proper Persons*, London, 1973

Herbert, G. *Pioneers of Prefabrication: The British Contribution to the Nineteenth Century*, London, 1978

Hewitson, A. *A History of Preston*, Preston, 1882. London 1969 edn

Hill, O. *Homes of the London Poor*, London, 1875

Hill, W. T. *Octavia Hill: Pioneer of the National Trust and Housing Reformer*, London, 1956

Hinz, G. *Peter Josef Lenné und Seiner Bedeutendsten Schöpfungen in Berlin und Potsdam*, Berlin, 1937

Hix, J. *The Glass House*, London, 1974

Holmes, Mrs Basil, *The London Burial Grounds*, London, 1896

Holroyd, A. *Saltaire and its Founder*, Bradford, 1873

Honeyman, J. *Open Spaces in Towns*, Glasgow, 1883

Hoskins, W. G. *The Making of the English Landscape*, London, 1977 edn

Hoskins, W. G. and Stamp, D. L. *The Common Lands of England and Wales*, London, 1963

Hughes, J. A. *Garden Architecture and Landscape Gardening*, London, 1866

Hunter, Sir R. and Birkett, P. *Gardens in Towns, being a statement of the law relating to the acquisition and maintenance of land for purposes of recreation*, London, 1916

Humphrey, N. (ed.) *Vital Statistics: Selections from the Writing of W. Farr*, London, 1885

Hussey, C. *The Picturesque: Studies in a Point of View*, London, 1977 edn

Hyams, E. *Capability Brown and Humphry Repton*, London, 1971

Izack, R. *Remarkable Antiquities of the City of Exeter*, Exeter, second edition, 1681

Jackson, A. *Semi-detached London*, London, 1973

Jackson, W. E. *Achievement – a Short History of the L.C.C.*, London, 1965

Jekyll, F. *Gertrude Jekyll: a Memoir*, London, 1934

Jekyll, G. *Colour in the Flower Garden*, London, 1908
  Public Parks and Gardens, Bromley, 1918

Jevons, W. S. *Methods of Social Reform*, London, 1883. Reprinted 1904

Johnson, J. *Parks for the People*, London, 1885

Johnson, W. *Battersea Park as a Centre for Nature Study*, London, 1910

Jones, G. P. and Tyler, J. E. *A Century of Progress in Sheffield*, Sheffield, 1935

Kaighin, J. R. *Bygone Birkenhead, Sketches Round and About the Sixties*, Birkenhead, 1925

Kemp, E. *How to Lay Out a Small Garden*, London, 1850, 1858, 1864
  The Parks, Gardens, etc. of London and its Suburbs described and illustrated, London, 1851

King, E. *The People's Palace and Glasgow Green*, Glasgow, 1988 edn

Knight, R. P. *An Analytical Enquiry into the Principles of Taste*, London 1805

Koppelkamm, S. *Glasshouses and Wintergardens of the Nineteenth Century*, London, 1982. Translated by K. Talbot

Langford, J. A. *Birmingham: A Handbook for Residents and Visitors*, Birmingham, 1879

Larwood, J. *The Story of the London Parks*, London, 1872

Laski, H. J., Jennings, W. I. and Robson, W. A. *A Century of Municipal Progress, 1835–1935*, London, 1935

Le Mire, E. D. *The Unpublished Lectures of William Morris*, Detroit, 1969

Leader, R. E. (ed.) *The Life and Letters of J. A. Roebuck*, London, 1897

Lewis, R. A. *Edwin Chadwick and the Public Health Movement, 1832–1854*, London, 1952

Lillie, W. *The History of Middlesbrough*, Middlesbrough, 1968

Liverpool City Council, *The Parks, Gardens and Recreation Grounds of the City of Liverpool, Official Handbook*, Liverpool, 1934

Livesey, A. H. H. *The Green Heart of London: the History of the Royal Parks and Residences*, London, 1937

London County Council, *London Parks and Open Spaces, Notes on Acquisition, History and Maintenance*, London, 1906

  Notebook of the Parks, Gardens, Recreation Grounds and open spaces of London, London, 1897

  Open-air London: an illustrated guide to some 480 open spaces in and around London, including the green belt, London, 1939

  Return of Outdoor Memorials in London, London, 1910

Loudon, J. *A Short Account of the Life and Writings of John Claudius Loudon*, London, 1847

Loudon, J. C. *The Derby Arboretum*, London, 1840

  An Encyclopaedia of Cottage, Farm and Villa Architecture and Furniture, London, 1836

  An Encyclopaedia of Gardening, London, 1822

  The Landscape Gardening and Landscape Architecture of the Late Humphry Repton Esq., London, 1840

  The Suburban Gardener and Villa Companion, London, 1838

  A Treatise on Forming, Improving and Managing Country Residences, London, 1806

McCrone, K. E. *Sport and the Physical Emancipation of English Women, 1870–1914*, London, 1988

MacDougall, E. B. (ed.) *John Claudius Loudon and the Early Nineteenth Century in Great Britain*, Dumbarton Oaks, 1980

Mackerness, E. D. *The Social History of English Music*, London, 1964

McKenzie, A. *The Parks, Open Spaces and Thoroughfares of London*, London, 1869

  'Private Notebook', Guildhall Library, MS 16,861

Major, J. *The Theory and Practice of Landscape Gardening*, London, 1852

Major, J. and Major, H. *The Ladies' Assistant in the Formation of their Flower Gardens*, London, 1861

Malcolmson, R. W. *Popular Recreations in English Society 1700–1850*, Cambridge, 1973

Malton, J. *An Essay on British Cottage Architecture*, London, 1798

Manders, F. W. D. *History of Gateshead*, Gateshead, 1973

Margrie, W. *London's Fairylands . . . Breezy Notes on Forty Parks, Commons and Beauty Spots*, London, 1934

Marples, M. *A History of Football*, London, 1954

Mason, A. *Association Football and English Society 1880–1939*, Brighton, 1980

Mason, W. *The English Garden: a Poem in Four Books*, London, 1777–81

Mate, C. H. and Riddle, C. *Bournemouth: 1810–1910, The History of a Modern Pleasure Resort*, Bournemouth, 1910

Matthews, J. *Historic Newport*, Newport-on-Usk, 1910

Mawson, T. H. *The Life and Work of an English Landscape Gardener*, London, 1927

Mayfield, J. W. *History of the Springfield Waterworks and How the Pearson Park was Obtained for the People*, Hull, 1909

Meller, H. *The Ideal City*, Leicester, 1980

Leisure and the Changing City, 1870–1914, London, 1976

Mellors, R. *The Gardens, Parks and Walks of Nottingham and District*, Nottingham, 1926

Metropolitan Free Drinking Fountain and Cattle Trough Association, *A Century of Fountains, 1858–1959*, London, 1959

Millington, R. *The House in the Park*, Liverpool, 1957

Milner, H. E. *The Art and Practice of Landscape Gardening*, London, 1890

Mitchell, B. R. and Deane, P. *Abstract of British Historical Statistics*, Cambridge, 1962

M'Lellan, D. *Glasgow Public Parks*, Glasgow, 1894

Morley, J. *Death, Heaven and the Victorians*, London, 1971

Morris, M. (ed.) *The Collected Works of William Morris*, 24 vols, London, 1910–15

Mortimer, W. W. *The History of the Hundred of Wirral*, Manchester, 1947

Muir, M. J. and Platt, E. M. *History of Municipal Government in Liverpool*, Liverpool, 1906

Murray, A. *The Book of the Royal Horticultural Society*, London, 1863

Newton, N. T. *Design on the Land*, Massachusetts, 1971

Newton, S. M. *Health, Art and Reason*, London, 1974

Olmsted, F. L. *Public Parks and the Enlargement of Towns*, New York, 1870

Walks and Talks of an American Farmer in England, London, 1852

Olmsted, F. L. and Kimball, T. *Forty Years of Landscape Architecture*, New York, 1928

O'Neill, D. J. *The Saving of Aston Hall*, Birmingham, 1909

O'Neill, E. *Extraordinary Confessions*, Preston, 1850

Owen, E. *Hyde Park. Select Narrative, Annual Events, etc. during Twenty Years Police Service*, London, 1909

Papworth, J. B. *Rural Residences*, London, 1818

Patterson, A. T. *History of Southampton*, Southampton, 1971

Peacock, W. F. *Abel Heywood's Series of Penny Guide-Books. A Guide to Blackpool and Fleetwood*, Manchester, 1864

Perrin, J. *The Manchester Handbook*, Manchester, 1857

Pettigrew, W. W. *Handbook of the Manchester Parks and Recreation Grounds*, Manchester, 1929

  Municipal Parks: Layout, Management and Administration, London, 1937

Pevsner, N. *The Buildings of England*, series, London, 1952 on

Phillips, P. K. *Crystal Palace Park: Draft Landscape Plan*, Bromley, 1986

Picton, J. A. *City of Liverpool: Municipal Archives and Records ... Extract*, Liverpool, 1886

  Memorials of Liverpool, London, 1875

Pimlott, J. A. R. *The Englishman's Holiday. A Social History*, London, 1976

Pollard, S. *A History of Labour in Sheffield*, Liverpool, 1959

Poulsen, C. *Victoria Park: A Study in the History of East London*, London, 1976

Prentice, A. *Historical Sketches and Personal Recollections of Manchester*, London, 1851

Price, U. *An Essay on the Picturesque*, London, 1794–8

Pückler-Muskau, Prince H. L. H. von, *Hints on Landscape Gardening, Tour in England*, 1832. Translated by S. Austin

Rae, W. F. *The Business of Travel*, London, 1891

Ransome, A. *The History of the Manchester and Salford Sanitary Association*, Manchester, 1902

Reach, A. B. *Manchester and the Textile Districts in 1849*, Manchester, 1849. Reprinted 1972

Redford, A. and Russell, I. S. *The History of Local Government in Manchester*, London, 1940

Redlich, J. and Hirst, F. W. *The History of Local Government in England*, London, 1858

Reilly, Sir C. and Aslan, N. J. *Outline Plan for the County Borough of Birkenhead*, Birkenhead, 1947

Repton, H. *Designs for the Pavilion at Brighton*, London, 1808

  An Enquiry into the Changes of Taste in Landscape Gardening, London, 1806

  Fragments on the Theory and Practice of Landscape Gardening, London 1816

  Observations on the Theory and Practice of Landscape Gardening, London, 1803

  Sketches and Hints on Landscape Gardening, London, 1794

Ricauti, T. J. *Sketches for Rustic Work Including Bridges, Park and Garden Buildings, Seats and Furniture, with Descriptions and Estimates of Building*, London, 1848

Richardson, B. W. *The Health of Nations: A Review of the Works of Edwin Chadwick*, London, 1887

Roberts, H. *Proposed People's Palace and Gardens for the Northern and Midland Counties to Employ Factory Operatives*, London, 1863

Robinson, P. F. *Rural Architecture*, London, 1823

  Designs for Ornamental Villas, London, 1827

  Village Architecture, London, 1830

  Designs for Gate Cottages, Lodges and Park Entrances, in various styles, London, 1837

  A new Series of Designs for Ornamental Cottages and Villas, London, 1838

Robinson, W. *The English Flower Garden*, London, six editions, 1883–1898

  The Parks, Promenades and Gardens of Paris, London, 1869

  The Wild Garden, London, five editions 1870–1903

Roddis, R. J. *The Law of Parks and Recreation Grounds*, London, 1974

Rowan, A. *Garden Buildings*, London, 1968

Samuel, R. *People's History and Socialist Theory*, London, 1981

Saunders, A. *Regent's Park. A Study of the Development of the Area from 1066 to the Present Day*, Newton Abbot, 1969

Scar, R. *The History of South Park*, Darlington, 1954

Scholes, J. C. *History of Bolton*, Bolton, 1892

Sexby, J. J. *The Municipal Parks, Gardens, and Open Spaces of London*, London, 1898

Simey, M. B. *Charitable Efforts in Liverpool in the Nineteenth Century*, Liverpool, 1951

Simmons, J. *Life in Victorian Leicester*, Leicester, 1971

Simo, M. L. *Loudon and the Landscape: from Country Seat to Metropolis*, London, 1988

Simon, Sir J. *Public Health Reports*, London, 1887

Simon, S. D. *A Century of City Government in Manchester, 1838–1935*, Manchester, 1838

Smith, C. H. J. *Parks and Pleasure Grounds: practical notes on country residences, public parks and gardens*, London, 1852

Smith, G. *Bradford's Police*, Bradford, 1974

Smith, M. A. *et al.* (eds) *Leisure and Society in Britain*, London, 1973

Smith, S. *History of Greenock*, Greenock, 1921

Southworth, J. G. *Vauxhall Gardens*, New York, 1941

Stainton, J. H. *The Making of Sheffield, 1865–1914*, Sheffield, 1924

Stevenson, E. *Park Maker: A Life of Frederick Law Olmsted*, London, 1977

Sturge, J. *The Birmingham Saturday Half-Holiday Guide*, Birmingham, 1879

Summerson, J. *Architecture in Britain, 1530–1830*, London, 6th edn, 1977

  The Life and Work of John Nash, Architect, London, 1980

Sunderland Central Library, *Mobray Park: History*, Sunderland, 1978

Sutcliffe, A. (ed.) *British Town Planning: the Formative Years*, Leicester, 1981

Sutcliffe, A. *Towards the Planned City*, Oxford, 1981

Tait, A. *History of the Oldham Lyceum*, Oldham, 1897

Tarn, J. N. *Working Class Housing in Nineteenth Century Britain*, London, 1971

Thompson, D. *The Chartists*, London, 1984

Thompson, E. P. *The Making of the English Working Class*, London, 1963
   William Morris – Romantic to Revolutionary, London, 1977

Thompson, P. *The Work of William Morris*, London, 1967

Thompson, S. C. (ed.) *Southampton Common*, Southampton, 1979

Thornton, C. E. *The People's Garden: A History of Birkenhead Park*, Wirral, undated

Thurston, H. *Royal Parks for the People*, Newton Abbot, 1974

Tiffany, T. *The People's Park, Halifax. Jubilee of Opening, 1857–1907*, Halifax, 1907

Triggs, H. I. *Formal Gardens in England and Wales*, London, 1902

Tweedie, E. B. *Hyde Park: its History and Romance*, London, 1908

Vaux, C. *Cottage Residences*, New York, 1869

Von Erdberg, E, *The Chinese Influence on European Garden Structures*, Harvard, 1936

Wagner-Reiger, R. *Der Wiener Ringstrasse: Bild einer Epoch*, Vienna, 1969–81

Walter Macfarlane & Co. *Architectural Ironwork*, Glasgow, c.1920
   Illustrated Catalogue, 2 vols, Glasgow, c.1880

Walvin, J. *Leisure and Society*, London, 1978

Wardell, J. *The Municipal History of the Borough of Leeds*, London, 1846

Watkin, D. *The English Vision. The Picturesque in Architecture, Landscape and Garden Design*, London, 1982

Whitaker, B. C. G. and Browne, K. *Parks for People*, London, 1971

White, B. D. *A History of the Corporation of Liverpool 1835–1914*, Liverpool, 1951

Williams, R. *The Country and the City*, London, 1973

Wirth, C. L. *Parks, Politics and People*, Oklahoma, 1980

Woods, M. and Warren, A. *Glass Houses*, London, 1988

Worsdall, F. *Victorian City*, Glasgow, 1982

Worth, R. N. *History of the Town and Borough of Devonport*, Devonport, 1870

Wright, D. G. and Jowett, J. A. (eds) *Victorian Bradford*, Bradford, 1981

Wroth, W. *Cremorne and the Later London Pleasure Gardens*, London, 1907
   The London Pleasure Gardens of the Eighteenth Century, London, 1896

Yeo, E. and Yeo, S. *Popular Culture and Class Conflict, 1590–1914*, Brighton, 1981

Zucker, P. *Town and Square. From the Agora to the Village Green*, New York, 1959

Index